In Praise of *Chiara*

"Madeline's biography is an imaginative way of entering into the life of Saint Clare. It brings to light the rich milieu of the Church, the culture and historical time that birthed forth Saint Francis and Saint Clare and the Franciscan family. It is an edifying read for the young reader, as well as for all ages."

—Sister Clare Hunter, FSE, Catholic speaker and Assistant Professor of Fundamental Theology at St. Vincent de Paul Regional Seminary

"Most works about Saint Clare in English are biographical or scholarly. This new book, more properly, tome, by Madeline Pecora Nugent is unique. Through exhaustive analysis and research, she has successfully recreated the milieu in which Saint Clare lived in a way no one else has. For anyone who wishes to truly know Saint Clare of Assisi, this book is a must-read."

—Bret Thoman, OFS, founder of St. Francis Pilgrimages and author of *A Knight and a Lady: A Journey into the Spirituality of Saints Francis and Clare of Assisi*

"Clare was one of my very first saint-friends as a young girl and pretty much the single-handed inspiration for my religious vocation. So if I had read a book like this when we were first introduced, I'd probably be a Poor Clare today! You see, like anyone else, I really loved a good story. When the story is as real as the Chiara in this book, it's absolutely unforgettable."

—Sister Julia Mary Darrenkamp, FSP, Catholic Instagrammer, book lover, and saint aficionado

"An amazing combination of fictional detail and historical fact, this well-researched and highly imaginative series of vignettes brings Saint Clare of Assisi and other personalities of her time out of the tomes of Franciscan history into the ambit of the twenty-first-century reader. Don't miss the end notes!"

—Mother Mary Angela, PCC, abbess of the Poor Clare Monastery of Our Lady of Guadalupe, Roswell, NM

CHIARA

CHIARA

A Story *of* Saint Clare *of* Assisi

By Madeline Pecora Nugent, *cfp*

*P*auline
BOOKS & MEDIA
Boston

Library of Congress Control Number: 2021951770
CIP data is available.

ISBN-10: 0-8198-1686-8
ISBN-13: 978-0-8198-1686-3

Originally published as *Clare and Her Sisters: Lovers of the Poor Christ* by Madeline Pecora Nugent, copyright © 2003, Daughters of Saint Paul

Cover design by Ryan McQuade

Excerpts are taken from *Clare of Assisi: Early Documents—The Lady* and *Francis of Assisi: Early Documents*, ed. and trans. by Regis J. Armstrong, OFM Cap., © New City Press, 202 Comforter Boulevard, Hyde Park, NY, 12538. Reprinted by Pauline Books & Media. Used with permission.

Excerpts are taken from the *Messenger of Saint Anthony*, © Edizioni Messaggero Padova, Via Orto Botanico 11, 35123, Padova, Italy. Reprinted by Pauline Books & Media. Used with permission.

Scripture quotations are from *The Catholic Edition of the Revised Standard Version of the Bible*, copyright © 1965, 1966 National Council of the Churches of Christ in the United States of America. Used by permission. All rights reserved worldwide.

"P" and PAULINE are registered trademarks of the Daughters of St. Paul.

Copyright © 2022, Daughters of St. Paul

Published by Pauline Books & Media, 50 Saint Pauls Avenue, Boston, MA 02130-3491

Printed in the U.S.A.

www.pauline.org

Pauline Books & Media is the publishing house of the Daughters of St. Paul, an international congregation of women religious serving the Church with the communications media.

1 2 3 4 5 6 7 8 9   26 25 24 23 22

To the sisters of the Monastery of Saint Clare in Langhorne, Pennsylvania,
and to Sister Mary Francis Hone, OSC.
Without the generosity, prayers, time, and patience
of these wonderful daughters of Saint Clare,
this book could never have been written.

Contents

Acknowledgments

Among the many people who helped make this book possible, the following deserve special thanks:

Many editors at Pauline Books and Media worked on the original publication of this book as well as on this revised edition. Thanks for your patience, editing, and support.

Father Regis J. Armstrong, OFM Cap., answered detailed questions about Clare and permitted the use of quotes in the original edition of this book from his translation of Clare's writings in *Clare of Assisi: Early Documents*. Claude Blanc, editor at New City Press, extended this permission to Father Regis' revised edition *The Lady: Clare of Assisi: Early Documents*, from which all of Clare's quotes in this edition are taken. In addition, New City Press, through Claude Blanc's permission, also granted permission to quote Francis' words and writings from *Francis of Assisi: Early Documents*.

In the original edition of this book, Mother Mary Francis, PCC, granted permission to use her translation from the booklet "Dance for Exultation: Letters of Saint Clare to Saint Agnes of Prague." Some of Clare's words in the original edition were taken from or adapted from Mother Mary Francis' translation.

Bret Thoman, OFS, director of Saint Francis Pilgrimages (www.stfrancispilgrimages.com), lent his expertise in knowing the lives and places of Saints Francis and Clare and shared his insights into the Umbrian language used during their lifetimes.

On a trip to Assisi, the following people were most helpful: Brother Jacopo Pozzerle, OFM, for a tour of San Damiano; Brother Gabriel Aceto, OFM, for a tour around Santa Maria degli Angeli and the Porziuncula; Brother Joseph Woods, OFM Conv., for sharing his insights on Francis and Clare; Father George Masler, OFM Conv., for a tour of the Basilica di San Francesco; the sisters and work staff at the Suore Americana convent were congenial hosts who also provided information on fall crops and farm work in Assisi (used in the chapter on Messer Ugolino); Brother Daniel Geary, OFM Conv., visited San Damiano to discuss the results of recent excavations with the friars there; Sister Chiara Anastacia, OSC, spent two hours sharing insights in person and then additional time answering many questions via mail.

Father William Lynn, SJ, of the Pontifical College Josephinum, answered questions regarding reception of the Eucharist and how the Mass was offered at the time of Saint Clare.

Sister Giacinta Zambonati and the community at the Monastery of Vallegloria in Spello kindly researched Abbess Suor Balbina and sent information about her.

Dr. Lubomir Gleiman explained how to say "Peace and blessings" in Czech for the chapters on Sestra Anežka.

Father Marino Bigaroni answered questions regarding an indulgence supposedly given to the oratory at San Damiano.

Dr. Robert Carrellas discussed some of the illnesses of the sisters at San Damiano and related other symptoms they may have had along with the ones described in the histories.

Maria Dolores Zannoni, a professional translator, translated three letters into Italian, without accepting any remuneration except gratitude.

Antonietta Calori translated another letter into Italian.

Much gratitude to all the sisters at the Monastery of Saint Clare, Langhorne, Pennsylvania, for allowing me to spend a week with them to experience the lifestyle of the followers of Saint Clare. The time spent with these delightful daughters of Clare meant a great deal to this book and to me personally.

Sister Mary Frances Hone, OSC, lent many of her materials on Saint Clare and was an invaluable resource. She spent hours discussing Clare, answering questions, checking details, and reviewing the manuscript. She is indeed the hidden author of this book, because without her it would never have been written.

Sister Ingrid Peterson, OSF, Sister Ramona Miller, OSF, Jean-François Godet-Calogeras, Father Cyprian Lawrence, and Father Conrad Harkins, OFM, shared many insights into Francis and Clare and their times and researched historical details. Sister Ramona and Father Conrad provided information about the layout of San Damiano, and Father Conrad also photocopied information and translated portions of the bulls *Etsi omnium* and *Quo elongati*. Sister Ingrid suggested giving the monastery cat an Italian name and conveyed the latest findings regarding Clare. Historian David Flood read the manuscript and provided tremendous help in checking its historical accuracy.

Father Claude Jarmak, OFM Conv., Father Julian Stead, OSB, Rita Maltoni, Fausto Devecchi, and Dr. Ascanio Dipippo provided on-the-spot translations of works and letters pertaining to Saint Clare. Father Claude also photocopied information regarding medieval liturgy. Father Julian discussed theological points, obtained various reference materials, and translated two letters.

Thanks to the librarians who assisted me, especially the staff at Salve Regina University, Theresa Shaffer and others at Saint Bonaventure University, and Beverly Wilson at Saint Hyacinth Seminary, Granby, Massachusetts.

Noel Riggs of the Franciscan Institute provided valuable information.

The Franciscan Friars of the Immaculate (New Bedford, Massachusetts), the Monastery of Saint Clare (Andover, Massachusetts), and Brother Gabriel at the Franciscan Retreat House (Andover, Massachusetts) provided various Franciscan publications.

Mary Lee Nolan shared her insights into medieval pilgrimages.

The historians at the Slater Mill, Pawtucket, Rhode Island, explained the operation of early mills and pointed out written references on them. This was useful in describing the mill owned by the Girardone family.

Linda A. Hughes, the admissions coordinator of Remuda Ranch Center for Anorexia and Bulimia, provided materials on anorexia and discussed how Clare's excessive fasting could have damaged her health.

Several members of the Franciscans of the Primitive Observance and Franciscan Friars of the Immaculate, especially Father David Engo, FPO, and

Brother Bonaventure, FFI, researched the thirteen wounds of Christ and came up with the final list mentioned in this book. Father John of the Trinity, TOCarm., explained how the Porziuncula indulgence might be obtained today.

In researching flora and fauna that existed in Assisi at the time of Saint Clare, used in Chapter 21 of this book, the following individuals were extremely helpful: Chris Nerone of the University of Rhode Island suggested nightshade as a poisonous, berry-growing vine of the region; Mark Schenck, proprietor of the Butterfly Zoo, Middletown, Rhode Island, identified a caterpillar and swallowtail butterfly that lived in Umbria.

Father John Broderick and Father Thomas Carnavale answered a variety of questions regarding Catholic customs, Mass rubrics, altar vessels, and so on.

Heather Minto spent a most delightful afternoon demonstrating the medieval spinning process using a drop spindle and flax. She also shared how thread is woven on a medieval loom.

The following individuals were especially helpful in trying to determine how Clare did her needlework: Norma Smayda, Susan Hay, Genevieve Hartigan, Barbara Gifford, and Leslie Tomaino.

Lee Depot articulated several insights into handwork at the time of Clare. Alda Kaye, curator of the University of Rhode Island's Historic Textile Collection, researched and photocopied information on drawn embroidery at the time of Clare. Joan Hitchcock explained the stitches in this article.

Thanks to those others who read the manuscript for the first edition of this book in whole or in part: Sister Ingrid Peterson, OSF; Mother Mary Francis, PCC; historian Jean-François Godet-Calogeras; history professor John Quinn; the Poor Clare community at Langhorne, Pennsylvania; the Capuchin Sisters of Nazareth in Tunkhannock, Pennsylvania; and my husband, Jim, who graciously encourages my writing and who picked up many library books for me. Jim also researched the dates for Easter in the early 1230s. Sister Eileen Heugh, OSF, proofread the manuscript for correct punctuation and grammar.

John Quinn checked the birth date of Pope Gregory IX, found a map of the Holy Roman Empire in 1250, and offered some valuable insights regarding Clare and her sisters.

Finally, thanks to all who prayed so fervently for this project. These include family (especially my husband and mother), friends, relatives, and others whom

I have never met. Their prayers meant everything, for God is the One Who is ultimately behind this book. Anything good herein is due solely to His boundless and undeserved grace. Therefore, it is to God and to Saint Clare, who shared herself through the research for this book, that I owe the greatest gratitude.

– MADELINE PECORA NUGENT, CFP

Introductory Material

Many people believe that Saint Clare of Assisi decided to follow Christ because she heard Saint Francis preach. He enclosed her in a convent where she lived a relatively uneventful life for forty years.

That is not the real Clare of Assisi.

This book attempts to present the real Clare from childhood to death, the many people she loved and influenced, and the complex, frightening, radical, disheartening, and joyful encounters of her life.

Clare began something revolutionary. During her time, convents were comfortable places for pious noblewomen who continued to have servants and property. Clare had a different vision. She created a monastery that would neither own property nor make money and in which all classes of women lived as sisters, serving each other.

Many excellent scholarly works have been written about Clare. Many of them were used in writing this book, which adheres to the primary sources (the first biography of Clare, her writings, and the testimonies of eyewitnesses) and to the life of Clare and the first Poor Clares, as many Poor Clares today understand them. However, *Chiara: A Story of Saint Clare of Assisi* goes beyond scholarly works to allow the reader to experience Clare and her sisters in a personal way. Thus, while sticking to historical facts, this work adds imagination, keeping the fiction as factual as possible. Chapter notes at the end of each chapter distinguish the factual from the fictional in this life of Saint Clare. They also note differences of scholarly opinion regarding certain parts of Clare's history.

God was Clare's first love. She challenges us to hold "fast to the footprints of Him" (CA:ED 47), the poor and humble Jesus Christ, so that we may join her sisters in "tasting the hidden sweetness that, from the beginning, God Himself has reserved for His lovers" (CA:ED 51). May this book teach us to do so.

Notes on Chronology

Certain dates in the life of Saint Clare, like the date for her flight from home on Palm Sunday, the date of the Fourth Lateran Council, and the dates of Francis' death and her own, are recorded in history, but the exact dates for many other events are uncertain. Her sisters in religious life remembered many incidents, but, as might be expected, they had difficulty pinpointing the exact time and year. The author has researched these undated incidents and selected reasonable times, as explained in the Chapter Notes. For other incidents, this book generally follows the chronology in the French edition of *Early Documents* with emendations suggested by Jean-François Godet-Calogeras, professor emeritus of theology and Franciscan studies at Saint Bonaventure University (Saint Bonaventure, New York) and general editor of *Franciscan Studies*.

Chiara: A Story of Saint Clare of Assisi helps the reader to see Clare through the eyes of her contemporaries. To obtain a fuller picture of the early Franciscan movement and its times and saints, the reader may also wish to read *Francesco: A Story of Saint Francis of Assisi* and *Antonio: A Story of Saint Anthony of Padua*. Although contemporary with these saints, Clare outlived both. With her death and the subsequent deaths of her first followers and those of Saint Francis, the early Franciscan movement ended. The Franciscan charism has continued, however, to this day.

Incidents covered more completely in the other books are:

1182–1199: Francis' early life; his part in city life and in the civil uprisings in Assisi. *Francesco*, Prologue, chapters 1–8

1190?–1226: Elia's friendship with Francis. *Francesco*, chapters 14, 20, 27, 88, 126

1202: The Battle of Colle della Strada and Francis' imprisonment. *Francesco*, chapters 11–13

1204–1206: Francis' gradual conversion, including his aborted try at knighthood, his dreams, his ministry to lepers, and his time at San Damiano. *Francesco*, chapters 14–34

1208: Francis' first followers. *Francesco*, chapters 48–51

1215?: Elia's reception into the Religio of the Lesser Brothers. *Francesco*, chapter 86

1220: First Franciscan martyrs and reception of Anthony of Padua into the Order. *Antonio*, chapter 1

1220: Cardinal Ugolino, at Francis' request, becomes cardinal protector of the Order. *Francesco*, chapter 98

1221: Gathering of friars in Chapter at the Porziuncula. *Antonio*, chapter 4

1224: Changes, unapproved by Francis, made to friars' lifestyle. *Antonio*, chapter 11

1224: Unrest over Elia's governance of the Lesser Brothers. *Francesco*, chapter 116

1224: Francis receives the stigmata. *Francesco*, chapter 118

1226?: Friar martyred with Rule in his hand. *Antonio*, chapter 15

1226: Francis' progressive illness and death. *Francesco*, chapters 123–127

1227: The papal election of Cardinal Ugolino as Pope Gregory IX. *Antonio*, chapter 20

1230: Elias' role in the construction of the Basilica di San Francesco, Francis' burial, and disruption of the 1230 chapter gathering. *Antonio*, chapters 25–27

1230: The bull *Quo elongati*. *Antonio*, chapter 27

1231: Death of Saint Anthony of Padua. *Antonio*, chapters 31–33.

Helpful Cultural Information

Biblical Quotations: At the time of Saint Clare, there were no standard verse divisions in the Bible and standardized chapter divisions were just being introduced. In this book, biblical quotes are taken from the *Revised Standard*

Version, Catholic Edition, except when they are part of a quotation from the writings of Clare, Francis, or another early source. The citations are given in the chapter notes at the end of each chapter.

Canonical Hours: Time was divided into three-hour segments. The sisters, like all penitents, clergy, and religious at the time, prayed, at specific "hours," certain set prayers called "offices." The modern name for the "hour" is given in parentheses:

> Matins (Office of Readings): First prayer of the morning, usually combined with Lauds
>
> Lauds (Morning Prayer): Prayer at dawn
>
> Prime (This office is no longer prayed): 6 a.m.
>
> Terce (Midmorning Prayer): 9 a.m.
>
> Sext (Midday Prayer): Noon
>
> None (Midafternoon Prayer): 3 p.m.
>
> Vespers (Evening Prayer): between 3 and 6 p.m.
>
> Compline (Night Prayer): 9 p.m. or when darkness was falling

Capitalization: All pronouns referring to God, Christ, and the Holy Spirit are capitalized except those that Clare or Francis or their copyists did not capitalize in their quoted writings.

Chapter Notes and Sources: The notes at the end of each chapter will help the reader separate fact from fiction in this biography. References are expanded in the bibliography.

All historical details in this book are accurate. Conversations, except where noted, are conjectural. All descriptions of Assisi (its buildings, monasteries, convents, architecture, streets, and outlying districts) are accurate unless otherwise noted. All other towns named existed and their history is portrayed accurately.

The names, backgrounds, occupations, relationships, and social standings of all characters are accurate unless otherwise noted. The ages of the characters, with the exceptions of Clare, Francis, and Clare's sister Catarina, are approximations based on available information.

Details regarding life in the comune of Assisi reflect Fortini's research, the primary sources, and the way that various social classes lived in twelfth-

and thirteenth-century Italy. Whether they lived in precisely the way presented is pure speculation, but the general outline of their lives is factual.

Characters: As close as we can tell, the names of the characters are as they would have been in their native tongue. People are named in relation to their ancestors. In Umbrian, Francesco di Pietro di Bernardone means "Francis, son of Peter who is the son of Bernard." The word "di" may be written as "de" or "dei" and in this usage means "child of" or "from." Other than Francis, Clare, and the popes, history records little, if anything, about the physical appearance of most of the people in this book.

Clare's Habit: Clare's habit is described in her *Form of Life* and in artwork by her contemporaries. Her mantle is on display in the Basilica di Santa Chiara. The earliest paintings of Clare show her dressed in a floor-length gray tunic that covers her feet, a hooded gray mantle (cape) that reaches to the floor in the back, a knotted rope cinched around her waist, and a black veil lined with white. Later artists depict Clare with a white wimple that covers her neck and throat. Clare and her sisters did not wear the wimple, which became popular after Clare's death.

Clare's Illness: Clare was so determined to be completely detached from the world and from sin that she undertook many bodily penances, including such rigorous fasting that her health was affected. Those who eat very little for a long time often lose bone mass and can sustain heart damage, electrolyte abnormalities in the blood, kidney problems, intestinal ulcers, loss of muscle, and depletion of body proteins. Clare's persistent illness had many of these symptoms.

Clare's Words: In this book, Clare speaks some of her own words. They are adapted or taken directly from her writings, or from words attributed to her in the *Process* for her canonization and in her first biography, *The Legend of Saint Clare*.

Eucharist: Clare and Francis both had a great devotion to the Eucharist because they recognized Christ in It. The consecrated Host was retained in pyxes, precious boxes, small cupboards, miniature towers, or dove-shaped receptacles, then placed in a niche in the church wall or suspended. In the Church of San Damiano, the Eucharist was kept in a suspended dove and, in the sisters' private oratory, in a small box in a wall niche to the left of the altar. The location of the Eucharist in other churches mentioned in this book is purely hypothetical.

Fasting: Fasting was a bodily prayer that was meant to eliminate natural faults and master the will, making the soul more receptive to grace. As voluntary suffering united to Christ's voluntary self-sacrifice, fasting was a powerful means of praying for the conversion of sinners. Both Francis and Clare granted dispensations from fasting to the weak, ill, or young. They also both fasted excessively, striving for the self-surrender and holiness gained by fasting for the sake of God's kingdom.

Locations: All places are in Italy unless otherwise mentioned.

Nuns and Sisters, Friars and Monks: A "nun" was a consecrated woman living in a convent, while a "monk" was a consecrated man living in a monastery. Most monks and nuns came from the upper classes of society. Convents and monasteries owned property, had servants, and were often rich.

Francis and Clare wanted their followers to come from all social classes and to live as family members in poor, simple communities. Francis called his followers "brothers" ("friars"), who were to pray, preach the Gospel, and work. Clare called her followers "sisters." They were to pray, work, and minister spiritually to others.

Physical Descriptions: The physical descriptions of Clare and Francis are taken from the primary sources (see bibliography), paintings of the period, and detailed studies of their skeletal remains. An anatomically accurate model of Clare's body, which holds her remains, can be seen in the Basilica di Santa Chiara in Assisi. The physical descriptions of other characters are conjectural unless stated otherwise.

Privilege of Poverty: Historically, Clare is said to have received the "privilege of poverty" at various times and from various popes. Currently, a difference of opinion exists among Clare scholars regarding whether this privilege was received and, if so, in what form and when. This book follows the traditional sources, but not all scholars will agree with its treatment of the "privilege of poverty."

Recluses: Also called anchorites, recluses were considered extremely holy penitents. During Clare's lifetime, nearly every city in Umbria supported recluses who were enclosed voluntarily in a small cell or cells, usually adjoining a church. A window in each cell looked into the church so that the recluses could participate at Mass. Recluses followed detailed rules of life, lived on alms, and spent most of their time in prayer—although they often gave spiritual counsel to visitors through a small, curtained window. The recluse was allowed a cat and a vegetable garden, tended by a servant. He or she could also stroll in a small, enclosed yard that might adjoin the cell. Some pious people lived reclusive, hermit-like lives at home. San Damiano was like a large "cell" where all the sisters together lived a poor lifestyle that had much in common with recluses. However, they did not have servants. The sisters themselves served one another and worked together.

Recluses around Assisi were called "Christianas" (*Cristiana* in Italian), or "Christian women," by the townspeople. As stated in the chapter "A New Fioretti" in Marion Habig's *Omnibus*, Francis nicknamed Clare "Christiana" (Cristiana), thus calling her a recluse. In this book, the spelling "Christiana" is used for Francis' name for Clare, to distinguish her from other sisters at San Damiano who were named Cristiana.

San Damiano: This book uses the word "monastery" for San Damiano to distinguish it from the rich "convents" of the time.

Archaeologists agree about some of the layout of San Damiano and speculate about the rest. The author has read various theories and archaeological studies and has pondered early Clare rules to determine a probable layout for the San Damiano complex. Not every scholar will agree with this book's conclusion. Moreover, the way San Damiano appeared in Clare's lifetime is not how it looks today.

Francis gave the sisters a Form of Life that Clare records as a single sentence. Was this Francis' entire Form of Life for the sisters? How did the sisters live? Scholars disagree on the answers to these questions.

In 1215, forced to choose a papally approved Rule of Life, Clare chose the Benedictine Rule. With this came a stricter enclosure than she may have been following. By 1219, she was given a Rule by Cardinal Ugolino. At that time, the speaking grill, Communion grill, choir, parlor, turn (if there were one), and so on would have been introduced if they were not already in place.

The author has studied the strictness of Clare's enclosure and has undertaken much prayer, reading, and counsel with Poor Clares and Clare historians to determine how Clare and her sisters most likely lived. Not all the people and sources agree with the conclusions in this book.

Social Class: Medieval people were honored according to their social class—for example, emperor, king, queen, lord, lady, baron, count. In the Church, clergy were also ranked: pope, cardinal, bishop, priest, deacon, cleric. The term "prelate" referred to any religious authority. The poor had no titles.

Social Mores: Power rested with the nobles, high religious leaders, and military. The merchants and middle classes were attempting to rise in power. The lower classes were powerless and generally disregarded. Below them were the beggars and then, at the lowest social level, the lepers, robbers, and other outcasts.

Clothing indicated social status and rank. The greatest scandal would be to go without clothing, not because nudity was sexually enticing (people slept in the nude, even in hospices where strangers shared beds) but because it indicated destitution and humiliation.

Stages of Becoming a Religious Order: Francis began his conversion as a voluntary penitent. His first brothers were also lay penitents. Clare followed this example as well as that of other penitents whom she knew. However, penitents generally lived in their own homes, not in community. As Francis gained followers who lived a common life with him, their group began to resemble a "*religio*."

"*Religio*" was the canonical term applied to a group of Christians who lived together a faithful life with certain common practices. The Church monitored a religio closely. Should it become sufficiently organized, a religio could become an approved "*ordine*" (religious order). The Church required a religio to submit a written rule of life, which the Church had to approve, before designating a religio as an ordine. Clare's religio became an ordine when the pope approved her Rule while she lay on her deathbed.

Time: In Clare's time, the new year began on March 25, the feast of the Annunciation. However, because that system confuses modern readers, the years in this book reflect current usage.

Titles: Titles for the major sections of this book are phrases from Clare's *Testament*.

Titles for Clare and Her Sisters: Primary sources and documents list several titles for Clare's sisters, including the Poor Ladies, the Enclosed Sisters, the Lesser Sisters, and the Ladies of Saint Mary of Saint Damian at Assisi. Papal documents called the sisters the Damianites of the Order of Saint Damian. Citizens of Assisi seemed to know the women by this term.

In the *Omnibus*, Habig states that Francis always called Clare's sisters "ladies," and Celano uses that term in his biographies. Francis, it seems, wanted his friars to use this term to preserve a respectful distance between the sexes.

Clare called the women "sisters," thus making them equal family members. In formal correspondence, she used the terms "enclosed Ladies," "Poor Ladies," and the "Order of the Poor Sisters," which is the term she uses in her *Form of Life* approved by the pope as she lay dying.

Titles for Francis and His Brothers: At some point, Francis was ordained a deacon, but he never became a priest. Out of respect, Clare often called Francis "Father" because she considered him a spiritual father to herself and to her sisters. Others called him "Brother Francis" (Fra Francesco). The friars were called Lesser Brothers (Friars Minor) from their beginning.

Tonsure: Hair was an object of beauty in the Middle Ages. Tonsure, involving cutting the hair in unattractive ways, was a sign that a person had abandoned a sinful life and was consecrated to God. A male religious kept his hair short and had a bald patch shaved in the center of his scalp. He went bareheaded except in inclement weather, when he might wear a cap or a hood. A female religious had her hair cut up to her ears, kept her hair short, and covered her "baldness" with a veil.

Translation of Italian Words Used

Addio: Goodbye

Bambina: Little girl

Bambino: Little boy

Comune: City-states that developed throughout northern and central Italy in the twelfth century

Consortium: A group of lords who, by mutual consent, shared property and power in a certain area

Del, della: "Of" ("the Piazza del San Rufino" means "the Plaza of the Cathedral of San Rufinus")

Dom: Title of respect for secular and diocesan priests

Fra (shortened from Fratello, Frate): Colloquial name for a religious brother

Grazie: Thank you. Mille grazie: many thanks.

Madonna (plural Madonne): Informal term for My Lady (My Ladies), used for noble girls and women

Mamma: Mommy, Mum

Mercato: Marketplace

Messer (Messers): Old Umbrian title of respect for a man: Mister, Sir, Lord (Lords)

Monte: Mountain

Ordine: Religious Order

Pace e bene: Italian for the Latin greeting *Pax et bonum*," which means "Peace and all good." This was the greeting that Saint Francis used.

Papà: Daddy

Piazza: A wide, open space where several streets come together

Podestà: The elected head of the comune, who had a council to advise him

Poggio: A hill, knoll. Umbria, the district around Assisi, is a series of hills. Many castles of Umbria were built on these hills.

Porta: City gate

Porziuncula: Little portion of land

Religio: An intermediary stage in becoming a religious order

Rivo: Stream, brook

Rivo Torto: Twisted Stream

San, Santa: Saint

Sì: Yes

Strada: Street

Suor (shortened form of Sorella): Colloquial name for a religious sister

Vescovado: Bishop's residence

Via: Street, road

Sometimes history did not record the name of a real character. At other times a character was created to illustrate a certain point. In these instances, the character was assigned an Italian name that indicates one of his or her qualities. The created names in this book are:

Bellezza (the beauty), Mattiolo's mother

Brontolone (the grouch), the grumpy, old beggar

Cappellano (chaplain), San Damiano's chaplain

Forte (the strong one), Lucia's father

Gatta (female cat), San Damiano's cat

Pia (the pious woman), the pious, demon-possessed woman from Pisa

Scherno (the scoffer), Pia's brother

Scuro (the dark one), Mattiolo's father

Penance—Then and Now

Penance means a conversion from sin to God. When people "begin to do penance," they begin their conversion. Saint Clare and Saint Francis began their conversion as penitents and always viewed themselves as such.

During the early 1200s, a great penitential movement swept Europe. The Church recognized the penitential life as a legitimate vocation for the laity, a vocation encouraged by the friars and sisters. Penitents followed rules that were written for them. This book contains some examples of the penitential practices they followed. Today some of these seem strange and masochistic, but they were common at that time. With the permission of a spiritual director or religious superior, penitents undertook these practices as a means of prayer, sacrifice, self-discipline, and identification with the poor and suffering Christ. The practices fostered surrender to God and its accompanying joy.

Fasting on bread and water is popular today. In medieval times, bread was made from whole grains; thus, with water, it could sustain health. Those who fast on bread and water today need to use the same whole grain breads.

Those who wish to undertake other types of penance should consult a spiritual director for guidance, as did Clare and Francis.

The Lay Franciscan Charism Today

An Internet search will reveal numerous Franciscan male and female religious orders. Some of these evolved from Francis' or Clare's original foundations, while others are trying to live his or her original expression today. Lay expressions of the Franciscan charism include not only the largest group, the Secular Franciscan Order (OFS), but also many smaller ones. Those seeking a lifestyle resembling that of Francis' first lay followers may wish to consult the Confraternity of Penitents, whose members "live the Rule of 1221 as closely as possible to its original intent." For more information, see www.penitents.org or write to Confraternity of Penitents, 1702 Lumbard Street, Fort Wayne, IN, 46803, U.S.

Abbreviations for Sources Referenced in the Chapter Notes

Early Documents regarding Saint Clare (as translated by Regis Armstrong in *The Lady: Clare of Assisi; Early Documents* [CA:ED])

1LAg: *First Letter to Saint Agnes of Prague* (CA:ED 43–46)
2LAg: *Second Letter to Saint Agnes of Prague* (CA:ED 47–49)
3LAg: *Third Letter to Saint Agnes of Prague* (CA:ED 50–53)

4LAg: *Fourth Letter to Saint Agnes of Prague* (CA:ED 54–58)

LEr: Clare's doubtful *Letter to Ermentrude of Bruges* (CA:ED 420–21)

FLC1: *Form of Life of Saint Clare* a.k.a. The Rule of Clare (1253) (CA:ED 108–26)

TestCl: *Testament of Saint Clare* (CA:ED 60–65)

BlCl: *Blessing of Saint Clare* (CA:ED 66–67)

FLHug: *Form of Life* provided by Cardinal Ugolino (1219) (CA:ED 75–85)

LRay: *Letter of Cardinal Rinaldo* (1228) (CA:ED 133–34)

PrPov: *Privilege of Poverty* by Pope Gregorio IX (1228) (CA:ED 87–88)

FLInn: *Form of Life* provided by Pope Innocenzo IV (1247) (CA:ED 89–105)

PC: *The Acts of the Process of Canonization* (1253) (CA:ED 141–96)

BC: *Bull of Canonization* of Saint Clare (1254) (CA:ED 263–71)

LCl: *The Legend of Saint Clare* by Friar Thomas of Celano (1255) (CA:ED 277–329)

Early Documents Regarding Saint Francis (as translated
in *Francis of Assisi: Early Documents* [FA:ED]:
The Saint [vol. 1], *The Prophet* [vol. 2], *The Founder* [vol. 3])

Adm: *The Admonitions* (undated) (FA:ED I 128–37)

2LF: *Later Admonition and Exhortation to the Brothers and Sisters of Penance (Second Version of the Letter to the Faithful)* (1220?) (FA:ED I 45–51)

1C: *The Life of Saint Francis* by Friar Thomas of Celano (1228) (FA:ED I 180–308)

AP: *The Anonymous of Perugia* composed by Friar John of Perugia (FA:ED II 34–58)

L3C: *The Legend of the Three Companions* composed by three of Saint Francis' early followers, Friars Leo, Angelo, and Rufino (FA:ED II 66–110)

AC: *The Assisi Compilation* seemingly compiled by Friars Leo, Angelo, Rufino, and possibly others (FA:ED II 118–230)

2C: *The Remembrance of the Desire of a Soul* by Friar Thomas of Celano (FA:ED II 239–393)

Other Biographies and Books

1.5C: *The Rediscovered Life of Saint Francis of Assisi* by Friar Thomas of Celano

13CC: *Thirteenth Century Chronicles*

1MP: *Mirror of Perfection* (Lemmens Edition) (FA:ED III 214–52)

3C: *Treatise on the Miracles of Saint Francis* (FA:ED II 399–468)

LMj: The *Major Legend* by Saint Bonaventure (FA:ED II 525–649)

Fioretti: *The Little Flowers of Saint Francis* (abbreviated *Fioretti*, its name in Italian) (FA:ED III 566–658)

24Gen: *Chronicle of the Twenty-Four Generals of the Order of Friars Minor*

Fortini: Arnaldo Fortini, Assisi mayor and historian, delved into Assisi archives and shared his research in *Nova Vita di San Francesco.* References in this book refer to Helen Moak's 1981 English translation unless otherwise stated.

PART ONE

Set Out on the Path of the Lord

1

Madonna Ortulana di Favarone

Bedroom, Offreduccio House, Assisi, Italy (Late January 1200)

In her dreams, Madonna Ortulana di Favarone smelled smoke. Despite the haze that engulfed her and her galloping chestnut palfrey, Ortulana could see herself clearly, her long, slender legs desperately gripping her mount; her firm, narrow nose, small chin, wisps of blond hair around her prim cap. A plodding line of ox-drawn carts, piled with goods and servants, magically kept pace with Ortulana's rushing steed.

She was racing toward the flame-engulfed, towering, red rock castle of Sasso Rosso, home of friends Messer Leonardo di Gislerio and his family. Flames turned everything red and orange as Ortulana dismounted and pulled loaves from her saddlebags while servants grabbed blankets, pottery, and weapons from the carts. Suddenly, Ortulana's servants changed into a mob of Assisi merchants and artisans. Shouting, they flung the goods at the castle, laughing as each item burst into flame against the walls.

Why were the merchants here instead of hawking their wares in the piazzas of Assisi's *mercato*? Why were they throwing grappling hooks over the walls of Sasso Rosso, climbing through flames, pulling down the house? In a billow of black smoke, Sasso Rosso crumpled like a child's tower of blocks.

The mob disappeared. Terror-stricken, covered with ash, Ortulana was standing in smoldering rubble with Messer Leonardo, his lady, children, and servants. Dainty, five-year-old Madonna Filippa was clutching a charred doll with which she and Ortulana's daughters often played. As Ortulana attempted to wipe it clean, the doll crumbled to soot.

The Gislerios disappeared. Now the smoking rubble was that of Ortulana's house and in it, as dumb-eyed as oxen, stood Ortulana, her husband Messer Favarone, and their children—six-and-a-half-year-old Madonna Chiara, almost-three-year-old Madonna Catarina, and toddler Madonna Beatrice. Instantly, pudgy, towheaded Chiara, wearing a scarlet dress, was alone in the prayer chapel, its fire-riddled wall tapestries wafting smoke into a clear sky as the chapel burst into flame. A bright spark floated upward from where Chiara had been. As Ortulana reached for the glowing cinder, it vanished against the sun.

Ortulana shrieked and awoke.

She was in her dark bedroom.

Through the cracks in her tightly shuttered windows came shouts and the dancing light of flames. The dream must be real.

For centuries, nobles and knights, like her own family and the family into which she had married, had ruled Assisi. Now the common people challenged that order. Barely two years ago, they had forged a new city government, a *comune*. Far more merchants, artisans, and farmers than nobles made up the comune. These lower classes had attacked and burned Sasso Rosso and several other castles and had chosen as governor their own consul in place of the emperor's appointed official.

Now the mob must intend to burn this immense Offreduccio house.

When his father, Count Offreduccio di Bernardino, died, Madonna Ortulana's husband, Favarone, had inherited this house and much of the count's huge estate. Daily, after early morning Mass in the prayer chapel, Favarone either visited his vast properties or hunted game. A quiet, stocky, raven-haired man given to squinting, Favarone could become an enraged bull if anyone threatened his household, but tonight he was away in Cannara.

Throwing back the feather coverlet and woolen blankets, Ortulana bolted out of bed, feeling for her gownlike chemise. Swiftly, she clad her body, not bothering to lace her sleeves or back. Unable to find her mantle, she ran into the torchlit hallway without it, bolting toward the main door that led into this second floor of the house. Young Ioanni di Ventura, his dark beard still fuzz, was supposed to be guarding that door. Ioanni was capable. Courageous. Alert. With deadly accuracy, he could aim his watchman's huge crossbow. Why hadn't he woken her?

Ortulana pounded at the front door. "Ioanni! Ioanni!"

"*Sì*, Madonna," came the puzzled reply.

"What's happening out there?"

"Madonna Savia escaped again. Her family is here in the piazza, trying to take her home."

Ortulana unbolted the door from the inside and cracked it open. A blizzard of driving snow swept across the Piazza del San Rufino. In front of the locked doors of the Cathedral del San Rufino milled a noisy cluster of servants and nobles, torches in their hands. Above the noise came a piercing, heartrending wail. "Let me alone! You're trying to keep me from my babies!" From the Offreduccio stable on the right, beggars, whom Favarone allowed to sleep in the stalls, were shouting, "Shut up! Go home!"

Madonna Savia. When her children and husband had died from plague, the noblewoman had become crazed. Despite having guards assigned to protect her, she sometimes managed to escape her household and wander pitifully through the city, crying for her dead children.

Ortulana closed the door and leaned against it, her knees weak. She was the Countess of Sterpeto, scion of the fearless Fiumi family, sister of bold Count Accarino, descendant of brave nobles and knights going back to Emperor Charlemagne. Possessing great energy and faith, she had made pilgrimages to Rome, Monte Gargano, and the Holy Land, her life endangered by harsh terrain, plague, and bandits. But, because of tonight's dream, the courage that surged in Ortulana's bloodline failed her.

Ortulana sometimes had vivid dreams, each containing some truth. Although Messer Favarone had forbidden her to ride to Sasso Rosso herself, he had agreed to send provisions. Servants had described the rubble, so she must have dreamed it accurately. Yet in her dream, her own house had been torched and Chiara had burned to a cinder.

Terrified, Ortulana hurried through cold halls to the unheated bedrooms. The door to the children's bedroom was open. Oil lamps in the room were lit.

Madonna Bona and Madonna Pacifica, the Guelfuccio sisters who served the Offreduccios, stood as Ortulana entered. In the stark light, the women, wrapped in dark fur mantles, looked exceptionally pale.

Two little bodies, one plump and one thin, each wrapped in a heavy, hooded cape, plunged into Ortulana's gown. Four little arms grabbed her legs. Madonna Chiara and Madonna Catarina.

Catarina was sobbing, her thin ribs heaving. "Mamma, they're gonna bun our house like they bunned Madonna Filippa's."

"We'll fight them off," Chiara declared, stamping her foot.

"No, *mi bambinas*." Ortulana stooped and stroked the children's heads. She had to be strong. "No one is burning anything. No one is fighting anything. Madonna Savia got away again. That's all."

"Oh, my God, *grazie*!" Pacifica dropped to her knees, her full mouth wide with a joyful smile.

Bona planted her fists firmly on her hips, her elbows jutting out from her big body like two wings. "I wouldn't put it past the mob to burn this place."

Catarina sobbed louder. "They're gonna bun us!"

"No one is burning anything," Ortulana said sharply to her lady-in-waiting. She glanced at the shutters. There was nothing beyond them but blackness. The night was still.

Ortulana put her finger to her lips. "Catarina, shh. Listen."

The only sound was Catarina's panting.

"They've gone home," Ortulana said gently. "Back to sleep." She kissed the girls, then looked up at Madonna Bona. "Madonna Beatrice didn't awaken?"

"One-year-olds sleep through anything," Bona said.

"Then good night. I'll put the girls back to bed." Ortulana paused before adding, "Grazie."

Bona and Pacifica nodded as they returned to their bedroom, which adjoined the children's room. Thank God for these sisters, distant relatives of Ortulana, who had served her ever since her marriage. She depended on Bona, big-boned, outspoken and gregarious, to accompany her and tell her everything that was going on in Assisi. Timid, chestnut-haired Pacifica deserved her name—woman of peace. Living as a penitential recluse and leaving the house only to pray, attend Mass, and accompany Ortulana on pilgrimage, Pacifica kept the household grounded in faith. Though both women's Roman noses betrayed their noble background, Pacifica seemed to have forgotten her lineage. She preferred to remain unnoticed, to speak little, and to not even look at men.

The sisters were irreplaceable. How could Ortulana manage this household without them? They could have put her daughters back to sleep. However, for her own peace of mind, Ortulana needed to do that tonight.

Ortulana slipped off the girls' capes, then tucked Catarina and Chiara into their shared bed. She wrapped her chilled body in a feather-stuffed quilt from a chest at the foot of the bed, then sat on the bed and stroked her daughters' foreheads.

Sandy-haired Catarina, worn out from sobbing, fell into swift, peaceful sleep.

Under the layers of warm blankets, Chiara was lying still, her eyes closed.

"Mamma, if they burn our house, I'm going to fight." The child's thin lower lip was firmly set.

"Shh, Chiara. Go to sleep."

"I'm going to fight with Papà and Messer Monaldo, Messer Ugolino, Messer Scipione, Messer Paolo." All her uncles. "And Messer Martino, Messer Giorgio di Ugone, Messer Angelo di Tancredi." Her cousins.

"Shh. Go to sleep, bambina." If Ortulana could sing, she would sing her daughter to sleep.

Chiara was quiet, her eyes closed. But her little body was tense. Ortulana stroked and stroked the child's forehead and patted the snug nightcap that covered Chiara's ash-blond curls.

If they burn our house . . . our house. The first-floor granary, storage rooms, kitchen. The second-floor bedrooms, ladies' sewing room, the great hall with its single hearth. The third-floor servants' quarters and family chapel.

If they burn our house . . . the flames will rise above the Piazza del San Rufino, threatening the adjacent Cathedral del San Rufino. Water in the nearby fountain would be useless against the blaze. Flames might leap across the piazza, destroy the stable, the canons' residence, the Guelfuccio home.

If they burn our house . . . our servants will be homeless. Watchman. Almoner. Maids. Cook. Stablehands. Steward. Squires. Kitchen workers.

If they burn our house . . . we will have to move. Familiar beggars will have to beg coins, food, and clothing elsewhere.

If they burn our house . . . what will happen to Madonna Chiara?

Like smoke, fear billowed up within Ortulana, the same fear that had swelled within her while she was pregnant with Chiara. As Ortulana stroked Chiara's cheek, the memory of her first pregnancy returned. She had feared that her unborn child would die, so she had prayed unceasingly for the baby to live.

One day Ortulana had been given a sign. The day had begun ordinarily enough. Prayer. Mass. Morning work. Prayer. Midday meal. *Siesta.* Then four ladies had assembled in Ortulana's sewing room to stitch, chat, encourage, and counsel each other.

Young, delicate-featured Madonna Alguisa, wife of Messer Giorgio di Ugone, dreamy-eyed, romantic mother of Messer Paolo and Madonna Emilia, anxious to have another girl and name her Ginevra after the queen of Camelot.

Domineering Madonna Bona, whose desire to marry had been thwarted since so many knights had died in war.

Sweet and gentle Madonna Pacifica, content in her secret, single life of penance.

And Ortulana.

After a few hours, the women had walked to the Cathedral del San Rufino for their daily prayers. The cathedral existed, Ortulana acknowledged, partly because of the families of these women entering it. Over sixty years earlier, Giorgio di Ugone's family had given property for the church's expansion. Fifteen years later, the consortium of which Count Offreduccio and Messer Guelfuccio were members did the same.

Above the altar hung a huge crucifix, Christ in glory suspended upon it, His gentle eyes smiling on those who came to worship. Ignoring the shouts and banging of workmen enlarging the cathedral, Ortulana knelt, her eyes fixed on the Lord's face, shadowy in the semi-darkness. On this hot, sultry day, Ortulana, big with child, was weary. Closing her eyes, she had let her silent heart speak.

YOU WILL BEAR A CHILD WHO SHALL BE A LIGHT FOR ALL THE WORLD.

From where had come the words, spoken in a masculine voice? Had only she heard them? Bona, Pacifica, and Alguisa were kneeling silently, their heads bowed.

To Ortulana, that promise became a rare jewel. She had repeated it to herself during labor and then each time plague touched Umbria or Chiara fell ill.

This child whose face she was stroking had been conceived in ardent love. Ortulana had stitched her baptismal gown, breastfed, bathed, and dressed her. She was teaching Chiara to sew, write, read Latin, pray. Servants would not rear Ortulana's children.

Chiara. The name meant "Brilliance."

YOU WILL BEAR A CHILD WHO SHALL BE A LIGHT FOR ALL THE WORLD.

In Ortulana's dream, Chiara had disappeared in fire.

Please, God, Ortulana prayed. *Whatever the dream meant, don't let it mean that.*

NOTES

History records the merchants' uprising and the destruction of Sasso Rosso. The Offreduccios and Gislerios may well have been friends. While Ortulana's fiery dream is the author's invention, she did, while praying before an undescribed crucifix, hear the words "Your child will be a light to all the world" (CA:ED 161). Some historians believe this happened at the shrine of San Michele in Monte Gargano, while others place it in the Cathedral del San Rufino. The postulated description of the San Rufino crucifix is likely for the time.

The wealthy Offreduccios owned all the lands attributed to them in this book (Fortini 329). Their large house, the exact size of which is unknown, was located next to the Cathedral del San Rufino (Fortini 327–28 and footnote). The house's layout and family's lifestyle are imagined from what was typical for the period. At some point, Count Offreduccio died and Favarone inherited the house. Chiara's family was wealthy and generous (CA:ED 195).

Most likely Ortulana was in her teens and Favarone in his twenties when they married. Most modern historians agree that Chiara was the eldest child. Ortulana was a pious, generous woman who went on the pilgrimages noted in this chapter (CA:ED 145), possibly all prior to Chiara's birth. The pilgrimage to the Holy Land must have taken place in 1192 because of unrest in the area prior to that year.

Ioanni di Ventura was the Offreduccio house watchman when Chiara was a young girl (CA:ED 195). Historians do not know when his employment began.

Without giving any other information about her, Fortini mentions an Assisi woman named Madonna Savia who was insane (Fortini 265).

A group of pious, unnamed women relatives used to meet in Ortulana's house. Presumably, Bona and Pacifica were among them. Alguisa, a relative and neighbor, could have been part of this group. Her two children Emilia and Paolo seem to have been older than Chiara.

Ladies-in-waiting were women of slightly lower noble rank who were companions to higher-ranking ladies. Pacifica lived across the piazza from the Offreduccios and accompanied Ortulana on her pilgrimages to Sant'Angelo and Rome (CA:ED 144–45). Bona stayed with Chiara in the Offreduccio house and "many times" brought to the poor food which Chiara had saved from her own meals. She "many times accompanied her to speak to Saint Francis" (CA:ED 192). Without being titled "ladies-in-waiting," Bona and Pacifica seem to have filled that role.

Pacifica was known publicly as a penitent who "had never seen" Favarone (CA:ED 145). Perhaps Favarone was away from home a great deal, hunting and visiting his properties. Men and women had separate rooms in noble houses, and this prevented mingling of the sexes. It's unlikely that Favarone was an invalid. He couldn't have been dead, because he fathered three daughters. When Chiara was seventeen, "her father, mother, and relatives" wanted her "to marry magnificently" (CA:ED 194). Could Pacifica have never seen Favarone because she had adopted a penitential, reclusive life and purposely attempted not to see any man? Public and private recluses were common in Umbria, the area of Italy where Assisi is located.

Pacifica and Bona are named as daughters of Guelfuccio, not as wives of this or that nobleman (CA:ED 144, 192). This may indicate that they never married.

The Cathedral del San Rufino was being enlarged in 1193, the usually accepted year of Chiara's birth. In *St. Clare of Assisi* Nesta de Robeck lists Chiara's traditional birth date as July 16, but this is not provable.

Mothers usually taught their daughters, so Ortulana probably did likewise. Women made their families' clothes; Chiara learned fine stitching from someone, most likely her mother. It seems plausible that Ortulana made Chiara's baptismal gown, whatever it looked like.

Priests were instructed to condemn the common practice of having servants care for the children of the nobility. Ortulana, being a pious woman, would likely follow this instruction and breastfeed and care for her own children.

2

Messer Favarone di Offreduccio

Piazza della Minerva, Assisi (Late January 1200)

R ound-faced Messer Favarone di Offreduccio and his brothers Messer Paolo and Messer Scipione eased their horses through the crowded Piazza della Minerva. Under his jaunty blue cap, Favarone's curly black hair plastered his forehead, while his fur cloak billowed about his blocky body.

Three days ago, the men had left Assisi on a wearisome journey down the Strada del'Arce to inspect Offreduccio lands near the leper colony by San Gregorio's and in the vicinity of Castelnuovo. Then they proceeded to Cannara, where a peasant was accused of stealing and butchering a neighbor's hog, a crime almost excusable during this unrelenting famine. The brothers had stayed two nights in the bailiff's house while deciding in favor of the noble.

Yesterday morning a snowstorm had swept down from the north, detaining the men until it ended and a warm wind, preceded by soft rain, blew in. Today the men had spurred their steeds along the muddy roads, eager to conclude a meeting with Messer Monaldo and return home.

"Messers!"

Favarone squinted toward the left, but his weak eyes could only recognize the blurry, colorfully dressed figure as young Francesco Bernardone approached.

"Messers, please tell your *Madonne* that the damasks from France have arrived." Francesco gestured toward blurred tables covered with indistinct cloth in the street just outside the Bernardone fabric shop.

Favarone nodded as the brothers continued inching their way through the crowd, and shortly they arrived at the less crowded Via San Rufino, where they could ride three abreast.

"Maybe someday he'll be riding with us." Large Paolo's voice and body dwarfed his steed.

"Who?" Favarone and Scipione asked together.

"Francesco."

"You're an *idiota*," Scipione scoffed.

"I heard that his father wants him to become a knight," Paolo retorted defensively.

"He can't. He's a merchant," Favarone argued.

Paolo shrugged. "Pietro has enough money to buy him everything he needs for knighthood and the means to train him for it."

"He could never become a knight like us. He's not born to this position," Favarone insisted.

"And he's too small," Scipione added.

Paolo shook his head. "Doesn't matter. Look at Messer Tancredi di Ugone's gate."

"What about it?"

"Tancredi was the city consul and he bowed to the merchants."

Favarone remembered the gate being broken through the city wall near Tancredi's house in the rich Parlascio section of Assisi. The gate provided a better route to the March via the Norcera and Gualdo roads. "We all benefit from that gate," Favarone said. "Don't we all buy from the merchants who use it?"

"Sure," Paolo agreed. "But Tancredi had the names of merchants and nobles etched together on the keystone."

"He added a cross," Scipione recalled.

"So isn't he saying that merchants and nobles are equal in Christ?" Paolo pressed.

No one replied as they reached Messer Monaldo's house and pulled up their muddy horses. Two squires appeared and took the reins. They would feed, dry, and brush the animals.

"So, what's the meeting about?" Favarone asked, changing the subject as the men clambered upstairs to the second floor.

"Only Monaldo knows," Paolo shrugged.

Resembling twin giants, Monaldo and Ugolino were waiting in the great hall. A blazing fire warmed the room, so Favarone and the others threw their fur cloaks across the far end of one of the long oaken tables. Sitting at another table, they watched Monaldo bolt the door.

Ugolino turned to Favarone. "Guilty?" he asked, his black eyebrows bobbing.

"He stole the pig," Favarone said. "We fined him."

"Pig business done." Ugolino slapped the table with his large, powerful hands and turned to Monaldo. "So, brother. Why this meeting?"

Broad-shouldered Monaldo eased onto the bench next to Favarone.

"I've taken up citizenship in Perugia."

"Come on," Paolo groaned, rubbing his huge hand through his thinning hair. "We want to get home. Stop making jokes."

"I'm not joking."

"What!"

"No!"

"Impossible!"

"Perugia!"

"Assisi's enemy!"

"Without consulting us?"

"Better to be a citizen in hell."

"Quiet!" Monaldo boomed.

The brothers fell silent.

"I became a citizen in Perugia and so will you."

"You can't make our decisions," Scipione decreed, his ruddy face ruddier with anger.

"You will become citizens in Perugia, or you will burn with Assisi."

"No one is burning Assisi," Ugolino noted.

"Look!" Monaldo pushed away from the bench and flung open the shutters of the window behind him. "Out there." In the distance, Favarone could see the fuzzy shape of Monte Subasio. "You see what Rocca Maggiore looks like?" Monaldo demanded.

"We can see it's a skeleton," Paolo replied. Favarone could see only a large, tan blob.

"The emperor's men ruled Assisi for centuries from the Rocca. Then, two years ago, Duke Conrad goes to Narni to meet with Lord Pope, and the people of Assisi—*Assisi*—destroy the Rocca, ignoring Lord Pope's envoys and the emperor's men who tell them to desist."

"Duke Conrad was vicious," Favarone said.

Monaldo stared at his younger brother. "He was the emperor's able captain."

"He did nothing to stop his men from raping and torturing," Favarone shot back.

"War is not nice, Favarone."

"Old Fly-in-the-Brain governed Assisi, Foligno, Spoleto, Norcera, and Rieti brutally and ineffectively. Where was the war then?"

"Don't be stupid, Favarone," Monaldo said. "We are discussing Assisi, not the Duke. Have you forgotten how the people destroyed the castles and towers? Sasso Rosso. Montemoro. Poggio dei figli di Morico. San Savino. Davino. Poggio San Damiano. Poggio di Bucaione. What next? Our castles?"

Monaldo looked from one brother to the next.

"Merchants, artisans, and farmers destroy castles because we ask for our due. Isn't it fair to charge tolls on roads that we build, repair, and patrol? Isn't it right to tax people who keep from starving because they live on our lands?"

"The people want fair treatment." Scipione pushed to his feet, towering over his seated brothers. "Then they will not bother us."

"The people are a mob," Monaldo said. "Merchants and artisans aspiring to be knights, wearing noble clothes, carrying swords. With money they buy titles, status, and respect. It isn't natural. Even angels are in hierarchy."

"Are we gods with rights over other men?" Scipione asked.

"Does it matter?" Monaldo asked. "Commoners outnumber us. We're not safe in Assisi."

"But Perugia?" Ugolino questioned. "Perugia has been Assisi's enemy for centuries."

"Assisi is now the enemy," Monaldo argued. "Messer Girardo di Gislerio of Sasso Rosso has become a Perugian citizen. So has his brother Messer Fortebraccio and his nephew Messer Oddo. The rest of the family will follow."

Favarone understood well the political wrangling. By becoming citizens of Perugia, which was loyal to Lord Pope, the Gislerios—who had property in Assisi, which was loyal to the emperor—had acted cunningly. Assisi collected taxes on property within its boundaries but kept only taxes paid by Assisi citizens. Assisi would never give Gislerio taxes to Perugia, so Perugia would declare war. If Perugia won, the Gislerios would recover their lands. If Assisi won, the Gislerios would switch their allegiance to Assisi and still recover their lands. The Offreduccios, as Perugian citizens, would do the same thing.

"Since we've been good to the people, they may not bother us," Scipione said.

"You have sons," Favarone declared. "Messer Rufino and Messer Paolo are almost knights. I have daughters. How safe would women be in war?"

The men were silent.

"Catarina has had night terrors ever since the castles were destroyed." Favarone looked at the men around him. "What can I do but leave Assisi?"

"Once the people find out that Monaldo has joined Perugia, none of us will be safe. We should leave within the week," Ugolino said.

Thus the decision was made.

The week was filled with packing, preparations, and archers at the windows in case their secret leaving leaked out. How stupid Favarone had been fifteen years earlier when a strange prophet had wandered through the streets, sing-songing, "*Pace e bene!* Peace and all good." Then, young Favarone had wanted war. Now, war wearied and frightened him.

Unlike Ortulana, who prayed before deciding, Favarone acted first and prayed later. Tonight, he would stop to ask God to bring his family safely to an enemy city.

A single candle on the simple altar lit the third-floor prayer chapel. In its ghostly glow knelt a small figure, her chemise almost translucent. Madonna Chiara. She turned toward Favarone as his slippered feet brushed the wooden floor.

"Papà, why can't we stay and fight?"

Favarone knelt and enfolded Chiara's plump body in his arms. The small stones on which she, like a little monk, counted her prayers tumbled out of her lap and clattered against the floor.

"Chiarita, some battles are fought, others avoided. This one we avoid. We will fight others."

Sitting back on his heels, Favarone drew Chiara to his chest. Her thick blond hair, pushed up into a snood, felt like a soft pillow on his breast. With his large hands, he rubbed her pudgy, icy fingers to warm them.

"Why can't we take the beggars with us?"

Favarone sighed at this Offreduccio persistence. For a week, she had been asking this question. "Chiarissima, we cannot take the beggars to Perugia."

"Who will feed them, Papà?"

"Let the merchants feed them." The bitterness in his voice surprised him.

"Some merchants never give the beggars anything."

"Francesco Bernardone is generous."

"Will he feed the beggars?"

"If they go there."

The child's hands felt warmer. Favarone stretched his overblouse over them.

"I'll tell the beggars to beg from Francesco."

Favarone began to rub Chiara's tiny, almost frozen bare feet. "You tell them, Chiarita."

"Is Madonna Ginevra going to Perugia?"

"I don't know. If Messer Giorgio leaves Assisi."

"Will they burn her house? Or ours?"

The child's toes were warming under Favarone's rubbing. "I don't know, Chiarita."

"Does God care about us, Papà?"

"God cares about everyone."

"But does He care about *us*?"

"Of course He cares about us." *I think.*

"Then why are these things happening?"

Favarone tucked the child's warmed feet close to her body and pulled her chemise over them. Then he wrapped his arms tighter around her. How cold she was in this unheated room! "Why do bad things happen, Chiarissima? Only God knows."

"Does God ever tell anybody why they happen, Papà?"

"Maybe. But He has never told me."

Two weeks later, in Perugia, word came that merchants and commoners had torched the Offreduccio house. Not long after, Perugia and Assisi were at war.

NOTES

Favarone is barely mentioned in the primary sources, yet he must have been a religious man because he permitted Ortulana's pious practices and seems to have given more generous alms than were expected.

Fortini (Chapter 4) details Assisi's violent climate and civil war. In 1182, about the beginning of a fifteen-year famine, a stranger went about the streets, calling, "Peace and all good" (Fortini 82–84). Yet civil war, not peace, came to Assisi. Sometime between 1198 and 1202, at the beginning of Assisi's civil war, Monaldo took up residence in Perugia. Chiara's family followed him (Fortini 333). Most likely the other Offreduccios, with the exception of Scipione, did the same.

This chapter postulates that Monaldo made his move after the nobles of Sasso Rosso switched their allegiance to Perugia, beginning with Messer Girardo di Gislerio's request for Perugian citizenship on January 18, 1200. On January 23, Girardo's brother Messer Fortebraccio and nephew Messer Oddo became Perugian citizens. Soon after, the other Gislerio family members followed suit (Fortini 148–49).

Medieval nobles visited their properties, stayed overnight with the managers of their lands, accepted tolls, tributes, and taxes from those who used their property, and saw that justice was done for their serfs and landlords. The fictional incident involving the thief illustrates how the nobility would have handled such a crime.

Francesco was five feet, two inches tall, as evidenced by his skeletal remains in the Basilica di San Francesco.

Chiara counted her prayers on pebbles (CA:ED 282), as monks did, and was known as a prayerful, holy child who sent some of her own food to the poor and who did penance (CA:ED 195). The primary sources give no other details about her childhood.

3

Madonna Benvenuta di Peroscia

Children's Playroom, Benvenuta's House, Perugia, Italy (Early Autumn 1205)

Hefty eleven-year-old Madonna Benvenuta di Peroscia sat on a large pillow in front of her puppet stage and picked at the tangled strings of a Mary Magdalene marionette. Benvenuta, Madonna Filippa, Madonna Ginevra, Madonna Chiara, and Madonna Balvina had been practicing a puppet show on the resurrection of Christ when Benvenuta had dropped the Magdalene. The puppet show was better, Benvenuta thought, than any performed by the canons of the Basilica di San Pietro.

Benvenuta's short, awkward fingers were so clumsy!

"Madonne," came a soft voice.

Benvenuta hadn't heard Mamma enter because Mamma always walked silently in her softly slippered feet. "Madonna Ortulana wants to go to the mercato to buy some vases from Deruta. All your mothers are coming and Catarina, Beatrice, Pacifica, and Bona, too. Do you want to come?"

"Are you going to buy sweets?" Balvina asked. Fat as a puppy, Balvina was two years older than Benvenuta.

"Not today," Mamma said.

Balvina shrugged. "Then I don't want to come."

Benvenuta looked at Chiara, Filippa, and Ginevra. They shook their heads.

"We don't want to come either," Benvenuta said. "We're trying to practice this puppet show for Madonna Catarina and Madonna Beatrice."

"Fine," Mamma said. "We'll see you later." She closed the door gently behind her.

Benvenuta admired Deruta ceramics splashed with dancing maidens, delicate ferns, and beautiful, shimmering flowers. Perhaps Deruta pottery was not sold in Assisi, so the ladies wanted to purchase some before returning home.

"Now we can make the cords," Chiara said. At twelve, Chiara was the tallest of the girls and, with her blond curls, oval face, and high cheekbones, maybe the loveliest.

Benvenuta shoved the Magdalene into Filippa's hands. "You untangle her." Running to the window, Benvenuta stood on tiptoe to watch the women.

"They're gone!"

"And the Magdalene is untangled." Dainty Filippa's melodious voice resembled a sweetly ringing bell.

Benvenuta hung the puppet on a peg behind the puppet stage.

Square-faced Ginevra straightened the puppet, then announced, "Now we can go to the stable."

So they did, with no one to stop them. At Chiara's request, the young, obese groom cut five lengths of rope, his onion-shaped nose bobbing as he sliced. He asked no questions, and soon the girls raced breathlessly back to the playroom, ropes in hand.

"Do you think the groom will tell anyone?" Benvenuta huffed.

"Why should he?" Balvina puffed.

"Penance isn't as good when everyone knows about it," Ginevra noted.

"Let's never tell anyone," Filippa suggested.

The girls agreed.

"Let's start tying," Chiara suggested. "Thirteen knots, one for each of Christ's wounds."

The girls recited the wounds as they tied the knots. Christ sweating blood in the garden of Gethsemane. Soldiers binding Him with rope. High priest slapping Christ. Scourging at the pillar. Crowning with thorns. Soldiers striking Jesus with a reed. Christ's shoulder wound from carrying the cross. Nails in His hands and feet. Gall that burned His parched tongue. Lance in His side.

Balvina extended her finished cord. "If we wear these, we'll be penitents."

"Wearing a cord doesn't make you holy." Chiara's deep voice was direct. "The cord must remind us to love God, to obey Him, to help others. Then maybe we will become holy."

"Let's put on our cords right now," Filippa suggested. So each girl did, hiking up her billowing gown and chemise and cinching the cord tightly around her waist, next to her skin. Each girl smoothed out her skirt, then looked at the others. The gowns hid the itchy cords perfectly.

"Aren't penitents supposed to offer their sufferings to God?" Benvenuta asked. "Let's pray."

As Benvenuta led the way to the chapel, she felt older, wiser, and holier. Penitents had seemed heroic and mysterious until she had met Madonna Pacifica, who laughed, sang, and liked candied oranges, but who secretly wore a hairshirt, prayed, fasted, and shared her food with the poor. Two weeks ago, Madonna Ortulana had the girls read a Latin commentary on the thirteen wounds of Christ. Pacifica, who was listening while she embroidered, casually commented that penitents sometimes secretly wore rough rope cords with thirteen knots to remind them of the wounds of Christ. Each girl had immediately thought of making such a cord, and, during playtime, they had agreed to do so. Today was the first time they had been alone to make them.

The girls knelt in the chapel to dedicate their penance to Christ. The cord was itching madly, but Benvenuta would not scratch. She had chosen this itching penance. *She would not scratch.*

Benvenuta raised her eyes to the tapestry behind the altar. On it, Christ was holding a lamb while a second lamb stood alongside, gazing at Him in adoration. *God, I love You*, Benvenuta began to pray. *Let these itches be little prayers of love.*

She tried to think of something else, but Christ and the lambs were distracting her. She imagined Madonna Chiara and Madonna Balvina as those lambs. Christ was taking them back to their flock in Assisi. Tomorrow the Offreduccios were going home.

When the Offreduccios had left Assisi, Chiara's family had moved in with Benvenuta's. Balvina's father, Messer Martino, the son of Madonna Chiara's uncle Messer Ugolino, had lodged two streets over. For the past five years, Chiara and Balvina had been part of Benvenuta's life.

Filippa and Ginevra were like Benvenuta's sisters, too, but Filippa's family might stay in Perugia forever. Her father, the dark-faced, lanky Messer Leonardo di Gislerio, was scary. He hated Assisi for destroying Sasso Rosso and for killing his son Messer Oddo and his brother Messer Girardo. He cursed Assisi for mutilating and dismembering the enemy dead. Yet Filippa said he wasn't scary to her. When she would wake at night, screaming from night terrors, then her papà would rush into her bedroom and rock her in his big arms, promising that they would never return to Assisi.

Although Filippa might stay in Perugia, Ginevra could return to Assisi. Her family lived near Madonna Chiara's. They were friends, and Ginevra's father, Messer Giorgio di Ugone, didn't hate Assisi.

The cord was itching. Benvenuta would not scratch. But she couldn't think about the thirteen wounds. She could only think of Chiara and Balvina. Balvina was kneeling on her heels, her head bent low. Chiara was lying on the floor, weeping silently. They always prayed that way.

She would never see Chiara or Balvina again. Tears squeezed out of Benvenuta's eyes and trickled down her cheeks.

Was suffering in the heart worse than suffering in the flesh?

How many goodbyes did Jesus say? Goodbye to God the Father when He came to earth. Goodbye to Bethlehem when He went to Egypt. Goodbye to Egypt when He went to Nazareth. Goodbye to Joseph when Joseph died. Goodbye to Mary when He left home to preach. Goodbye to John the Baptist. Goodbye to disciples who deserted Him and to relatives who did not understand Him. Goodbye to those He cured. Goodbye to Lazarus, Martha, and Mary. Goodbye to Judas. Goodbye to His Mother and to His apostle John at the cross. Goodbye to those in the afterworld who saw Him after He died. Goodbye to everyone when He ascended into heaven. Thirteen goodbyes. Like thirteen knots on the cord. Like thirteen wounds of Christ.

Saying goodbye was like a wound.

But goodbyes didn't have to be forever. Wouldn't Chiara and Balvina always be part of Benvenuta's life? Weren't all the girls one in Christ?

Benvenuta rubbed the irritating cord. The girls had pledged to wear their cords always. The ropes bound them to God and to each other. Bound them together like sisters. Forever.

NOTES

Chiara's family lived with Benvenuta's family in Perugia (CA:ED 150, Fortini 333). In *Clare: Her Light and Her Song*, Sister Mary Seraphim records Benvenuta's family name as Peroscia. However, Peroscia is an old name for Perugia. The primary sources do not mention Balvina's or Ginevra's families relocating to Perugia, although they probably did. Filippa did relocate with her family (Fortini 333–34). History records no other details of Chiara's stay in Perugia.

Fortini speculates that Oddo and Girardo di Gislerio were killed in the war with Assisi, because their names disappear from the archives at that time. But this could be a false supposition, as historian David Flood pointed out to the author. Using Assisi archives, Fortini gives 1205 as the year when Chiara's family returned to Perugia. Other historians give other years.

Deruta, a town in the outlying districts of Perugia, is still recognized for its fine ceramics. Whether these were sold in Perugia and not in Assisi is unknown.

Chiara, in religious life, wore a cord with thirteen knots, representing Christ's thirteen wounds, underneath her habit. No one knows when she adopted this penitential cord.

Chiara prayed while prostrate (CA:ED 146) and frequently cried profusely while praying (CA:ED 156, 168). Apparently, she had "the gift of tears," a spiritual gift to release intense emotions in prayer through spontaneous weeping.

Marionettes were popular children's toys. Canons (clerics) in several medieval churches, possibly including San Pietro, used marionettes and puppets to teach Bible stories. Using puppets to dramatize non-religious tales came later.

4

Madonna Pica

Bernardone House, Assisi (Early Autumn 1205)

At the hour of Sext, stoop-shouldered Madonna Pica locked the doors to her husband Pietro Bernardone's basement cloth shop and wearily climbed the stairs to the family's living quarters. After the midday meal and rest, Assisi shops would reopen. Too tired to work at standing erect, she entered the dining room hunched but relaxed.

As usual, Francesco was littering the table with bread. Before Pietro had left on this buying trip to France, he had tried to stop Francesco from giving the beggars so much food. "Give them trenchers only," he had ordered. That attitude befitted Pietro. Let the family eat their saucy, juicy meals on fat slices of bread, and then, like everybody else, give the sopping dough to beggars. So Francesco was serving food on many sliced loaves, creating many trenchers.

Quick, sturdy footsteps sounded on the stairs; then Pica's lithe, dark-haired son Angelo bounded into the room. "Messer Tancredi di Ugone wants fine silk for thirty banners," he whooped. "Perhaps the other city consuls will want new banners also. Won't Papà be delighted?"

Angelo bent to lightly kiss Pica, then playfully slapped her back. "Straighten up, Mamma. You look like an old woman." Then he sat at the table and picked up a loaf in each hand. "So, Francesco, you're still crazy."

"Angelo, you mustn't say that," Pica scolded.

"Mamma, he's only joking," Francesco said.

Pica wasn't so sure.

"No need to put all this bread out tomorrow," Angelo said, slicing one of the loaves in two and putting it on his platter. "Tomorrow you can send all the San Rufino beggars back to San Rufino. The Offreduccios returned last night." Angelo scooped some eel onto his trencher. "You must go to see them, Mamma."

"Angelo, we haven't said a blessing," Pica reminded.

Angelo bowed his head. Pica and Francesco settled into their seats. Together the three recited the Our Father.

"Amen."

Angelo smacked his lips. "The Offreduccio nobles have absolved the comune of any responsibility to rebuild their homes." He set aside his slightly soiled trencher and put a fresh one on his platter. "Messer Aguramonte di Giovanni di Matteo, Messer Andrea dell'Isola, and several others have done the same thing." Angelo laughed. "The nobles say that Assisi has already compensated them for their damages." Angelo looked from Pica to Francesco, then broke into a detestable, know-it-all grin. "They have never been compensated. But the nobles wish to return so badly that they will say anything. Five years ago, they left Assisi fast enough. Now they scramble to return."

All because of Philipp of Swabia.

Would war never end? Pica was weary of hearing endless political discussion at the dinner table. If only her family were as concerned about God as they were about government. She had heard the convoluted story so many times. And it just kept going on and on. First the commoners had rebelled. Now they ruled Assisi through their elected consuls. The war with Perugia had been bloody. In 1203, Perugia declared that it would make peace if Assisi repaid damages to the nobles who had left. Messer Leonardo di Gislerio and Messer Monaldo di Offreduccio each claimed thirty *libbre* in damages. Where was Assisi to get that amount of money?

Assisi wrote its own "peace paper," levying heavy penalties against the deserting nobles. The comune would confiscate their goods and appropriately punish any turncoats who returned to Assisi.

Philipp of Swabia changed the stalemate. Since Emperor Heinrich VI died in 1198, Philipp and Otto of Brunswick had been vying for the empire. They challenged each other and Lord Pope, who claimed several cities for the Church. Last year, Philipp sent his forces into this part of the empire to reconquer papally occupied cities. Perugia remained loyal to the papacy, but Assisi swore allegiance to Philipp. Philipp recognized the city's comune government led by the common people and the guilds as long as their elected consuls pledged allegiance to him. Philipp threatened to revoke privileges of nobles who opposed this arrangement.

Philipp was strong. Surely he would conquer the Church-controlled cities, because God seemed to have abandoned the corrupt Church. Many priests kept mistresses. Some were drunkards, others more concerned with acquiring money, land, and honor than with God. The majority knew nothing about preaching.

Papally-controlled Perugia had evaluated the situation and issued a peace treaty on August 31. As before, the treaty ordered Assisi to compensate the nobles for damages and to rebuild their homes, but the nobles claimed that Assisi had already compensated them and did not have to rebuild their homes, leaving Assisi no reason to punish them when they returned.

When a noble returned to Assisi, Pica, under orders from Pietro, was to forget that her sons had helped destroy the nobles' homes. She was to welcome the nobles back, bring a few sweet cakes, and remind them that Pietro's shop supplied the best cloth to remake ruined wall hangings, bed coverings, banners, and pillows.

So, after a midday rest, Pica planned to go to the Offreduccios. Angelo would manage the shop. What Francesco would do, Pica didn't know. Sometimes he worked with Angelo. Other times he disappeared, and he might not return home until dawn pinked the sky. He said he was praying through the night in abandoned churches.

What had happened to Francesco? As Pica walked through the streets of Assisi, she reviewed his life, trying to make sense of it.

Francesco had always wanted to become a knight. In the war with Perugia, Pietro had equipped him with the best armor. Francesco had been confident in Assisi's eventual victory until November three years ago, when the cities had clashed at Colle della Strada. What brutality had Francesco witnessed on that knoll that marked the border between the two cities? The Perugians, who mutilated, dismembered, and disemboweled the dead, had captured twenty-one-year-old Francesco, imprisoning him in a dirty, dank cell with the nobles. What he had experienced there, Pica shuddered to imagine.

When, after a year, Perugia finally agreed to Pietro's negotiations for his son's release, a near-dead Francesco was carted home. For weeks, Francesco fought sickness, delirium, madness, and death. Pica had lived at his sweat-sopped bedside, begging heaven for his life and his sanity. Life had been granted, but sanity?

By mid-spring, a stronger Francesco took to walking, first in Assisi and then outside. A restless uncertainty gripped her son; where he went, Pica didn't know. When he began to work in the shop, he did so without his characteristic flair. Sometimes illness would recur, sending him to bed and Pica to her knees.

Francesco's vigor returned when he heard that the noble, victorious knight, Sir Gautier de Brienne, was coming to Apulia. Pietro had outfitted him gloriously as a knight. Francesco set off and returned the next day. Why? Because of some dream he had about an enchanted castle filled with armor and weapons and housing a beautiful bride. Somehow, he thought this would be his. But he wasn't making any effort to make the dream come true. Instead, he was back with his friends, throwing big parties and dancing through the streets at night. Then he had another dream where he saw that bride again, but now in rags and barefoot.

Why did he even care about these dreams? Pica hated to admit that maybe the townspeople were correct when they whispered that Francesco had gone mad. Poor Francesco! What was happening to him? *Lord, take care of him*, she prayed. It had become her constant prayer.

Praying it over and over, she soon was crossing the Piazza del San Rufino, walking toward the severely damaged Offreduccio house. Forcing herself to stand erect, she made her way up the half-collapsed stairs and found Madonna Ortulana attempting to bring some order to the charred master bedroom.

The women hugged a bit self-consciously. Pica shared the sweet cakes and invited Ortulana to peruse Pietro's fabrics to redecorate the house. Ortulana sent Madonna Bona and Madonna Chiara, now a tall young maiden with an oval face and a husky build, to buy inexpensive cloth to cover the walls.

After Pica had visited other homes, persuading other ladies to purchase Pietro's goods, she returned to the shop. As she entered, Francesco, his eyes shining, grabbed her hands and pressed them to his face.

"Mamma! You remember my dream about the castle and the beautiful lady? And then the lady came again, barefoot and in rags?"

Pica nodded.

"Madonna Chiara came today to purchase cloth. Mamma, she reminded me of the lady in my dreams! What do you think it means?"

"I don't know," Pica said, stunned. Could some significance underlie such strange visions? "Perhaps God will explain things to you." She certainly couldn't.

NOTES

The civil war between the nobles and the common people established Assisi as a comune, that is, a city-state ruled by citizens elected by the people, not by the nobles. Upon their return to Assisi, Monaldo and Favarone absolved Assisi from making restitution to them, as did the other nobles mentioned in this chapter. Favarone's and Monaldo's homes were damaged (Fortini 333–34).

The history regarding the war with Perugia, the treaties, and the jockeying of Philipp, Otto, and the pope is accurate. At that time, the papacy, holding cities and lands, was a political as well as a religious institution.

Francesco's birth, activities, illnesses, and visions follow the primary sources. He had at least one brother, Angelo. Francesco spread extra bread on the table for the poor when his father was not home (FA:ED II 73), and Pietro seems to have been away a good deal. If the San Rufino beggars begged from Francesco, he would have fed them.

Pietro could certainly have instructed Pica to welcome the nobles back to Assisi, because he was always looking for ways to please his customers and increase business. It is possible that Chiara visited the Bernardone shop.

Francesco had a vision of a bride in an enchanted, armor-filled castle (FA:ED II 245). No mention is made of a woman in Francesco's ecstasy in the street, although at this time he told his friends that he was thinking of taking the most beautiful, noble bride in all the world (FA:ED II 72). Biographers believe that he had in mind the woman of the first vision, whom historians consistently identify as Lady Poverty. Could Lady Poverty have resembled Chiara? Noble Chiara lived in a large, palatial house filled with the armor of knights. She eventually relinquished this to embrace Gospel-inspired poverty, to become

Lady Poverty in the flesh. After his conversion, Francesco consistently hesitated to become involved with women, yet he sought out Chiara to preach to her (CA:ED 167, 183). God gave Francesco a vision about noblewomen living at San Damiano (CA:ED 60–61). How did Francesco know which noblewoman to entrust with this vision? Did God use Francesco's visions to pave the way for his acceptance of Chiara?

Together Francesco and Chiara begot many spiritual children. These followers turned to Chiara as "mother" when their "father" Francesco died.

5

Madonna Balvina di Martino

Offreduccio House, Assisi (Late January 1206)

Fourteen-year-old Madonna Balvina was leaning over a small table in one of the women's rooms in the Offreduccio house. She had angled her bulky body to keep her shadow from falling across the parchment on which Madonna Chiara was writing. The letter was going to Madonna Benvenuta and Madonna Filippa in Perugia. Balvina was supposed to be think-ing of news to share. So were Chiara's sisters, Catarina and Beatrice, who were seated on pillows on the rush-covered floor.

Brrr! Despite the tightly closed shutters on the narrow windows, the room was cold. Heat radiating from fireplaces in the great hall and the kitchen was minimal here. Balvina pulled her fur-lined mantle tighter about her and tugged her cap over her ears.

"Did you tell them how Madonna Amata looks all over and how she holds onto your finger?" Balvina asked.

"I'll tell them."

Balvina's big-eyed, tiny-fingered sister Amata had been born at the family's castle, Correggiano, but Balvina's mother had come to the Cathedral del San Rufino to be churched and blessed after giving birth. The family was staying with their Offreduccio relatives to celebrate.

What was that clatter? As Balvina looked toward the doorway, into the room burst Madonna Ginevra, her solid, square face red with exertion, her mantle cockeyed.

"Come on! Now! Or we'll miss it!" Ginevra panted.

"Miss what?" Balvina asked.

"Francesco Bernardone is on trial at Bishop Guido's. For stealing. Now, come on!"

"How do you know?" Balvina asked.

"Because my big old brother Messer Paolo was talking with the other knights and they told him. He and Madonna Emilia are at the bishop's palace already. Now *come on*." Ginevra tore out of the room. The girls followed, bounding through the hall and clattering down the stairs.

"Ioanni," Ginevra called to the house watchman, "we're going to the bishop's. Tell Madonna Ortulana." And the girls were racing across the piazza and down the steep, winding streets to the bishop's court, the Vescovado, their luxuriant mantles billowing behind them.

In the January air, the piazza in front of the bishop's palace was misty with human breath. Even the balconies were packed. All of Assisi seemed present.

"I can't see," complained seven-year-old Beatrice.

"Excuse us," Ginevra said, elbowing through the crowd, making way for the girls. They pushed forward to the extreme left of the bishop's stairs. A few snowflakes drifted down. The girls tugged their mantle hoods over their hats.

"Oh, there's Francesco," Ginevra said, pointing to their far right.

There in a tight circle stood the Bernardone family. Smiling Francesco. Scowling Pietro. Worried-looking Pica. Self-assured Angelo.

"Don't Francesco look happy?" a man behind the girls sniggered.

"Crazy, you mean," a woman's high, thin voice responded. "That green cloak and tunic he's wearing are beggar garb."

"I seen him wearing worse than that, going about the streets half-dazed."

"People say he's praying." The voices behind came quick and sharp.

"I seen kids sling stones at him. He bows to them like they was little princes."

"Went on a pilgrimage to Rome."

"Been tending the lepers at San Lazzaro d'Arce. Gotta be crazy to do that."

"I seen Pietro try to beat some sense into Francesco. Didn't work."

"Pietro even imprisoned him in his house. No use. Madonna Pica let him out."

"Shhh." A great hush swept the crowd as Bishop Guido, wearing his immense mitre and wrapped in a blue velvet mantle, emerged from the doorway of his house. With great dignity, he maneuvered his huge body to sit in the bishop's chair placed at the top of the stairs. Around him swarmed the canons of the bishop's church, Santa Maria Maggiore, as well as the acolytes, assessor, vicar, notary, and knights.

Snow was drifting lightly earthward. Balvina pulled her hood far over her head to keep the snow out of her face.

A bell rang.

"Shhh."

Silence.

"Pietro, what is the problem?" Bishop Guido's voice thundered across the piazza, a huge puff of steam coming from his mouth.

"Messer Bishop, my son is a thief." Richly dressed Pietro grabbed Francesco by his thick, dark hair and dragged him to the stairs. "He took my horse and bolts of cloth from my shop, then sold them in Foligno and gave the money to the priest at San Damiano."

"Is this true, Francesco?" Bishop Guido asked, his eyes widening in his rotund, beardless face.

"Sì, Messer Bishop."

Pietro shook Francesco violently.

"Francesco, does the priest have this money?" the bishop asked.

"No, Messer Bishop," Francesco grunted. "He wouldn't take it. It's here." Squirming under Pietro's grip, Francesco patted the pouch attached to his belt.

"Good." Bishop Guido settled back in his chair. "So, what do you want, Pietro?"

"I want my money back." Pietro shook Francesco again and lifted his massive hand as if to strike his son, then thought better of it and released his grip on Francesco's hair. Francesco rubbed the sore spot.

"Francesco, why would you steal your father's goods and sell them without his permission, then give away the money that was rightly his?"

"Messer Bishop," Francesco said, straightening up, "the crucifix at San Damiano spoke to me. 'Francesco, rebuild My house, which, as you can see, is falling into ruin.'" Francesco's voice was exultant. "The money was to rebuild San Damiano."

"Who in God's name is San Damiano?" asked a raspy voice behind Balvina.

"Him and his brother San Cosmas was famous doctors. Don't you know nothing?"

"Where the hell is San Damiano?" the voice croaked.

"Down in the woods near the Via Cupo di San Petrignano. In the Balia di Genga. You go out the Porta San Giorgio."

"The road past them old Roman tombs and funeral monuments. Down the steep hill of San Feliciano."

"That old church? He gotta be crazy. Why'd God tell anyone to rebuild that dump?"

"Did God tell you to steal?" The bishop's voice boomed across the piazza.

"No, Messer Bishop." The answer came softly, contritely.

"Francesco," the bishop continued, "a disobedient son may be banished from Assisi at his parents' request. No one may feed or help him in any way. Upon the request of two of your relatives, you could be imprisoned until your family chooses to release you."

Francesco squared his shoulders. "Messer Bishop, those laws don't concern me. By the grace of God, I've become a servant of the Most High by living as a lay brother with Dom Pietro, the priest at San Damiano."

"Do you presume to tell me what I already know?"

"No, Messer Bishop, I was merely pointing out. . . ."

"Francesco," the bishop interrupted, "you have been brought before this episcopal court precisely because you have declared yourself to be a lay brother. Had you taken the money and horse under other circumstances, you would be subject to the penal laws."

"I know, Messer Bishop."

"Do you know, too, how wrong it is for a man dedicated to God to do what you've done with another man's goods?"

"I hadn't thought of it, Messer Bishop."

"Well, think now, Francesco. You have greatly upset your father. Give him back his money. God will provide other means for the restoration of the church."

Quickly, Francesco removed the pouch from his belt. "Messer Bishop, I will gladly give back to my father all his gold." He handed the pouch to Pietro, who grabbed it forcefully. "In fact, I will happily give back to him everything that belongs to him." So saying, Francesco bounded up the stairs past the bishop and into the bishop's residence, leaving shoe prints behind on the snow-dusted steps. An acolyte bounded after him.

"Wait," the bishop called to the acolyte. "Let him go."

Moments passed before Francesco, holding his clothes and shoes, reappeared. But for a sleeveless hairshirt, he was totally naked, as destitute as the poorest beggar.

The crowd gasped.

The bishop bolted to his feet. "Francesco, what are you doing?"

"Listen to me, all of you, and understand," Francesco called out, his gaze sweeping the crowd. "Until now I have called Pietro di Bernardone my father. But, because I have proposed to serve God," he continued joyously as he ran down the stairs, "I return to him the money on account of which he was so upset, and also all the clothing which is his, wanting to say from now on: '*Our Father who art in heaven,*' and not 'My father, Pietro di Bernardone.'" Then Francesco knelt before Pietro and held the clothing toward his father, who snatched it fiercely.

Quickly Bishop Guido descended the stairs, then deftly undid the golden clasps of his mantle and tenderly draped the cloak over Francesco's shoulders. Wrapping the mantle around the young man's wiry body, the bishop helped him to his feet and guided Francesco back up the stairs. Then he turned toward the crowd and called in a loud but tremulous voice, "This trial is concluded. Francesco has declared publicly his desire to follow God and to relinquish all that his family could give him. Pietro, take what is yours and go."

Lifting his right hand, the bishop traced a silent sign of the cross over the piazza. In a giant, sweeping motion, the crowd crossed themselves. Then the bishop put his arm around Francesco's shoulders and led him into the bishop's house. The acolytes, canons, knights, notary, assessor, and vicar silently followed. The door closed. The light snow fell.

The speechless crowd parted to let Pietro stalk through, followed by straight-backed Angelo and stoop-shouldered, weeping Pica. Then the spell of disbelief began to lift. Here and there whispering began, snickering, jeers. Suddenly everyone seemed to be talking.

The girls were stamping their feet to get warm when the door to the bishop's house reopened and finely dressed Bishop Guido, minus his mitre, appeared in the doorway. Beside him walked Francesco, barefoot and clad in a long, ragged farmer's tunic. Bishop Guido must have given the tunic to Francesco—the bishop's farmland lay just outside the wall.

Francesco fell to his knees. The bishop made the sign of the cross over him, then laid his big hands on Francesco's head. After a few moments, the bishop raised Francesco to his feet, hugged him, and kissed him on one cheek and then the other. Francesco bowed slightly, then skipped down the stairs, bowed to the girls, and called, "Pace e bene!" Dancing and singing, he wove through the laughing, jeering crowd, bowing to those on his left and right, prancing toward the Piazza del Santa Maria Maggiore exactly as he had done when he led his friends dancing in the streets.

Soon, Francesco was out of sight.

"Let's go home," coaxed Beatrice. "I'm cold."

The crowd had thinned enough for the girls to push their way through. They had made their way through the Piazza del Santa Maria Maggiore when Balvina realized something.

"Where's Madonna Chiara?"

"She was still standing in the Vescovado when we left," Ginevra said.

"What was she doing?"

"Looking at where Francesco Bernardone had gone. Don't worry about her. She knows how to get home."

Balvina felt odd heading home without Chiara. But Balvina was hungry, and it was time for the evening meal. The girls chattered about Francesco, how he would survive, and whether he was crazy or holy to do what he'd done.

On the stairs of the Offreduccio house, Balvina hesitated before following the other girls inside. She was starving, and she could smell roasted peppers, garlic, and savory sauce—dinner in the warm great hall. But what about Madonna Chiara?

Before she could decide whether to look for her, she spotted Chiara, her mantle pulled tight around her, walking briskly into the piazza from the Via San Rufino. Her gaze was cast downward, as if she were deep in thought. Chiara hurried past the Offreduccio house, tugged open the door of the Cathedral del San Rufino, and disappeared inside.

How could Chiara pray when it was time to eat?

Impulsively Balvina scurried down the stairs and ran to the cathedral.

Inside, in front of the wall niche holding the ornate silver box that contained the Body of Christ, Chiara, clad in her mustard-colored dress, was kneeling, her head almost to the floor.

Brrr. It was cold in here. Why had Chiara taken off her mantle?

From the shadows, a hand poked at Balvina. Startled, she turned and caught the gaze of a grimyfaced beggar. Having no alms to give, Balvina turned away, then gasped as she realized that the beggar was snuggled in Chiara's mantle.

Christ's words flashed across Balvina's mind. I WAS NAKED AND YOU CLOTHED ME.

Something of grace was happening here. To disturb that would be wrong. Quietly, Balvina opened the cathedral door and backed out into the lightly falling snow.

NOTES

Chiara seems to have kept in touch with her friends in Perugia.

Balvina and Amata were Chiara's cousins, daughters of her cousin Martino (Fortini 352 footnote). Possibly Amata was born at Correggiano and her mother churched at San Rufino.

The exact date of Francesco's disrobing in 1206 or 1207 is unknown. Historians generally agree that this happened in winter or early spring. The activities of Francesco, his parents' reactions, the unfolding of the trial, and the bishop's response are in the primary sources. No account mentions snow, although heavy snows occurred around this time in Assisi (Fortini 226).

The Legend of the Three Companions records Francesco's words to the crowd (FA:ED II 80).

Prior to reaching marriageable age, children were given complete freedom to play in the streets. When girls attained marriageable age, they were then kept indoors, out of danger and away from prying eyes. As a child, Chiara could have witnessed Francesco's disrobing. If she did not, she certainly heard of it because it became the talk of the town.

Francesco's action had an immediate, profound effect on Chiara, who stated that shortly after his conversion, she herself began to do penance (CA:ED 61). She did not detail what she meant.

Francesco's disrobing broke no moral or civil laws, because people were not prudish about nudity. Men and women slept nude, except for hats that they wore to bed. Maids assisted noblemen and women at their baths, often taken together. Within the home, people often saw each other without clothing. Clothing was not worn for modesty; it was worn to indicate social class. Only those who had nothing to wear appeared unclothed in public. To appear naked in public was a disgrace because it indicated the depth of the individual's poverty and his or her exclusion from a clothed society.

The words of Jesus, "I was naked," are taken from Matthew 25:36.

PART TWO

The Lord Gave Us the Light of His Grace

6

Messer Ranieri di Bernardo

Piazza del San Rufino, Assisi (May 1210)

Beneath his shirt of scarlet silk and his fine gray cape, Messer Ranieri di Bernardo's heart was pounding. He plucked off his small cap with its upturned brim and ran his fingers through his curly black hair. Again he checked the four bulging saddlebags. Each was securely fastened. His angular, lightly bearded cheeks and strong forehead felt tense. Never had he been this nervous. Fighting for love was worse than fighting for life.

How intensely he loved his distant cousin, Madonna Chiara! Polite. Pleasant. Beautiful. Good. People said that she was a saint because she fasted, prayed, and sent choice food to the poor.

Ranieri's tension was spooking his dappled-gray mount, so he slacked the reins. The knights accompanying him fell into line on either side. Hooves beat an uneven staccato on the stone Piazza del San Rufino.

Messer Rufino di Scipione maneuvered his horse alongside Ranieri's. The short knight's broad face was earnest. "Don't worry. Madonna Chiara always used to tag behind you at family feasts. She likes you."

"She's rejected so many other suitors," Ranieri said.

"She's not yet seventeen. She doesn't know whom she wants," Messer Ugolino di Pietro Girardone commented. The knight's statuesque posture lent credence to his words.

"The others were not as wealthy as you," remarked Messer Martino di Ugolino di Offreduccio, the creases on his forehead arching.

"Or as good-looking!" Rufino's gentle eyes sparkled.

"Good-looking is a matter of opinion," Ranieri said.

"But wealth is not," Martino pointed out. "Messer Rufino and I know that our uncle Messer Favarone wants Madonna Chiara to marry well. You're well-off indeed, my cousin."

"Madonna Chiara will obey her parents," declared Messer Ugolino di Pietro Girardone. Naturally Messer Ugolino would think of obedience. Years ago, he, wed barely six months, had sent his disobedient and willful wife Madonna Guiduzia back to her parents. He had refused to see her since.

"My sister Madonna Ginevra says, 'Talk to Madonna Chiara about God,'" Messer Paolo di Giorgio di Ugone offered, his dark eyes flashing.

"And about Fra Francesco Bernardone," Rufino added. "He's often spoken to her about Christ. Madonna Chiara follows all that Francesco does."

The Offreduccio stable doors creaked open. At last! Here came the women. Messer Paolo's sister, girlish Madonna Emilia with a splash of freckles across her nose. Messer Bernardo da Suppo's doe-eyed daughter Madonna Cristiana, who was living as Chiara's companion. Chiara's constant escort, the imposing Madonna Bona. Messer Martino's daughter, the incredibly plump Madonna Balvina. Chiara.

The women were seated discreetly, their colorful gowns draped across their legs, covering even their feet, their dainty caps perched on their heads. Although the older Bona's hair was caught up at her neckline in a pouch of thick net, the younger women had let their long hair cascade across their shoulders to their breasts and beyond. In her saffron gown and deep blue mantle, fastened with a golden brooch, blond-haired Chiara rivaled the sun and sky in radiance.

Ranieri bowed to Chiara and she, smiling daintily, bowed back. Ranieri spurred his horse into an easy walk. Chiara urged her walnut-colored palfrey to keep pace with Ranieri's. The others stayed behind, out of earshot, for Ranieri had planned this excursion to court Chiara.

"God has answered my prayers for a perfect outing, Madonna Chiara."

"God be praised for this beauty." Chiara's voice was lilting, almost a song.

I praise Him especially for you, Ranieri thought. *You are more beautiful than anything else in God's creation.*

Ranieri led the way to the Porta San Giorgio, then down the wide, gravel-lined path that soon led into the Via Cupo di San Petrignano. The horses walked lazily down the steep hill of San Feliciano. Ranieri's conversation was light. What were they even discussing?

Chiara was so beautiful, her complexion flawless, her body well-rounded in all the right places. If only they were wed. Then, alone in this quiet forest, he would remove Chiara's cap and run his fingers through her long golden curls, pushing them away from her spacious forehead. He would stroke her soft, flushed cheeks and kiss her full pink lips, and love her. How badly he wanted to make her his wife!

Ranieri caught himself. He could see, farther down the steep incline, the pinkish-white stone of San Damiano. How many times had he rehearsed what he was about to say?

"Madonna Chiara, just ahead is San Damiano, the church that Fra Francesco first repaired." Ranieri always passed San Damiano on his way to the Strada Francesca, the road that led to France. "Would you care to go in to offer a prayer?"

Chiara broke into a grin. "Most happily."

Ah, things were going as planned. The riding party reined their horses in front of the chapel. Ranieri dismounted, then helped Chiara from her saddle. Taking her by the hand, he led her into the dimly lit church.

Who was leading whom? Chiara was walking ahead of him, directly to the front of the church, where steps led up to a raised altar. Other steps led down to the dark crypt below it. Chiara fell to her knees directly in front of the altar. Ranieri knelt beside her, with the other nobles clustered about them on the rose-colored pavement.

Behind the altar was a huge crucifix of the glorified Jesus. On a red, gold, and black background, Jesus' thin arms were stretched over the faithful. His eyes were wide open, His face serene. A golden halo protruded from the background so that Jesus' face tipped forward. The crucifix was teeming with angels and human figures. At its top, a miniature risen Jesus stepped into glory.

Lord, let her consent to marry me.

Ranieri's gaze strayed to Chiara. She was kneeling sturdily, a few tears snagged on her long lashes, her eyes fixed on a wooden dove suspended above the altar. The Body of Christ was reposed in the dove.

He should not stare at her beauty, so he closed his eyes and bowed his head. In his imagination he could still see her shapely, kneeling form.

When Ranieri finally heard Chiara shift and stand, his knees were stiff. He led the way out of the chapel and helped her mount, then swung into the saddle and returned to the road.

"I was down this way when Fra Francesco was up on that outer wall, and he called out in very poor French to some poor people who were watching, 'Come and help me in the work on the monastery of San Damiano, because there will as yet be ladies here who will glorify our heavenly Father throughout His holy, universal Church by their celebrated and holy manner of life.' I sent him some stones and my workmen to help him."

"God will bless you for that," Chiara smiled.

"And He will bless Francesco for carting those stones down that steep hill."

Chiara laughed lightly. How musical her voice was!

The horses plodded as the road became swampier. Through the thick trees to the left, the Rivo Torto was twisting its lazy way through the low-lying forest. Eventually the Via Cupo di San Petrignano veered away from the river and became drier. "There is San Pietro della Spina, which Fra Francesco also rebuilt. Would you like to go in?"

"Of course. Messer, how kind of you to take me here."

After praying at the small chapel, built for the countryside folk, the group headed west on the Via Antica before turning north on the Strada della Porziuncula. Immediately ahead, in a small clearing in the twisted, wild oak forest, stood the small, pinkish-gray stone chapel: Santa Maria degli Angeli. The country folk, for whom it was built, called it the Porziuncula.

"People say angels often visit this church," Ranieri said.

Chiara smiled agreeably.

A glimmer of movement near the shaky reed huts surrounding the church caught Ranieri's attention. A gray tunic. Another. Another. Good. The friars were here. Last year the men had gone to Rome to see Lord Pope, who had approved their way of life. Ranieri knew these men: their once trim, flowing locks shorn, their beards untidy, and their scalps shaved in the center in clerical tonsure. For Chiara's sake, he would overcome his unease in their presence.

A friar came striding toward the group. His scraggly thin beard bobbed as he called out, "Messer Ranieri! Messer Rufino! Messers! Madonne! Pace e bene!"

The friar was Pietro di Catanio, the former lawyer who had once won a lawsuit for Ranieri's father.

Pietro grasped Ranieri's palm. Turning toward the church, he called out, "My brother, look who's here!"

A tall, vigorous man in a ragged gray tunic turned from the church toward the group. "The Lord be praised!" With his head held high and his spine straight, easy-going Giovanni di San Costanzo sprinted toward the group. Last year after Lord Pope had approved Francesco's *Form of Life*, Francesco or another friar had preached every Sunday in the Cathedral del San Rufino. Vannie, as Ranieri called him, had captivated this audience by preaching with energetic excitement.

Vannie was beaming with exuberance. "So, my neighbor, you are no longer angry with me for coming here?"

Ranieri was no longer angry, just puzzled. Here stood an admirable, aristocratic noble who now labored with his serfs and who would get only stale bread for his labor. For Chiara's sake, Ranieri would accept Vannie even if he couldn't understand him.

Leaping from his horse, Ranieri enthusiastically threw his arms around his friend and kissed him on both cheeks. The other knights followed, sweeping Vannie up in a great surge of hugging, back patting, and exclaiming.

"Pace e bene!" Two other friars approached the group. Ranieri instantly recognized that black hair peppered with gray. Bernardo di Quintavalle! The lawyer all of Assisi once consulted. When he sold his goods, gave away all his money, and joined Francesco, the citizens of Assisi had been incredulous.

As Bernardo grasped Ranieri's shoulders in a tight hug, the younger, beardless friar called exultantly, "Messer Rufino!"

"Fra Egidio!"

Egidio and Rufino embraced heartily.

"So, are you going to stay with us this time?" Egidio asked, his innocent face aglow.

A hearty laugh bubbled out of Rufino's expansive mouth. "You always ask that! I prefer partying. This life is boring."

The four friars burst into laughter.

"If only you knew," Egidio grinned. "The world is boring. Not God."

"Pace e bene!" The cheer came from the church roof. A tiny gray figure was inching along the roof line. Francesco.

Ranieri took Chiara's hand. "Come."

As the couple approached, Francesco looked down and pursed his lips. "Messer, I thank you for the roof tiles." Francesco tapped the tiles directly in front of him. "We have placed them next to those Madonna Chiara bought for us." He pointed to his right, then leaped to the ground. "Come, see the chapel, rebuilt in part with donations sent from both of you and from many other good people of Assisi."

"Gladly, brother," Ranieri said.

When Chiara had finished praying in the chapel, Ranieri led her back to the horses and undid the four fat pouches on his saddle. They were plump with fresh bread, which he handed to the friars before bidding them farewell.

Ranieri led the way along the Strada della Porziuncula, toward Assisi. The sun was low in the sky, the shadows long.

Nervousness again swelled Ranieri's chest. *Get over your fear, Ranieri.* "Madonna." The words were sticking in his throat. He forced himself to go on. "I was most delighted when your father granted me permission to court you. I would be honored to wed you."

At last! It was out.

"Messer," Madonna Chiara replied in her deep, firm voice, "any woman would be honored to wed you. But I cannot."

Ranieri groaned. He had feared this answer. His pounding heart rivaled the plodding of the horses' hooves.

"Madonna, both your parents wish to see you magnificently wed. I have lands. Jewels. Servants. Houses." Ranieri's voice was trembling. "Gladly would I fight any battle to give you all you wish. You will be highly honored. I know that you're devoted to God, generous in alms and prayer. My money and power will be yours to use as you wish for our Lord Jesus Christ."

Chiara gazed at Ranieri, her blue eyes full of sympathy, her voice tender. "My dear Messer Ranieri, Jesus said that it's easier for a camel to go through the eye of a needle than for a rich man to enter the kingdom of God. I love worldly things too much. I must leave earthly things and seek heavenly ones."

Ranieri reached for Chiara's hand. The touch of her soft skin sent a thrill through his heart. "Madonna, can one not seek the kingdom and still live in the world?"

"Of course. But not me. The world tugs at me, Messer. It is a great struggle."

"As my wife, you could serve God as you wish." The horses were walking so close together that Ranieri could have leaned over and kissed Chiara, had he been so bold.

"Messer, my heart is with another Lord."

Ranieri was quiet. What could he possibly say?

"Messer Ranieri, isn't that another church up ahead?"

"The monastery of San Nicolo dell'Orto."

"May we go in? I'd like to offer a prayer for you."

"As you wish, Madonna Chiara."

Chiara spurred her horse and it trotted ahead, breaking pace with Ranieri's mount.

The party stopped at the small chapel and entered the dim coolness. Before the altar with its bold wooden crucifix, Chiara knelt. Taking Ranieri's hand in hers, she bowed her head and prayed silently, her lips moving slightly, her eyes closed. Finally, she opened her tear-filled eyes and looked directly at Ranieri. "Oh, gentle Messer Ranieri, let's always pray for each other."

"I'll pray for you, Madonna Chiara." Ranieri's voice was barely audible. *And I'll court you until you consent. I love you so much.* Ranieri lifted his eyes toward the crucifix over the altar. *I can't let you go, even to Him.*

NOTES

Intermarriage among distant family members maintained social standing and property within the family. Chiara's parents wanted her to "marry magnificently"

(CA:ED 194). However, she rejected all her suitors, including Messer Ranieri di Bernardo, a distant cousin, who remembered her beauty even in his old age. Ranieri had many times asked Chiara to marry him, but she always refused and even preached to him about leaving the world (CA:ED 193). History does not record how Chiara's courtship took place, but any courtship would have been in a group setting such as a riding party.

Most people who initially thought that Francesco was crazy eventually became supportive. Ranieri may have been one of these people.

Francesco most likely had volunteer work crews helping him rebuild abandoned churches.

At this time, Francesco was also tending lepers at the leper hospital of San Lazzaro. Chiara sent food to the poor and possibly to lepers (CA:ED 17, 192).

Since Chiara's penitential practices and holiness were well known (CA:ED 144–96), Francesco went often to preach to her (CA:ED 183), and she secretly and frequently went to speak to him (CA:ED 192).

What San Damiano looked like before Francesco renovated it, how many times he worked on it and when, and what renovations he made are all speculative. Father Marino Bigaroni believes that San Damiano originally looked as this chapter describes it. Bigaroni believes that Francesco renovated it twice, once prior to the incident in this chapter and then again, more extensively, a few years later. San Damiano's cross and its location in the church are accurately described.

For an unknown reason, Cristiana, daughter of Messer Bernardo da Suppo, seems to have lived with Chiara for an unspecified length of time (CA:ED 185).

In an unrecorded year and for an unknown reason, Messer Ugolino di Pietro Girardone sent away his wife, Madonna Guiduzia (CA:ED 191).

Prior to his conversion, Francesco was friendly with many young men of Assisi, possibly including Rufino and Egidio (Giles). In "The Life and Sayings of Brother Giles" (*Fioretti*), Egidio stated that life in the world was boring.

At the time of this chapter, all the friars mentioned had joined Francesco. Their backgrounds are accurate. Vannie's background is unknown.

The descriptions of all places, objects, and activities associated with Francesco are correct. The chapels San Pietro della Spina and the Porziuncula, both of which Francesco rebuilt, were for rural people (Fortini, footnotes 248, 249).

From the primary sources and from their skeletal remains in the Basilica di San Francesco, we know that Angelo di Tancredi was tall and robust and Rufino shorter and presumably delicate-looking.

Francesco rebuilt the churches mentioned and was working on the Porziuncula during the spring of 1210. Chiara held dear Francesco's prophecy about San Damiano (CA:ED 60–61). Whether Ranieri heard him make this prophecy is conjectural.

The Scripture passage, "It is easier for a camel . . ." is from Matthew 19:24.

7

Madonna Bona di Guelfuccio

Offreduccio House, Assisi (Late Autumn 1210)

In the sewing room of the Offreduccio house, the ladies were chatting as they stitched. Ortulana. Pacifica. Chiara. Cristiana. Catarina. Beatrice. Alguisa. Emilia. Ginevra. Bona.

Bona wasn't paying close attention to the conversation, so intent was she on the bodice of the olive-colored gown in her lap. Her specially designed, intricate pattern must be perfectly stitched. Shoving annoying strands of prematurely graying hair under her small cap, Bona carefully took another stitch.

"Madonne."

The servant's deep voice startled Bona, who jerked, almost bungling the stitch.

"Madonna Chiara is asked to come to the great hall at the request of Messer Rufino di Scipione."

Bona gasped. Messer Rufino? Here? After what he'd done!

Almost too quickly, Chiara hurried out of the room. Apprehensive, Bona put down the gown and hurried after her. Bona always accompanied Chiara.

A few weeks ago, Bona had returned to Assisi after a pilgrimage to the shrine of Santiago de Compostela. Chiara had urged her to make the penitential journey to gain the special indulgences given to pilgrims during this jubilee year, four hundred years since the discovery of Saint James' body in that far western corner of Spain. What graces Bona had received! She had touched the apostle's staff. Marveled at the church's elaborate sculptures. Prayed before the gold-adorned altar. Begged Saint James to deepen her faith. With the Compostela pilgrim's traditional scallop shell fastened to her bread pouch, she had returned, full of peace and joy.

Then she had heard what Messer Rufino had done, and her joy had died.

As Bona entered the great hall behind Chiara, she caught sight of two youthful, barefoot friars in coarse, penitential tunics, awkwardly waiting. Rufino. And another young man.

The friars were bowing. Chiara was curtsying. With disdain, Bona curtsied, too.

Then Chiara threw her arms around short, fine-featured Rufino, who pressed his face against Chiara's shoulder and began to sob. After several minutes, his weeping subsided.

"It's good to see you." Chiara's voice was quivering, her arms tight around her cousin.

"And you." Rufino's words were husky.

Slowly the two broke their embrace and gazed at each other. "You're beautiful, Fra Rufino," Chiara observed.

"To you. Not to the other Offreduccios. They loathe what I've done."

"They don't understand that you've chosen to serve the noblest Lord." Taking his hand, Chiara led Rufino to the benches around the massive table. "Sit and introduce your brother. Share what life with Fra Francesco is like."

Bewildered, Bona sat next to Chiara and tried to sort her thoughts. This—this beggar—was a noble. Messer Rufino. Gentle. Courtly. Refined.

"This is Fra Barbaro." Rufino introduced his grinning, wiry, baby-faced companion. "An Assisi man whose hot temper helped bring me to Francesco." Rufino smiled at the women's startled expressions. "About a year ago, I was riding to Limigiano to visit the Scipione castle. In the piazza I saw Fra Barbaro and another friar arguing!"

"Francesco preaches peace," Bona objected.

"True," said Rufino, "so why were the friars about to swing at each other? Suddenly Fra Barbaro drops to the ground and stuffs donkey's dung into his mouth."

"Ugh!" Chiara and Bona grunted.

"The argument was my fault," Barbaro said.

"Do you remember what you said?" Rufino asked. "I remember it exactly."

Barbaro shrugged.

"You said," Rufino quoted, "'Let the tongue that spat the poison of anger on my brother now chew manure.'"

"Sì. It was something like that."

"Madonne," Rufino said, nodding at the women, "I was amazed. Who were these friars? So I went to Rivo Torto where Francesco and his friars were living in an abandoned stable."

How sickening! Bona thought.

"When a peasant moved his donkey into the stable, the brothers moved to the Porziuncula."

"During this past summer, he visited so often," Barbaro smiled, "that we called him 'our rich friar.'"

Rufino's voice began to tremble. "There is so much love with Fra Francesco. If an Offreduccio offends an Offreduccio, there is yelling and arguing. But if one brother offends another, the offender prostrates himself on the ground. He asks the one whom he offended to put his foot on his mouth."

"Have you done this?" Bona asked.

"Since joining three months ago, I have offended three times."

"Did you think that you had offended me," Chiara asked, "that you haven't visited?"

"I saw my father's face and my uncles' when I preached in San Rufino in my breeches. They were offended."

"Disgraced is the word," Bona retorted.

Barbaro lay his hand on Rufino's shoulder. "Fra Francesco had ordered my brother to preach, but he's shy and not good with words. So he begged Fra Francesco to excuse him."

"I was disobedient," Rufino said quietly. "Prideful, afraid of appearing a fool. How could I obey God if I couldn't obey Fra Francesco? So he ordered me to preach in my breeches."

Bona remembered the jeering congregation, who had thought that Rufino had gone mad with penance.

Rufino found Chiara's eyes. "Only your father, Madonna, seemed compassionate. I think he would have thrown his cloak over me had Fra Francesco not come in." For Francesco, also clad only in breeches, had entered the church and had begun to preach about penance, poverty, and humiliation for the kingdom of God. As Francesco clothed himself and Rufino in tunics, the jeers turned to weeping.

"How are you serving God this way?" The words burst from Bona before she could stop them. "You and Messer Angelo di Tancredi could buy bread for every beggar in Assisi, yet you have become beggars. Why?"

"Who can understand?" Barbaro asked. "For some of us, poverty is God's way."

"Madonna Chiara," Rufino said softly, "Fra Francesco would like to speak to you privately about matters of the spirit, about penance."

Chiara leaped to her feet. "Fra Rufino, I've been praying for months for this."

"Tomorrow at the hour of Terce at the Porziuncula?"

"Sì!"

"No!" Bona blurted. Chiara gave the friars goods and money for Masses and candles. What more did Francesco want? "Your parents won't permit it."

"We won't tell them," Chiara said.

"We have to tell them."

"No, we don't. I'm of age to do as I wish." Chiara's voice was firm.

Bona groaned. As a lady-in-waiting, she was to obey her mistress.

Rufino stood. "Tomorrow, then."

"Now you must meet the others!" Chiara's voice was eager as she started out the doorway. "About this meeting, we will say only that we visited."

Awkwardly, Bona and the friars silently waited until the other women burst into the room, chattering, questioning, giggling, hugging Fra Rufino.

Finally Rufino raised his hands. "My dear relatives, we must beg yet today."

"You have already begged," Ortulana remarked. "Wait here." She strode out of the room, returning with four servants carrying figs, bread, and meat.

"For the friars," Ortulana said.

Grinning, Barbaro and Rufino dropped the food into huge, deep pouches sewn into the sides and chests of their tunics and even into their hoods.

The women curtsied to the lumpy men. The friars bowed.

"Come again. Soon," Ortulana said, grasping each of their hands.

"We will. Grazie, all."

NOTES

Before Chiara was tonsured, she sent Bona on a pilgrimage to Santiago de Compostela, Spain (CA:ED 193). Perhaps this occurred in 1210, which was a jubilee year for the shrine, with special indulgences for pilgrims.

Barbaro's abusive attack on a fellow friar and his self-rebuke are accurate (FA:ED II 143, 347). Any friar who got angry followed the prescription of prostrating himself and begging the offended party to put his foot on the bad-tempered one's mouth. Barbaro went beyond this by impulsively chewing ass' dung to curb his temper. Fortini (p. 335) speculates that this incident occurred at Limigiano and that Rufino was the nobleman who witnessed it.

Rufino di Scipione, Chiara's first cousin, joined Francesco and his friars sometime in 1210. The Offreduccio family's reaction to this is unknown.

The *Fioretti* tells how Francesco sent timid Rufino to preach in his breeches. The account does not name the church nor does it state that Rufino's family saw him preaching. Those who saw him jeered until Francesco, clad in his own breeches, preached as well. Then the congregation's attitude changed.

The description of the friars' tunics is accurate.

Chiara sent votive offerings and alms to the friars working on the Porziuncula (CA:ED 193).

8

Fra Filippo di Lungo

Porziuncula, Assisi (Late Autumn 1210)

Raven-haired Fra Filippo di Lungo heard bells before he heard clumping hooves. Putting down the wooden bowl into which he had been picking parsley to garnish tonight's meal, he hurried toward the Strada della Porziuncula and met Madonna Chiara and Madonna Bona in the clearing.

The tall, slender friar, barely twenty, bowed graciously to the women dressed in matching green. Helping the women from their lavishly outfitted palfreys, he then tethered the animals, offered the women a seat on rude benches at the foot of a gigantic oak, and went to fetch Francesco.

Two years ago, Filippo, a native of Costa di San Savino, had left his sheep to another shepherd and had joined Francesco who, just now, was praying beside his straw bed in one of the narrow, poorly constructed huts that encircled the Porziuncula.

"Madonna Chiara is here," Filippo said softly.

Breaking into a grin, Francesco bounded past Filippo as Filippo held aside the drape that served as a door.

"Pace e bene!" Francesco called to the women. He straddled an empty bench as Filippo sat on another bench across from him. Francesco allowed no friar to speak alone to a woman. The presence of a companion preserved virtue and reputation.

So this was Madonna Chiara who, so Fra Rufino claimed, was pious. In his worldly life in Mandria within the comune of Assisi, Filippo had never heard of her. But he had heard of the Offreduccios, a family of twenty or so who held great power and wealth in the comune.

"So, Madonna Chiara," Francesco said, smiling, "I hear that you are a holy woman."

The lady's face reddened. "Perhaps you can help that come true."

Francesco grinned. "Have you ever thought of leaving the world?"

"Frequently."

Filippo caught his breath. Perhaps Francesco was right in thinking this woman might share his vision.

Francesco cocked his head. "Why haven't you?"

"Because I don't want what the anchorages and convents have. I want what you have. Or don't have. I want to give myself to Jesus in His poverty. Can you help me?"

"Perhaps." Francesco propped his elbow on his knee and leaned his chin into his fist. "We must observe the commands and counsels of our Lord Jesus Christ. We must also deny ourselves and place our bodies under the yoke of service and holy obedience. Can you embrace this?"

"I'm not afraid of poverty, hard work, or difficulty, brother. Nor do I care about public opinion."

Francesco arched his eyebrows. "It's more than that. We must not be wise and prudent according to the flesh, but, instead, we must be simple, humble, and pure. And let us hold our bodies in scorn and contempt because, through our own fault, we are all wretched and corrupt."

Chiara was nodding solemnly. "I am familiar, brother, with the subtleties of our crafty enemy, the pride that destroys human nature, and the vanity that infatuates human hearts. I see that by humility, the virtue of faith, and the arms of poverty, you have taken hold of that incomparable treasure hidden in the field of the world and of the human heart. Can you help me do as you have done?"

Filippo's heart skipped a beat. This was exactly what Francesco had hoped to propose.

Francesco furrowed his brow. "Would you meet weekly with me to discuss it?"

Chiara's face lit up. "Sì."

"Surely you're not thinking of joining the friars?" Bona burst out.

Chiara rolled her eyes. "That would be indecent."

"Nor would we permit such a thing," Francesco noted.

"Then what will you do?" Bona asked.

"Fra Francesco will have to tell me, because I don't know."

Madonna Bona leapt to her feet. "You cannot come here again. If the Offreduccio knights knew you were here, talking like this, they might kill you."

Francesco whistled. "Really?"

"Quite possibly," Bona said.

"They won't know," Chiara declared. "We'll continue to meet secretly."

"Your parents would disapprove," Bona objected.

"My parents have taught," Chiara said, "that, ultimately, one must obey the Father of our Lord Jesus Christ."

NOTES

Filippo di Lungo's origin and the date he joined Francesco are controversial. This text follows Fortini's research (280 footnote).

Possibly through the intermediary Fra Rufino, Chiara and Francesco arranged to meet. These secret meetings took place for over a year, with Bona accompanying Chiara and Filippo accompanying Francesco (CA:ED 192). We do not know where or how these meetings took place.

Francesco's words about obedience, poverty, and contempt of the world are from his *Letter to All the Faithful* (FA:ED I 48).

Chiara's words about the "subtleties of our crafty enemy" are from her *Third Letter to Agnes of Prague* (CA:ED 50).

9

Madonna Beatrice di Favarone

Piazza del San Rufino, Assisi (January 1212)

Thirteen-year-old Madonna Beatrice and her older sister Madonna Catarina had made ten snow figures beside the steps of the Offreduccio house. Now they were finishing a chambermaid.

Wouldn't Papà and her uncles be surprised when they arrived home!

From the snow-covered Via del San Rufino came the muffled plod-plod of horses' hooves. Oh, no. The hunting party was home! The snow servants weren't finished.

At the steps, Messer Monaldo leaped from his chestnut steed. "Out of the way! Get back!" he barked at the girls. In his dark furs, striding into the clump of fast-moving, grunting uncles milling around Papà's horse, Monaldo looked larger than usual.

Messer Scipione was at Beatrice's side, his long, perfectly shaped fingers dark with blood and grime, probably from disemboweling a boar or stag. Fresh meat for dinner tonight!

"Move back, Madonne," Scipione said softly. "Papà has been gored."

Catarina screamed.

"Papà!" Beatrice cried.

She tried to run after him, but Messer Scipione was blocking her way. "Let him in the house. He needs a doctor."

Her sturdy uncles were carrying Papà up the stairs. The belly of his blue tunic was stained red. A huge red blotch smeared his fox-fur cape. Often Papà came home splattered with animal blood. But these blots were huge, solid patches.

"You may go now," Scipione said.

Beatrice threw a swift glance at the snow people. A drop of fresh blood had bored its way into the chambermaid's head.

The girls raced upstairs, dotted with red.

Everything was out of kilter. The hall, dark and long. Mamma and Papà's bedroom, crowded. Messers, blood flecking their clothes. Servants. Confusion. Shrieking. Cursing. Papà, lying on his back in bed. Chiara kneeling at Papà's side, holding one of his bloody hands. Mamma crouched on the other side, her small, fine chin trembling, her gentle hands carefully rolling Papà's clothing away from his wound.

Beatrice threw herself down beside Chiara while Catarina fell to her knees next to Mamma.

Papà's life was seeping out of his belly in a widening red circle. The room shifted, expanded outwards. Beatrice clutched at her consciousness. *Oh, God, don't let me faint!*

"Everybody stay back but the family! Get back!"

The doctor's harshness startled Beatrice, cleared her head.

The doctor was hurrying, cutting away the bloody tunic. The room was flying away from her.

I will not faint.

Beatrice felt a firm hand squeeze her shoulder. "Take deep breaths, Madonna Beatrice." The voice was Chiara's.

One deep breath. Two deep breaths. Three. *I will not faint.* She could hear scissors cutting, could smell blood.

I will not faint.

A bandage of undyed cloth covered Papà's belly, a pinprick of red in its center. Papà's eyes were closed. Under his cockeyed cap, his gray-flecked black hair was plastered against his pale forehead.

Beatrice stroked back Papà's hair. Papà felt cool.

Papà, speak to me. Are you dead?

If only she could think of a story, a poem. He used to tell her stories when she was sick.

The doctor was speaking to Mamma. "Boar must have been huge . . . very long tusks . . . wounds very deep."

No! Papà, wake up. You're not dying. Talk to me.

"Move back. Give him air."

Beatrice recognized Canon Crescenzio's commanding voice. Messers and servants backed from the bed, making room for the youthful altar server and the grim-faced canon in his violet stole.

The canon was blessing the house, the people. A drop of holy water landed on Beatrice's forehead. *Why don't You heal him, God?*

"Messer Favarone!" Why was Canon Crescenzio shouting at Papà?

Papà's whisper was barely audible. "Sì."

"Do you wish to confess?" The words were softer.

"Sì."

The canon turned to the group. "Everyone out. Messer wishes to confess."

The murmuring crowd pressed out of the room. Messer Paolo lifted Beatrice to her feet and guided her backwards, away from Papà.

"Papà!"

This was a bad dream. Beatrice would awaken, go outdoors, and complete the snow people with Catarina. Papà would come home and praise their artistry. This confused, deadened crowd in the hallway—this was not real.

"He is absolved." Canon Crescenzio appeared in the doorway.

The people filed in, encircling the bed. The canon was opening a little wooden box, removing the Body of Christ, placing it on Papà's tongue. More prayers. Canon Crescenzio dipping his finger into a vial of holy oil. Anointing Papà's eyes. Ears. Nostrils. Mouth. Hands. Feet. "May the Lord forgive you by this holy anointing whatever sins you have committed. Amen."

God, do not let him die.

Canon Crescenzio scanned the room. "Messer Favarone wants to speak to Madonna Ortulana, his daughters, his brothers."

Shivering, cold, Beatrice moved as though in a dream. She and Chiara knelt on Papà's right, Mamma and Catarina on his left. The uncles clustered around.

Mamma's tiny, slender hand clasped Papà's large fist. "We're here, Messer."

Papà's eyelids flickered open. "Madonna," he whispered, turning slowly to Ortulana, "Forgive me my faults, for I have always loved you." Slowly he lifted his right hand to her face, tenderly stroked her cheek. "Pray for me."

"Until the day I die, I will pray for you." Mamma's voice was deeper than Beatrice had ever heard it.

"Bicetta." Papà called Beatrice by his pet name for her. "And Catarina. Do good in your studies and your duties. Obey your mamma and uncles." Papà stroked a lock of Catarina's sand-colored hair that was tumbling across her cheek. Then his blood-blackened fingers pushed Beatrice's auburn hair away from her face. "May you marry fine, loving Messers. Pray for me, eh?"

Beatrice nodded. Words would not come.

"Chiarita." Papà slowly reached toward Chiara and flicked her blond curls away from her forehead. Chiara took his hand and pressed it against her cheek.

Papà's breaths came deeply. "Chiarita, you wish . . . to remain a virgin for Christ. . . . May God bless you. . . . When you give your life to Jesus . . . pray for me."

Trembling, Chiara pressed Papà's hand to her lips and kissed it tenderly. "Grazie, Papà. I will always pray for you. I love you."

Papà nodded weakly. "Messer Monaldo . . . will be Papà to you now. . . . Treat him with respect . . . love . . . obedience . . . as you would treat me."

Papà coughed, caught his breath. "Monaldo," he whispered, "you are now Messer . . . of this household. Promise . . . that you will care always . . . for my family."

Monaldo knelt by Papà's right side and placed his massive right hand over Papà's heart.

"I promise."

"Promise . . . that you will not oppose . . . Chiarita."

"I promise."

"And that . . . you will support . . . Bicetta and Catarina . . . in whatever they wish to do."

"I promise."

Papà coughed, caught his breath. The red blotch on the bandage was widening.

"All my brothers," Papà gasped, "support my household. . . . Care for them. . . . Be generous to the poor. . . . Manage the estates well.

"All here," Papà's voice rose in volume as he slowly looked about the room. "Forgive . . . my offenses. Continue . . . faithfully. . . . Pray for me."

Staccato-like assent came from around the room.

Papà's gaze lifted upward. "Our Father . . . who art in heaven . . . holy is Your name." A spasm shook him. A gasp broke from his mouth. Then Papà's eyes closed; his head fell back and turned slightly to the left.

Catarina screamed.

"Damn!" Monaldo cursed, his hand still over Papà's heart.

Canon Crescenzio dropped to his knees. The others followed. "Come to his aid, O saints of God. Come forth to meet him, angels of the Lord, receiving his soul, presenting it to the Lord Most High."

NOTES

Favarone disappears from the histories about this time, although Fortini, in "New Information about Saint Clare of Assisi," lists a 1229 document that mentions a Favarone without giving an ancestral name. Favarone di Offreduccio was not the only Favarone in Assisi, as evident from a 1233 document that mentions Favarone di Cannara. About this time, Monaldo and the other relatives assume authority involving Chiara and her sister Catarina, even to the point of Monaldo intending to kill Catarina when she, having gone to join Chiara, refused to relinquish her vocation (CA:ED 304). If Favarone were alive, they could only have assumed this authority if he had been incapable of making decisions. This is possible but not likely. If Favarone had opposed Chiara's vocation as Pietro opposed Francesco's, biographers would have certainly emphasized it because it would make Chiara's story parallel Francesco's. The fact that Favarone is not mentioned and that other relatives had authority to act in his place suggests that Favarone must have died. But when?

Bona testified that she "many times accompanied her to speak to Saint Francis. She went secretly so as not to be seen by her parents" (plural) (CA:ED 192). Therefore, Favarone was alive when Chiara and Francesco first began to meet.

It seems that Favarone must have died sometime between Chiara's first meeting with Francesco and her total embracing of religious life.

Part Three

I Bend My Knee to the Father

10

Bishop Guido

Sasso del Maloloco, Comune of Assisi (Early March 1212)

B ishop Guido and his servant were guiding their mounts along a winding, rocky path that led to a hodgepodge of grottoes in the steep, mountainous area called Sasso del Maloloco. Francesco and his friars had made hermitages of the caves, calling them their *Carceri*, their holy prison, where, periodically, they came to be alone with God.

On this cool spring morning, the two men kept their horses to a slow walk, pushing out of their way the branches that overhung the path, which was puddled with melting snow and pocked with hoofprints. Who had ridden this way earlier? They had to be part of the secret meeting that Francesco asked Guido to attend.

Self-assured and confident, Guido owned and managed half of all the comune's land. Often he browbeat into submission anyone who disagreed with him. Once he used his fists to get his way. He coordinated an entire retinue of servants, farmhands, canons, knights, and policy makers. He had overcome a great many irate nobles and powerful merchants. Yet he was soft where Francesco was concerned.

Guido had liked Francesco the merchant for regularly praising Guido's choice of cloth. He had admired Francesco the religious that snowy day six years ago when he had given up everything for God. Now he loved Francesco like a son.

Unlike other self-styled reformers, Francesco did nothing without his bishop's permission. Yet he wouldn't allow Guido to make life easier for the friars. Francesco insisted on being as poor as Christ and trusting God. Therefore, he refused to take sides in Guido's political battles. He preached peace based on equality instead of on treaties, concessions, and pacts of protection. Guido had innumerable concerns and obligations, it seemed. Francesco had one—to serve God in humility, poverty, and love. No wonder Guido often envied the friars.

Ahead through tangled, bare holm oak branches, Guido spied two tethered horses. He recognized the trappings. Offreduccio horses. Now what?

"Pace e bene, Messer Bishop."

Guido returned the greeting from diminutive, gray-haired Dom Silvestro, whose quick, sharp steps always reminded Guido of a hopping sparrow. The former canon of the Cathedral del San Rufino looked healthy and happy in his patched tunic. Silvestro tethered the bishop's horses, left the servant with them, and led Guido to a grotto in the cliff. Just outside the grotto, four figures stood chatting. Fra Francesco. Fra Filippo. Madonna Chiara. Madonna Bona.

Smiling and greeting Guido, Francesco led the way into the torchlit, smoky cave. Guido and Chiara followed while Filippo and Bona remained outside.

A distance into the grotto, a crude stool sat in the center of a straw pile. Knowing that it was for him, Guido straddled the stool and plopped his huge frame onto it, then drew his fur-lined green cloak around his arms and chest to keep warm. Like eager students, Francesco and Chiara sat on the straw, directly in front of him.

"Messer Bishop," Francesco began, "Christiana . . ."

Francesco's pet name startled Guido. An eighteen-year-old noblewoman familiarly called Christiana—Christian woman—by a man her social inferior? The term referred to women recluses who lived in and around Assisi, enclosed in tiny cells adjoined to churches and devoted to prayer and counsel.

". . . begs your blessing to begin a public life of penance."

Madonna Chiara a public penitent, in a sackcloth tunic?

Guido slowly shook his head. "No, Madonna. Women of your class embrace penance at home, as your mother has done. Or they enter convents for women of your class."

"Messer Bishop, the convents are too rich," Chiara politely pointed out.

Guido felt the hair on his neck begin to rise. Many of the convents were under his control. "Noble virgins enter convents. Or they are penitents at home or in an anchorage or a community such as that at Panzo."

Chiara shook her head. "I want poverty and my God, like Fra Francesco."

Guido turned to Francesco. "Have you proposed this?"

"I have proposed it," Chiara said.

Guido grunted. He leaned forward and looked Chiara directly in the eye. "Madonna, do you know what can happen if you wander about as the Lesser Brothers do? Lustful men don't honor a penitential habit."

"Christiana wishes to be enclosed in a convent," Francesco said.

"A poor convent," Chiara added.

"Impossible," Guido said. "There are no poor convents."

"We wish to create one," Francesco offered. "At San Damiano."

The abandoned church belonged to Guido. "San Damiano is no place for a woman to live."

"Religious consecrated to God lived there once," Francesco said. "Builders tell me that we can lower the church floor and build a dormitory above the church. We can construct a few other necessary buildings, all poor. Some of my friars will go and beg for the women and say Mass for them."

"What women?"

"The ones who will join Christiana."

"Who would that be?"

"God knows," Francesco said.

Was this God's new revelation?

"You want me to give you San Damiano."

"I don't want to own it," Chiara qualified. "Just use it."

Guido slapped his hands against his thighs and rose. He looked at Chiara's idealistic young face. "Madonna, your uncle Messer Monaldo is one of the most powerful men in the comune. He was your family's most angry member when Fra Rufino gave up all to join Fra Francesco. How do you suppose he will react to your decision?"

"Before he died, Papà made my uncle promise not to oppose my vocation."

"Messer Favarone would have assumed that you wish to enter one of the convents of Assisi."

"Papà would not oppose me."

"Sì, he would. So will Messer Monaldo, no matter what he promised. Women are physically weak, silly, and feeble of mind. They cannot live as the Lesser Brothers do."

"Please, Messer Bishop," Chiara pleaded, "do not oppose God's plan. Permit me to embrace poverty as Christ did."

Guido pounded a fist into his palm. How could he control this woman?

"You don't need my permission to embrace a public life of penance."

Chiara's gaze was penetrating. "I would like your blessing. I don't wish to do anything against the Church."

"This isn't against the Church," Guido said.

"Will you tonsure her, Messer Bishop?" Francesco asked.

"No, I won't tonsure her. She may tonsure herself. Or you may do it, or your friars. If God is calling Madonna Chiara into this, I cannot oppose it. But I will have nothing to do with it. If Messer Monaldo comes to me, as he did about Fra Angelo and Fra Rufino, I'll send him to both of you. I accept no responsibility for this decision."

"Palm Sunday is the beginning of Holy Week, of Jesus' Passion," Francesco said. "Christiana would like to begin her life of penance then."

Palm Sunday was two weeks hence.

"How is this to happen?"

"One of my friars and I will accompany Madonna Chiara to Santa Maria degli Angeli. At night, when her family is asleep."

"How is she to leave the city? The gates will be guarded and locked."

"Your own palace adjoins the wall, and your own watchmen guard your gate," Francesco said.

Guido shook his fist at Francesco. "So you want me to tell my guards to open my gate for Madonna Chiara! For certain Messer Monaldo will show up at my palace."

"I want you to tell the watchmen to open the gate for some friars."

Francesco was amazing. "Madonna Chiara in friar's garb? You haven't forgotten a detail, have you?"

Francesco was grinning.

Guido tried to look severe. "Where is she to stay after you receive her at Santa Maria degli Angeli?"

"At the monastery of San Paolo delle Abbadesse until San Damiano is ready. That is, if you'll ask the nuns there to accept her temporarily—as a servant, Messer Bishop."

San Paolo, a monastery of nuns under Guido's control. And one that had the privilege of asylum. If Chiara's family tried to take her from San Paolo, they would suffer automatic excommunication. They would be placed outside the Church and unable to receive its sacraments. San Paolo also commanded armed forces to defend anyone seeking sanctuary. Francesco was smart to think of taking Chiara to San Paolo.

"I have to think about this."

"Will you know by Palm Sunday?" Francesco could be so persistent.

"Let me think." Guido paced the cave. *Lord, give me an idea.* And, just like that, an idea came. An idea that would buy him time.

"Madonna, you will be in the Cathedral del San Rufino on Palm Sunday. Fra Francesco, you must be there as well. When I distribute the olive branches, do not come up, Madonna."

"Do not come up?" Chiara asked, incredulous.

Of course, the suggestion was startling. All the women came up for olive branches.

"If I agree to these plans, I will bring a branch to you. That will be a sign that I have told my watchmen to let friars through my gate and that the nuns at San Paolo have agreed to accept you. But if I don't give you a branch, you'll have to think of an alternate plan."

"Grazie, Messer Bishop," Francesco said. "May we begin the renovations on San Damiano tomorrow?"

Guido grabbed Francesco by the shoulders and shook him playfully. "I haven't yet decided to give you San Damiano. Let Madonna Chiara live at San Paolo first. Maybe she'll want to stay."

"Messer Bishop," Chiara protested, "San Paolo is rich."

Guido cleared his throat. "If I approve this plan, you will stay there out of obedience. If you don't like convent life under the Benedictine Rule, I will permit you to transfer to the community at Sant'Angelo in Panzo. You've heard of them, haven't you? The women are a holy community of penitential recluses who support themselves by selling cheese and wool from their flocks and farms." The women had no definite rule but were subject to Guido.

"Sant'Angelo isn't poor," Francesco offered.

"Poverty isn't the only virtue, brother." Guido tried to look stern as he stared down into the two young, disappointed faces. "Obedience is the most salutary form of penance, Madonna Chiara. If both San Paolo and Sant'Angelo are unsuitable, we'll discuss San Damiano. That is, if I approve this plan, which," he emphasized, "I haven't yet done."

Chiara looked from Francesco to Guido. "Messer Bishop, I will go anywhere as long as I may observe the holy poverty that I have promised to the Lord and to Fra Francesco."

NOTES

The *Carceri* or caves of San Francesco are located in a rocky, mountainous area known then as Sasso del Maloloco.

Bishop Guido was the most powerful noble of the comune of Assisi. He owned half the comune's property, including the monasteries and convents mentioned in this chapter (Fortini 27–28). In his article "The Church of San Giorgio in Assisi and the First Expansion of the Medieval City Walls," Father Marino Bigaroni states that Guido physically beat and wounded the nuns of the community of San Donato di Flebulle. In this chapter, Guido's spiritual life is postulated from what we know of him and his admiration for Francesco.

Guido appears to have been Francesco's friend, probably knowing him quite well during his merchant days. Likely many of Pietro Bernardone's fine cloths graced the bishop's household.

In his *Testament*, Francesco wrote, "And after the Lord gave me some brothers, no one showed me what I had to do" (FA:ED I 125). Yet he subjected himself totally to Church authority so as not to be branded a heretic or a madman. Thus, he certainly seems to have sought Guido's permission for his lifestyle.

No historical source tells of a meeting such as the one portrayed in this chapter. Yet it seems that such a meeting would have taken place. Francesco would probably not have taken responsibility for Chiara without the bishop's knowledge and at least his tacit permission.

How did Chiara leave Assisi at night when the gates should have been locked and guarded? Did she bribe the guards to let her out? Was the city gate in the vicinity of the Porta Moiano left open because of renovations on the luxurious baths and fountains there? Father Rene Charles Dhont includes a footnote on page 7 of his book *Clare among Her Sisters* that reads, "Clare profited from the plan to open the gates of the city which, in the Middle Ages, were closed and guarded during the night." Were the gates left open on Palm Sunday so that those celebrating with their families could return to their homes in the villages after dark? Or was Bishop Guido part of the plan to let Chiara escape? When Chiara's relatives attempted to make her renounce her vocation, the Church did not support their efforts. Does this mean that Guido, as the Church's representative, had taken Chiara under his protection?

The order of penance was an approved ecclesiastical form of life that the laity could embrace. Because Chiara's tonsure took place during a penitential season and at the hands of the friars (not the bishop), it was not a juridical act of consecration of a virgin. The tonsure signified Chiara's entry into a life of penance and could have been administered by anyone, even by Chiara herself.

In his article "San Damiano—Assisi: The First Church of Saint Francis," Father Marino Bigaroni states that San Damiano, which was under Bishop Guido's control, had previously been a monastic foundation, probably set up as a satellite monastery to a larger abbey where monks could pray and work. History does not record when Francesco and Chiara first conceived the idea to send Chiara to San Damiano or when they first asked the bishop for use of the complex. The renovations Francesco suggests in this chapter were later made by him.

11

Fra Francesco Bernardone

Offreduccio House, Assisi (Palm Sunday Night, March 18, 1212)

In the darkness, Francesco and Fra Leone sat with their backs against a corner wall of the Offreduccio house. They'd come here at dusk when the city was falling asleep after a day of Mass, processions, and feasting. They had tried to doze, waiting.

How Francesco's heart had leaped when, at today's Palm Sunday Mass, Bishop Guido had descended from the altar and given Chiara an olive branch! After Mass, Francesco remained in the cathedral to pray in gratitude. Chiara had remained too, kneeling before the altar with Madonna Pacifica beside her, for Madonna Bona was spending Holy Week in Rome. How right that Chiara's espousal to the poor Jesus should take place this holy night on which Jesus had begun His suffering, culminating in His death and resurrection!

"Fra Francesco."

The light whisper woke him. Before him stood two women, their faces well hidden by the hoods of their penitential habits.

"Fra Leone." Francesco shook the shoulder of the square-headed priest from Assisi. Leone awoke with a start and leaped to his feet.

In silence the four made their way across the torchlit Piazza del San Rufino. They walked in the light so that watchmen could see them. No one stopped them or called for them to halt.

Francesco marveled at what was happening. This must be the woman he'd seen in that long-ago vision, walking these same streets. The daughter of a knight, barefoot and in rags. *Grazie, my Lord.*

They came to the bishop's palace. Guido's watchman nodded to them. His guard unlocked the bishop's small personal gate, letting the four out of the city. On the other side of the wall Fra Bernardo and Fra Pietro waited, bearing torches.

Wordlessly, the group began the steep descent from the city to the plain, moving toward the Strada Francesca. They would follow the Strada Francesca northwest until it fed into the Strada della Porziuncula. They would follow that road south to the church of Santa Maria degli Angeli.

The ladies, like the friars, were barefoot. Giving no sign that their feet hurt, the women were keeping pace with the men. Down, down. They had reached the Strada della Porziuncula a while ago. The incline began to level off as they approached the plain. The friars' torches cast light across the road and on the trees looming on either side. The group seemed to be hurrying through a black tunnel, illumined by the fire of God.

The party reached the little church of Santa Maria degli Angeli. From this torchlit chapel across the dark clearing came the deep, melodious chanting of the friars.

The men led the women to a small hut. Lighting a candle from one of the torches, Francesco dripped a bit of wax onto the single table in the hut, then stuck the candle into it. He nodded at the women, then left the hut, proceeding to the chapel with his men.

Moments later, Chiara appeared in the chapel doorway, the light from the candle in her hand casting her in an angelic glow. Her face was radiant, her smile brighter than Francesco had ever seen. She was dressed as magnificently as a bride, as Francesco had directed, in the same deep scarlet gown, studded with sapphires, that she had worn to the Palm Sunday Mass. Jewels and ribbons wove through her long blond curls. Pacifica, in a simple mustard-colored gown, accompanied her.

As rehearsed, Bernardo and Pietro, each carrying candles, approached Madonna Chiara and led her to the candlelit altar of the russet-walled church. There, Chiara knelt at the foot of the image of the gentle Virgin surrounded by angels, glorious in her blue mantle and corona of stars as she entered eternal glory. The friars began to chant the Office of Vigils. Chiara raised her eyes to the little tower in which the Eucharistic Lord resided.

The chanting for Vigils ceased. In a deep, resonant voice, Fra Angelo began to read. "From the Gospel of John." Everyone made the sign of the cross. "Mary took a pound of costly ointment of pure nard and anointed the feet of Jesus and wiped his feet with her hair; and the house was filled with the fragrance of the ointment. . . ."

Joy surged through Francesco's heart. Mary had given her best to Christ. Now Chiara was about to give Him herself.

The cantor began to chant. Francesco nodded to Bernardo, who handed him the scissors they had borrowed from one of the farmers who lived nearby. Taking Chiara's stubby candle, Francesco dripped wax onto the altar and stood the candle in it. In a smooth motion, Chiara plucked the jewels and ribbons from her hair, dropping them to the floor. Then, with her face lifted to her Eucharistic Lord, she waited.

Pietro and Bernardo came forward and stood, one on either side of her with Francesco behind. Francesco placed his hands on Chiara's head and prayed silently. *Lord, thank You for this moment. Bless our sister Chiara. May she be Yours forever.*

As Pietro and Bernardo lifted the ash-blond locks, Francesco began to cut, dropping great, soft clumps to the floor. Quickly Chiara's hair was cut above her ears. Francesco's heart throbbed with joy at this visible sign of penitence and consecration to God. Raising her to her feet, he handed her the candle from the altar and two lengths of cloth—one black, one white. He glimpsed her expansive smile, the tears on her cheeks glistening like flecks of gold.

Carrying a candle, Fra Leone came forward and, wordlessly, led Chiara, followed by a weeping Pacifica, out of the chapel. In the chapel, the friars knelt in silent prayer. Leone returned and joined them.

Moments later, Chiara appeared again in the doorway, dressed in the rough, shabby tunic she had worn out of the city. The rim of a white veil peeked out from beneath a black veil, totally covering her cropped hair. White for virginity. Black for penance.

As Chiara knelt at the altar, Francesco moved forward to speak.

"Let us look, this night, to the Good Shepherd who bore the suffering of the cross to save His sheep. The Lord's sheep followed Him in tribulation and persecution, in shame and hunger, in weakness and temptation, and in other ways; and for these things they received eternal life from the Lord. Let us praise the Lord this night for Suor Chiara and her decision to truly be a lamb of His flock."

The friars began to chant their final prayers. As they ended, Chiara rose and silently left the chapel. Pacifica, Francesco, and Filippo followed, each taking a torch from the outer wall braces of the Porziuncula. The quartet started down the road. The air was crisp and tinglingly cool. A pale frost sparkled on the rutted road and the dried leaves. They would reach San Paolo delle Abbadesse before dawn.

NOTES

Chiara sold her inheritance and gave all the money to the poor (CA:ED 162, 187), although historians dispute if she did this before or after entering religious life. Chiara's actions angered her family.

Bishop Guido presented an olive branch (or, in some translations, a palm) to Chiara on Palm Sunday (CA:ED 283–84). Was this the bishop's signal to Chiara and the friars that he approved their plans?

Chiara "embarked upon her long desired flight with a virtuous companion" (CA:ED 286). Scholars identify this companion as Madonna Pacifica rather than a friar. For Chiara to have run off with a man would have scandalized her family and cast suspicion on the friars at a time when sexual misconduct among the clergy was common. Bona had always accompanied Chiara on her visits to Francesco, but Bona was on pilgrimage to Rome (CA:ED 192–93). For propriety's sake, Francesco always sent his friars out in pairs, and he most likely would have wanted Chiara to have a female companion whenever she came to see him.

The hypothetical idea that Pacifica accompanied Chiara as her lady-in-waiting accounts for the facts as Pacifica herself stated them. She said that she "always" served Chiara and entered the order "at the same time" (CA:ED 145). However, most historians believe that Chiara alone was tonsured at the Porziuncula on Palm Sunday night 1212 (or 1211, as some scholars believe) and that Chiara's sister Catarina, not Pacifica, was the first one to embrace Chiara's form of religious life. Pacifica's attendance on

Chiara as a lady-in-waiting would be historically possible and would be consistent with this commonly accepted information.

Francesco tonsured Chiara (CA:ED 183, 191, 192, 196). The names of the other friars who were at the Porziuncula that night are not listed, but those named in this chapter had joined Francesco at that time. Quite likely Filippo accompanied Francesco and Chiara to San Paolo delle Abbadesse, since he had accompanied Francesco to all his meetings with Chiara. Leone's physical description is based on an examination of his skeletal remains, venerated in the Basilica di San Francesco in Assisi (Padre Anacleto Iacovelli, "Le Tombe dei quattro [Cavalieri della Tavola Rotonda] e quella della [Dama Romana]").

Chiara put aside her fine clothing once her hair was cut (CA:ED 286). Perhaps she acquired her own penitential tunic or perhaps the friars gave her one. What happened to Chiara's discarded clothing? Possibly Francesco or another friar returned it to her family or gave it to the poor.

The Scripture quoted in this chapter is John 12:3. Francesco's words about the Good Shepherd are from his *Admonitions* (FA:ED I 131).

12

Messer Monaldo di Offreduccio

Offreduccio House, Assisi (Monday of Holy Week, March 19, 1212)

As he approached the stairs to the Offreduccio house, Messer Monaldo sensed something amiss. When he had left his steed at the stable, the grooms had averted their eyes, as they had done when Messer Favarone had died.

Monaldo dashed upstairs, the wood thudding under his heavy boots. Dwarfing the well-muscled house watchman Ioanni di Ventura, Monaldo shot him a question. "Is something wrong?"

"Last night Madonna Chiara left ... secretly. Through the door of the dead."

The door of the dead! That obscure, barricaded door was opened only to carry a corpse feet-first out of the house, to send a bride to her wedding, or to flee an enemy.

Monaldo threw open the door of the Offreduccio house and raced down the corridors until he came to the seldom-used hall of the dead. The hall led to a small second-story door that had no steps to the street. To exit the door of the dead, one had to leap. Those who left by this door were, in a real or symbolic sense, dead to the family.

The door was ajar. The light streaming in teased him closer. He walked slowly, trying to absorb what he saw. The thick wooden beams that had barricaded the door from the inside had been moved aside. The door was pulled open against the rubble. Monaldo stepped over the mess and peered outdoors into the empty street.

"Damn!" Monaldo slammed the door shut. He rammed into place the ponderous iron bar that bolted the door, then heaved the wooden beams against the door, barricading it again. How could a young woman have the strength to unblock that door, leap down into the street, and disappear?

He flung himself through the halls to the women's sewing room and threw open the door. Madonna Ortulana, Madonna Beatrice, Madonna Catarina, and Madonna Cristiana, visiting daughter of Messer Bernardo da Suppo, were sitting there, their sewing idle in their laps. They turned to him, conversation dying on their lips, horror spreading across their faces.

"Who helped Madonna Chiara out?" he demanded.

No one had. Even the servants had been questioned. Chiara had left behind a note saying she had taken Jesus as her spouse. About an hour ago, Fra Bernardo di Quintavalle had returned her clothing.

Madonna Pacifica was also gone from the Guelfuccio house.

Monaldo sent for the other Offreduccio knights. Messer Ugolino and his son Messer Martino. Messer Paolo and his son Messer Bernardino. Messer Scipione and his son Messer Paolo. Messer Ranieri. Others. They would ride to the Porziuncula and bring her back.

Monaldo did not have to threaten Francesco for information. "She's consecrated to God and has sanctuary at San Paolo delle Abbadesse in Bastia," Francesco told him.

The knights galloped to Bastia. Monaldo tried to calm himself. If Madonna Chiara had gone to San Paolo, the situation wasn't so unthinkable. San Paolo was a powerful Benedictine monastery whose nuns, all members of the highest nobility, lived in wealth and influence. The opulent stronghold that stretched along the banks of the deep Chiagio River was the perfect place for an Offreduccio who insisted on marrying God.

The abbess, in her tasteful black habit, politely instructed the knights to wait in the little pink-and-beige stone church of San Paolo, but to tether their horses outside. The knights, who usually rode their steeds into church, complied.

The men were standing awkwardly in the white-plastered church when the abbess entered through a small door on the left. With her came a black-veiled, limping penitent clothed in the poor gray tunic of the Lesser Brothers, a rope knotted around her waist, her feet bare against the red stone floor.

Madonna Chiara.

Every bitter emotion that Monaldo ever felt toward this niece surfaced. Her childish insistence on taking beggars to Perugia. Her weird, extreme fasting that had thinned her plump and pleasant face. Her rejection of marriage that would have allied another powerful family with the Offreduccios. Her refusal to sell her inheritance to the family, defrauding them of what was theirs and giving it to the poor. Now, dishonoring her family further by making herself a pauper.

Monaldo tried to calm himself. "We've come to take you home."

"You're ill," Messer Ugolino said kindly. "We'll obtain the best doctor."

"I need no doctor," Chiara said firmly. "I'm not going home."

"Your mother is worried," Messer Paolo noted.

"Tell her that I'm fine."

Monaldo stuffed down his impatience. "Madonna Chiara, your place is at home."

"You've always wished to become a nun," observed Messer Ranieri, one of Chiara's rejected suitors. "Why not as befits your class? You appear a pauper."

"Messer, this dress befits a spouse of the poor Jesus," Chiara tenderly replied. "And your wife is well?"

"Very well."

"No noblewoman would do what you've done." Monaldo's patience was waning.

"We care about you," Ugolino said. "Perhaps your fasting or your father's death has affected your mind. Come with us and recover."

Just then a bell pealed, its rich tones reverberating through the chapel. The side door opened and the abbess appeared. "I hope that you had a lovely visit," she said sweetly. "Madonna Chiara must come now for prayers."

Chiara bowed to the knights. "*Addio*, Messers. Please tell my household that I'm well." Limping slightly, she followed the abbess through the side doorway and closed the door.

Monaldo slammed his fist into a thick pillar. "Tomorrow, we return."

The knights returned Tuesday, Wednesday, Thursday. Each day they argued with Chiara. Each day she disappeared through the door with the abbess.

Then came Good Friday. Chiara needed to be home for Easter. On Easter, noble maidens dressed in their finest clothes to impress the young noblemen at Mass. If she didn't return home by Easter, she'd be lost forever.

The altar was draped with a plain white cloth. Gone was the little tower, off to the side, that held the Eucharist. The red cross traced on the pedestal of the altar appeared to be painted with blood. The church was as still as death.

Again, the abbess ushered Chiara through the side doorway. "Please respect the solemnity of the day on which Jesus was crucified," she requested. "Keep your visit short and your voices down."

Down? How? For four days Chiara had refused to listen to common sense. She was a stubborn and spoiled child. She needed to know what she'd done.

Monaldo stared at his niece, standing so tall and unshakable next to the white-draped altar. "You have done a detestable thing," Monaldo hissed. "You have made yourself a slave of these nuns who are less well-bred than you. You are more repulsive than pig's dung. You have dragged the Offreduccio name through mud and cast it upon a manure heap."

The words were spilling out, intense with fury, disappointment, and shock. "You—the one your father spoiled, his little Chiarita. You have sullied his memory. This is no honor to God. This is defiant idiocy. You have made the Offreduccios the target of Assisi gossip, the point of the crudest jokes."

Chiara began to tremble.

"You despicable and unruly child. Do you know how many people you have wounded? Even if you came home now, you could not fully undo the destruction. I'm ashamed to call you my brother's daughter. You're unworthy of Messer Favarone."

Chiara's face was blanched, tears streaming down her cheeks. Blinking, she turned briefly toward the crucifix behind her, then dropped to her knees. She took the altar cloth in her right hand and lifted her sorrowful face toward the knights.

Monaldo knew what she meant by touching the cloth. She was claiming the right of sanctuary. To touch her now would be to commit sacrilege, to incur excommunication.

Sacrilege and excommunication could be lifted. Would Bishop Guido hold Monaldo's taking of Chiara against him? It was Monaldo's duty to uphold the family's reputation. If Chiara wouldn't be sensible, he'd use force. If the knights who were pledged to defend this monastery tried to interfere, the Offreduccio knights would fight.

Monaldo leaped up the pink-and-white marble steps that led to the raised altar. Grabbing Chiara's right arm, he yanked her to her feet, pulling the altar cloth awry.

In one swift motion, Chiara raised her left hand and tore the veil from her head. Her eyes and Monaldo's met in a frigid stare.

Her head was practically naked.

Monaldo dropped her arm as if it were a snake. He recoiled from her, stepping backward from the altar, almost tripping down the steps, staring in horror at her intense, tear-streaked face.

Never had Monaldo looked upon a woman's naked head. A woman's flowing hair was her crown, her riches, her beauty, her modesty, her wealth.

Chiara's right hand slipped from the altar cloth, now skewed crazily across the altar. She joined both hands in front of her chest and bowed her head.

Was this the woman who had never tarried near windows lest she spark lustful thoughts in passersby? The woman whose sleeves had always modestly covered her wrists and whose train hid her feet? Only a woman consecrated to God would cut off her hair. The tonsure was a definitive act, placing Chiara securely under the guardianship of the Church. Because Chiara was tonsured, Church law forbade the knights to take her home. Nor would they wish to. A woman without hair was as worthless as a lame steed.

"You should be ashamed." Monaldo spat out the words as if they were flaming embers. "You have destroyed your beauty and your value to any man and to your family. You are no longer an Offreduccio or the daughter of Messer Favarone."

He turned to his wide-eyed knights. His voice was quavering with rage. "Let's go home. From now on Madonna Chiara is dead to this household."

NOTES

Chiara escaped through the "door of the dead," having removed by herself the rubble blocking it (CA:ED 185).

What was Chiara's status in the San Paolo community? Was she considered a postulant (person discerning a vocation to religious life) sent there by the bishop? Were the nuns willing to accept her as a member of their community although she had no dowry? Did she become one of the monastery servants? Did she live as a hermitess or a penitent? History gives no answers.

Although we do not know how Monaldo learned of Chiara's disappearance, he and other unnamed family members rode to San Paolo to confront her. Messer Ranieri di Bernardo seems to have witnessed the Holy Week struggle (CA:ED 183, 194).

In an unspecified year, Ranieri (CA:ED 193) married one of Chiara's relatives.

13

Madonna Catarina di Favarone

Strada di San Martino, Assisi (April 4, 1212)

Madonna Catarina and Madonna Bona left after Mass and headed out the Porta San Giorgio toward Panzo. They walked past fields of fresh grass, grazing sheep, and poor, scattered cottages. For the first time in sixteen days, fourteen-year-old Catarina felt hopeful. Until Chiara left, Catarina had never spent a day without her. The past two weeks were a bad dream. Chiara gone as if dead. Pacifica, too. Her uncles furious. When Madonna Bona had arrived home from Rome, Catarina had requested her company in walking to Sant'Angelo d'Panzo, south of Assisi where, as all Assisi knew, Fra Francesco had moved Chiara.

Above the road, the women saw a foreboding cliff: the Sasso Cupo, the cliff of dark stone. They passed the crumbling ruin of the Church of San Martino. Below, the dry streambed of Rigo Secco twisted like a scar. The women arrived at the monastery, which clung to the side of Monte Subasio.

All was quiet. Bona and Catarina walked up to the first building and peeked in at long dining tables.

"Are you looking for someone?" A gray-robed woman in sandals and black veil had come up behind them.

"For Madonna Chiara and Madonna Pacifica," Bona said. "We're their sisters."

The penitent burst into a smile. "I see resemblances. Come."

The woman led the way to a large garden struggling for growth beyond the buildings. Several women in gray tunics were hoeing or pulling weeds. One weeder, Madonna Pacifica, was dressed in a prim cap and mustard-colored gown.

Within moments, Chiara was embracing Catarina, and Pacifica and Bona were hugging.

The superior sent the women to the refectory until prayer time.

So much love to share! So many stories to tell! Chiara and Pacifica told of scrubbing floors, planting vegetables, making cheese. Bona told of her pilgrimage. Catarina told how the Offreduccio women spoke of Chiara, although Messer Monaldo had forbidden it.

The stories and the laughing went on until prayer time, which was followed by a light meal of eggs, spring greens, and cool water. The superior allowed the women to continue to visit.

"What is it like to be married to Jesus?" Catarina asked. "I've always dreamed of marrying a noble. But now I sometimes think of marrying Jesus."

"I've prayed for this!" With her face glowing, Chiara tried to explain her peace and joy. Love of Christ was like a sweet fragrance, a breath of air, a powerful embrace! "Do not be afraid. Run to Him joyfully, swiftly; abandon yourself totally to the Lord Jesus Christ, Whom in loving, you are chaste, in touching, you become more pure, in embracing, you are a virgin. He will give you the grace you need." Chiara squeezed Catarina's hands warmly. "Fra Francesco will visit us tomorrow. Do you wish him to tonsure you?"

Catarina wasn't sure. Yet she stayed behind while Bona, accompanied by Pacifica and two other penitential women, returned to Assisi. By the time for evening prayer, Pacifica and the other two were back at Panzo. Then a light supper. Night prayer. Dusk. Silence. Chiara led Catarina to a small, tight hermitage where, after the two embraced, her sister went off to her own hut.

Lying on straw, Catarina drew two shabby blankets over herself. How could she sleep? Being tonsured tomorrow was thrilling, frightening. Did she want to be married to a noble or to the Lord?

Catarina was accustomed to plump mattresses and quilts, not straw and thin blankets. She was used to hoofbeats, clamorous "Goodnights," and beggars arguing in the piazza, not to shuffling leaves, peeping frogs, and mournful, distant wolf howls. She always slept through the nightly ringing of the cathedral bells that called the canons to Matins, but tonight she was still awake when Sant'Angelo's bell rang. She arose with the bell to pray Matins.

In the chapel, aglow with oil lamps, the women's chanted prayers graced the night with praise of God. Catarina could have this every night. She could have Jesus. Whom else did she need?

When Matins ended, the women filed silently back to their hermitages. Whispering Christ's name, Catarina fell asleep.

Dawn came. More prayer, Lauds and Prime. Mass with the priest who lived at the hermitage. The end of silence. The women had a drink of water and went to work. Catarina and Chiara were sent to weed the herb garden. The two sisters were chattering about Francesco when Catarina heard the frenzied pounding of many boots.

Her heart froze.

"Madonna Catarina. Get ready to return immediately with us."

Messer Monaldo's huge frame seemed bigger than the garden. As Catarina backed away from his looming shadow, she could barely speak. "I don't wish to leave my sister."

Monaldo moved toward her. Other knights emerged from the forest. Monaldo's son Messer Francesco. Messer Ugolino and his sons Messer Monaldo and Messer Martino. Messer Paolo and his son Messer Bernardino. Messer Scipione and his son Messer Paolo. Messer Giorgio di Ugone and his son Messer Paolo. Messer Ranieri. Twelve Offreduccio knights.

To the left there was a swift flash of blue wool and brown fur as a huge hand smashed into Catarina's cheek, knocking her to the ground. Instinctively she covered her face. Fists were pummeling her, feet kicking her. She shrieked, her face still covered. Someone grabbed her hair, banged her head against the soil. The pain in her scalp was unbearable. She was being dragged by her hair.

Cursing. Shouts. High-pitched, pleading women's voices.

Huge, thick arms were grabbing her, hoisting her. "Dear sister, help me!" she screamed. "Do not let me be taken from Christ the Lord."

She kicked and fought the knights as they dragged her through the brambles to the steep bank of the dry Rigo Secco. Above the cursing and shrieking, like a sweet, angelic song, Chiara was pleading, "God, protect Madonna Catarina! Keep her constant in her resolve! Protect her from these violent men!"

Something hard slammed into Catarina's chest with a terrific force. She caught her breath and everything went black.

She felt herself coming out of darkness the way one comes out of sleep. She could hear voices through her grogginess.

"I can't lift her."

"All together!"

"You! Farmers! Help us lift her."

Hands were grabbing her everywhere. She was groggy, throbbing with pain.

"There're twelve of us. Five peasants. Lift her!"

More pulling, grabbing.

Chiara's voice again, strong. "God, give Madonna Catarina your strength and perseverance! Protect her from these violent men!"

Messer Ugolino's voice. "She has been eating lead all night; no wonder she is so heavy."

Monaldo's demand. "Get up! Now. Or you die."

Catarina would die. *Oh, my Jesus, forgive me. Into Your hands I commend my spirit.*

"Arragh!" The shriek was unearthly, prolonged.

Men's voices. "What's the matter?"

Monaldo's anguished groan. "I can't ... move ... my arm. No! Don't touch it! The pain. You'll break it. I ... can't ... move it!"

"Go home." Chiara's voice was commanding. "God wants my sister here. You cannot lift her. You cannot strike her. Go home."

Silence.

"Entrust Madonna Catarina to my care and to God."

Muttering.

"Go home."

"Let's go." Monaldo's words were trembling. "No! *Don't touch my arm!*"

Shuffling. Boots moving away.

A gentle hand on her forehead, brushing her hair aside. Chiara's soothing voice. "Dear sister, are you all right?"

Women's voices, all asking how badly she was injured.

Quite suddenly, Catarina felt strong and pain-free. She pushed herself into a sitting position.

Beyond the clucking cluster of women, down the path away from Sant'Angelo, the knights retreated. Messer Monaldo's right arm was raised, bobbing along with him.

Catarina stood and brushed off her tattered gown. She managed a grin. "Now I have to become a penitent. I can't wear this."

"Our relatives have halfway tonsured you." Chiara plucked a great clump of sandy brown hair from some brambles.

"You're more than half bald," Pacifica remarked.

"I must thank God for delivering me," Catarina said in awe.

"We'll all thank God," the superior announced.

In the chapel, the group fell to their knees; then, one by one, the women left to return to work.

Catarina felt a sturdy hand on her shoulder. Fra Francesco and Fra Bernardo were standing beside her. *Oh, sweet God, now I shall become only Yours.* With her heart thumping, Catarina began to rise. Francesco shook his head.

"Madonna Catarina, do you wish to embrace the penitential life?"

"More than ever."

"Christiana, stand next to your sister."

Chiara stood and placed her hand on Catarina's shoulder. Catarina knelt erect, her chin firm, her eyes closed. *Jesus, make me true to You, worthy of You, loyal. Make me Your spouse.*

Her hair was being lifted, cut. She tried to concentrate on her praying and on the cutting, so that she'd forever remember this moment.

Hands pressed her skull. "Christ, the innocent Lamb of God," Francesco was saying, "was beset by a pack of vicious men and killed for the world's sins. In memory of today's battle against vicious men who wished to tear you from Jesus and take your life, you shall henceforth be named after *Agnus Dei*, the Lamb of God. Madonna Agnese."

Agnese. She had not expected a new name. But it seemed perfect. She liked it.

NOTES

Catarina initially had her mind set on "carnal marriage." After Chiara became a penitent, she began to pray that Catarina would join her. Sixteen days after Chiara's consecration, whether alone or with a companion, Catarina came to Chiara. By then, Chiara was at Sant'Angelo in Panzo, where Francesco had moved her a few days after the confrontation with her relatives.

In *Without Turning Back: Life of Saint Agnes of Assisi*, Sister Chiara Lucia Garzonio states that Catarina made three visits to Chiara before the Holy Spirit inspired her to join. Other writers imply that Catarina came to Chiara only once.

For many years, historians believed that Sant'Angelo was a Benedictine monastery for nuns, similar to other Benedictine foundations around Assisi. Modern historians such as Marco Bartoli (*Clare of Assisi* 55), Jean-François Godet-Calogeras (*Out of the Shadows* 106–107), and others believe that Sant'Angelo was more likely a community of female penitential recluses in the model of the Beguines. The Beguines were groups of pious women in the area of Belgium who supported themselves through their cloth trade and who lived together without a common rule.

History records no details of the Sant'Angelo community. In this book, the Sant'Angelo women are imagined as living as penitential hermits and generally following a lifestyle that would be described in the Rule of 1221, which Cardinal Ugolino composed for the Brothers and Sisters of Penance (Habig, *Omnibus* 168–73).

The violent confrontation of twelve Offreduccio knights (some unnamed), led by Monaldo, and Catarina's pleas and her miraculous deliverance follow the history (CA:ED 303–04).

The legal age for entrance into religious life was twelve. At some time shortly after this chapter's savage episode, Francesco tonsured fourteen-year-old Catarina and renamed her "Agnese" (CA:ED 304, 24Gen 237–39).

Chiara's words to Catarina beginning with "the Lord Jesus Christ, Whom in loving" are from her *First Letter to Agnes of Prague* (CA:ED 44).

PART FOUR

To Dwell in the Church of San Damiano

14

Madonna Pacifica di Guelfuccio

Sant'Angelo d'Panzo, Panzo, Italy (May 1212)

Madonna Pacifica threw herself to the rough wooden floor of her tiny hut and wept. Madonna Chiara and Madonna Agnese had just left with Fra Francesco to live as enclosed sisters at San Damiano, where they would have no servants, not even Pacifica.

She felt for the cross, two knotty sticks that she had bound together at right angles with a length of lace from one of her gowns. Pacifica clenched the cross tightly, squeezing her fingernails into her palms. Her mind swirled with thoughts of Chiara and Catarina, now Agnese, whom she had known since birth. Her chest seemed about to split with sobbing.

YOU DON'T HAVE TO LEAVE THEM. YOU CAN BE A SISTER.

Pacifica gave a little gasp of surprise at this quiet inner prompting. She had several times rejected the notion, but here it was again, like a mouse come out of hiding when the household sleeps.

She was already doing penance, but secretly. Was God now asking her to make her penitential life public? To be, in others' eyes, more than a pious lady who went to Mass, made pilgrimages, and prayed? To become a public penitent?

How could she ever do that?

Some people shunned, berated, and ridiculed penitents. Others extolled them. Penitents were to model holiness. Those who set a poor example gave scandal to the Church.

Pacifica shuddered, her hands still digging into her palms.

I am a sinner, a bad example of someone who follows You.

The Church had enough bad examples. In Assisi, some clergy were addicted to fornication, drunkenness, gambling, greed, or usury. Wealthy religious houses engaged in lawsuits. Grouchy, stingy, and harsh religious bickered among themselves. Some preached heresy or toyed with schism. No wonder most churches were nearly empty and many were abandoned. Assisians mocked religious even while claiming to practice their faith. Why would she become visibly religious in such an atmosphere?

Sì, Francesco and his friars were converting many. Some priests and nuns were growing holier. They were great lights in the darkness, but Pacifica wasn't as good as they were. She was only a pinprick of light. What good was that?

IT'S ENOUGH LIGHT TO SEE THE CROSS.

The revelation startled her.

Madonna Chiara is starting something very different. You don't want me to join up with that, do You?

The thought came quickly. I HAVE ASKED FOR SURRENDER, NOT QUESTIONS.

Pacifica objected, *Lord, You said that prayer and fasting must be done secretly.*

He had an answer. RELIGIOUS GARB DOESN'T REVEAL PRAYER OR FASTING. IT REVEALS ME.

Pacifica knew what the internal voice meant. In contrast to the clergy and even to Bishop Guido—who dressed like nobility, concealing their tonsures with caps so as to appear as nobles—penitents and friars wore poor, ash-gray robes of *lazzo*, the homespun, woolen cloth of peasants. Their tonsures were evident. Garb became a sermon, proclaiming that Christ was important enough to follow radically.

Those who visibly displayed their religion were either praised or rebuked. What would her father, Madonna Bona, or her other relatives say if Pacifica went public with her penance?

God, give me courage.

Courage to do God's will, not hers or someone else's. Only doing God's will would make her holy.

For twenty years, Pacifica had toyed with the idea of entering a convent. Something always held her back. Now she was faced with a decision. Assisi? Or San Damiano?

Surrender means total surrender.

Pacifica laid the cross on the floor. In the light coming through the cracks, she could see the cross clearly. She looked for the chink in the wall that was letting in light. Small as a pinprick, it helped light the darkness. That was about all her life as a sister would be.

Pacifica pressed her hand over the cross before rising. She pushed back the reed door and her vision was flooded with light.

She would walk to San Damiano and ask Madonna Chiara to accept her as a sister.

NOTES

Scholars disagree on the date Chiara went to San Damiano, giving dates anywhere from May through October 1212 (or 1211, depending on the historian's choice of year for her tonsure).

Pacifica seems to have joined Chiara in the religious life about the time she went to San Damiano or shortly thereafter (CA:ED 145). The reasons for Pacifica's decision are not known.

15

Giovanna

San Damiano, Assisi (Late Autumn 1212)

Giovanna was curled against the wall of the Church of San Damiano. The unbolting of doors awakened her. Tucking her mouse-colored braids beneath the hood of her shabby brown mantle, Giovanna stood and blessed herself with water from a large basin near the church door. Timidly she descended into the dark church, her sturdy bare toes tickling the cool floor. In the apse, a short, silver-haired friar bustled to prepare for Mass. Two noble couples, one old, one young, strode into the church and stood near the altar. Peasants, including Giovanna, a few servants, and farmers, stood in the back.

Giovanna was shepherdess for a Perugian noble whose daughter, Madonna Benvenuta, had come two months ago, in late September, to this convent. Benvenuta's becoming a recluse pauper had baffled her household but encouraged Giovanna. Over a week ago, Giovanna had received permission from her noble's bailiff to come to Assisi while her father tended her sheep and his. She had promised to be back before the full moon.

She wanted to ask these pauper ladies if they would accept her as a pauper servant. Other convents had rejected her because she had never learned to cook the meats, sauces, and sweets that ladies liked—nor could she mend, launder, and scrub to a lady's satisfaction. Pauper ladies, however, might welcome a pauper servant.

Please, Lord. Giovanna sent her prayer toward a carved white dove pressed against the ceiling above the altar. Therein reposed the Eucharistic Lord. God, who whispered to Giovanna in nature, dwelt totally in that Holy Bread, the Lesser Brothers preached. How badly Giovanna wanted to be near Him!

Mass began, proceeded, ended. The noble couples approached a speaking grill in the apse and pulled a cord. On the other side of the wall, a bell chimed. The snap of a bolt. The sliding of a door. Unintelligible low voices.

After some time, the couples left the church while a waiting farmer approached the grill, rang the bell, spoke to someone. He chatted a bit, then left—on a rotating turn in the wall—a plump sack. The turn swiveled into the monastery, revealing its curved outer side, then rotated outward again, the empty sack returned. The farmer took his sack and left.

Giovanna was alone. She had waited for this moment. She had dreaded it.

With her eyes glancing at the dove, Giovanna cautiously approached the black-curtained grill and pulled the bell cord. The sounds of a shutter unbolting, sliding, came from the other side of the grill.

"Pace e bene. May I help you?" The voice came through the black curtain.

Giovanna swallowed. "Would you be in need of a servant, Madonna?"

"Just one moment. You must speak to Suor Chiara."

The unseen shutter slid shut, was bolted.

Please, God.

The unbolting, sliding sound drew Giovanna's attention from the dove. The black curtain at the grill was being lifted. Giovanna looked into the beautiful oval face of a black-veiled penitent. The woman was erect, her gaze direct, unwavering, and confident.

"Pace e bene. I'm Suor Chiara. And you, little one?"

"Giovanna of Perugia, Madonna." Giovanna curtsied shakily.

Chiara smiled and glanced at a taller penitent who stood near her. "Suor Benvenuta is from Perugia."

The other sister was tall and sturdy, her deep, dark eyes set close to her nose. So like Giovanna's nobleman master. So this was Madonna Benvenuta. Giovanna had never met her. "My father and I tend your father's sheep," Giovanna offered.

"Does my father mistreat you?" Madonna Benvenuta asked, her dark eyes tender.

"Oh, no, Madonna." Giovanna curtsied again. "I ask to be a servant here to be near my Lord Christ." She glanced at the dove.

"We have no servants here. All we sisters serve each other." Madonna Chiara's deep voice was gentle, her blue eyes kind. "Do you wish to become a sister, Giovanna?"

Anguish swept Giovanna. Only ladies could become nuns. "I have no dowry," she stammered.

"You yourself are your dowry. Will you give God yourself?"

Wonder rose in Giovanna's throat. "Is it possible, Madonna?"

"Certainly. Do you know how old you are?"

Giovanna calculated quickly. She had begun to tend sheep when her flock's big, spotted ewe, now fifteen years old, had been born. "I am some years older than fifteen."

"Old enough. Giovanna, we sisters wish always to observe the Holy Gospel of our Lord Jesus Christ, by living in obedience, without anything of one's own, and in chastity. We have promised reverence to Lord Pope Innocenzo, to the Roman Church, and to our gracious father Francesco, who brought us here. Do you believe all that the Catholic Church teaches? And all the sacraments? Do you use them?"

"Oh, sì."

"Are you married?"

"No, Madonna."

"Would you wish to marry our Lord Jesus and live with us, in prayer, penance, and service?"

"That must be like living in heaven!"

Chiara laughed. "To us, it seems so. Not to others. We own nothing."

"I have only what I'm wearing. Gladly will I discard it."

"Can you stay to see how we live?"

Giovanna had until the full moon. If she didn't return, she would send Papà a message. Someone else would shepherd her sheep. "I can stay!"

"Good. Now go out of the church and we'll lower the staircase into the monastery. Climb up, and we'll get to know each other."

Giovanna darted out so quickly that she forgot to curtsy.

NOTES

A document that names all the sisters in San Damiano in 1238 mentions three Giovannas (CA:ED 429–30, listed as the Latin Ioanna in CA:ED). We know nothing of these women.

The Giovanna in this chapter typifies women of the lower social classes whom Chiara accepted and even invited into her community at a time when convents were strictly for noblewomen. This chapter also attempts to explore how women were received into the community, following guidelines in Chiara's *Form of Life* (CA:ED 108–26), from which Chiara's words "to observe the Holy Gospel..." are taken (CA:ED 109).

The black curtain-covered grills were part of the traditional enclosure for anchorites. At San Damiano, the curtain could be lifted at the speaking grill when talking to someone, but it was never to be removed in the parlor (CA:ED 116–17). The speaking grill most likely opened into the very public church, while the parlor was probably a separate room for lengthier, private conversations. Always keeping the parlor grill covered with a curtain would preserve the good reputations of those speaking in the parlor.

16

Madonna Ginevra di Giorgio di Ugone

Bedroom, House of Messer Giorgio di Ugone, Assisi (Late Summer 1214)

Twenty-year-old Madonna Ginevra, daughter of Messer Giorgio di Ugone, was lying in her silk-covered bed, trying to sleep. Neither the heat nor the humidity were keeping her awake. Her thoughts were.

This morning, at Mamma's insistence, she had sorted through her gowns, discarding the ones she no longer wanted. Some she had sent to the lepers at San Lazarro, but the better ones she had taken to the Damianites, who would refashion them into priestly vestments and altar trappings given free to the churches of the region. She had kept five gowns for herself, and even those she didn't like. Who was she trying to stun with her beauty? Every nobleman whom Papà was considering as her mate was boring. Ginevra wrinkled her nose, thinking that in two months she might be sleeping next to one of them.

Ginevra shifted her broad shoulders and lay on her side. Her freckle-faced sister, Madonna Emilia, was happily married and mother to a new baby. Her brother, Messer Paolo, seemed quite content to be a husband. The problem with Ginevra was God.

Today at San Damiano the crucifix that had spoken to Francesco had spoken to Ginevra. And a miracle had happened.

Bored with nobles, tournaments, feasts, and silks, Ginevra had walked with her servants and her lady-in-waiting to the convent. What had Chiara said there? "It's not where you go that's exciting. It's whom you're with. God is here. And He isn't boring."

How could that be? Only the new sisters, Giovanna and Felicita, left the convent at all, and they to beg. The others stayed in an expansive area of sloping ground, behind high walls, curtained grills, and bolted doors. Even Ginevra had to speak to Chiara, her best friend, through a black curtain. The big news at the convent was that the new cat, fondly named Suor Gatta, had knocked over a candle, alighting Suor Pacifica's blanket while she slept beneath it. Suor Balbina had smothered the flames with her own blanket, so the damage had been slight. That was the extent of excitement at San Damiano.

Like her namesake, Queen Guinevere, Ginevra craved excitement. Suor Agnese's litany of people prayed for and lives changed at San Damiano may have excited Agnese, but not Ginevra.

But then there was that incident with the oil jar. Ginevra had seen the empty jar on the turn for old Fra Bentevenga to take to beg for oil. She had been speaking to Chiara when he had limped into the parlor, chastising Chiara for playing a joke on him and putting a full oil jar on the turn. Ginevra's servants, who had been waiting by the turn, swore that no one had filled the jar. However it was filled, Chiara now had olive oil for the ill sisters without lame Fra Bentevenga begging for it. He had oil too, for himself and the other three grumpy, elderly friars Francesco had assigned to the monastery.

Ginevra pressed her hands against her soft mattress. Had the filled oil jar been a miracle?

Miracles happened. Here, in the Cathedral del San Rufino, the relics of Assisi's patron, Saint Rufinus, had recently been unearthed. Berta, a possessed child, had been dragged kicking and screaming to the crypt, where she was released from her demon. Madonna Savia had climbed down into the crypt and had been cured of hysteria. Dropsy, fevers, scrofulas, fistulas—healed.

Then there was that voice from the crucifix. Ginevra had been kneeling, gazing up at it. *Why do I keep coming here?* she had asked. *What is there about this place?*

I AM ABOUT THIS PLACE, the voice had said.

What had Suor Agnese said? "In the silence and privacy of this place, we can speak to Him, know Him, serve Him."

From behind the curtained grill in the parlor, Chiara had almost sung. "May you totally love Him Who gave Himself totally for your love, at whose beauty the sun and moon marvel, Whose rewards and their uniqueness and grandeur have no limits." Chiara's full, deep voice had trembled with passion. "Whose strength is more robust, generosity more lofty, Whose appearance is more handsome, love more courteous, and every kindness more refined." The words had spilled from Chiara like a hymn. "The kingdom of heaven is promised and given by the Lord only to the poor because she who loves what is temporal loses the fruit of love."

What was love? Or Who? Did Love live at San Damiano?

I AM ABOUT THIS PLACE.

Over the next two months, Ginevra often visited San Damiano. There she found Love, and so she chose Him as her spouse. In His honor, she renamed herself Benedetta, "Woman blessed by God."

How blessed Suor Benedetta felt to live where God was!

NOTES

In 1214, Ginevra changed her name to Benedetta (sometimes written Benedicta) and joined Chiara and the other sisters named in this chapter (Fortini 350). No other details are available. Nothing indicates that the miracle of the oil jar, which occurred in 1214 prior to Ginevra's entrance (CA:ED 148), figured in her conversion.

San Damiano stood on about six acres.

No dates are preserved regarding the marriages of Emilia and Paolo and the births of their children.

The miracles at the tomb of Saint Rufinus are on record in the Cathedral del San Rufino (Fortini 370–71).

Since medieval people thought that light frightened away demons, they kept their sleeping quarters well lit. The Benedictine Rule, which Chiara was later made to adopt, stipulates that the dormitory must be lit by candles. Yet a cat, which Chiara at some point obtained, can leap up on a ledge and knock over a candle. Later rules for the Clares, including Isabella's Rule of 1259 and Urban's Rule of 1263, stipulate that a lamp (not a candle) must be kept burning all night in the dormitory. Was this done at San Damiano? Most likely, yes.

The Damianites used cast-off clothing to make priestly vestments and altar linens, which they gave away, just as the friars gave away sacred vessels and irons for making altar breads.

Francesco intentionally chose elderly, reluctant friars to serve the sisters. The begging friars at San Damiano were certainly Franciscans, but the chaplains may have been Franciscans or Cistercians. The first visitator to the San Damiano community was a Cistercian.

As a medicinal, olive oil was taken by mouth and also gently rubbed into wounds and sores. The wall on which Chiara left the jar was "near the entrance of the house." For years, monasteries have used the turn to exchange goods between the inside and the outside of the monastery. The "wall near the entrance to the house" may have been the turn. Fra Bentevenga went to get the oil jar and found it filled (CA:ED 148, 295–96).

Some sisters at San Damiano served outside the monastery. When they began to do this is not known, nor are the names of the serving sisters recorded. Two Felicitas appear on the 1238 document that lists all the San Damiano sisters (CA:ED 440), but we know nothing about them.

Chiara's words to Ginevra are from her *First* and *Third Letters to Agnes of Prague* (CA:ED 44, 46, 51).

17

Fra Francesco Bernardone

Church of San Damiano (December 1215)

wo friars—homely, scraggly-bearded Francesco Bernardone and tall,
swarthy, black-haired Masseo di Marignano—were praying prostrate
below the white dove in which rested the Eucharistic Body of their
Lord. Before them loomed the huge golden crucifix that had called Francesco to
conversion. Francesco's thin fingers pressed against the stone floor. Chilling
dampness seeped through his worn, much-patched tunic.

My God, is there another way? As one of the huge number of religious delegates to the Fourth Lateran Council last month, Francesco had been unable to
sway the council regarding the Poor Ladies. How was he to tell Christiana?

Francesco respected Christiana. When he had considered retiring from
preaching to live a contemplative life, he had consulted Christiana and Fra
Silvestro, both of whom told him that God intended him to preach. So Francesco
had preached throughout the beautiful Romagna countryside north of here and
throughout most of the Roman peninsula. Periodically he prayed at hermitages,
yet he still managed to preach in France and Spain, where he had contracted a
persistent illness sometimes so severe that Bishop Guido often made him recover
in the bishop's palace. Today, feeling stronger, he had come to San Damiano.
God was silent. Francesco pushed to his feet. Within moments, the dreaded
meeting began, with Francesco and Masseo seated on two rude wooden benches

in the parlor and Christiana, Madonna Pacifica, and Madonna Agnese greeting him from behind the black-curtained grill.

After offering a prayer, Francesco began. "I've come to tell you about the council, Christiana."

"Oh, Fra, we've been praying for the council ever since Pope Innocenzo convened it." Christiana's voice was eager. "Were our prayers answered?"

"Some were." He would tell the good things first. "The faithful must now confess and receive the Body and Blood of Christ at least yearly, at Easter. But the council urged more frequent reception, even several times yearly."

"Praise God! We will receive the Body and Blood of our Lord on every solemnity!" Christiana said joyfully.

"The perpetual virginity of Mary is to be stated in the profession of faith."

"God be praised." The voice was Agnese's.

"So that priests will not be ignorant, schools to teach them about the faith will be established. No man may pay to become a priest. Nor can bishops accept money to fill a position. Sacraments must be freely given, with no donation required, although one may give money freely as an alms or thank-offering. Nor may relics be sold. No money is to be demanded of anyone wishing to enter religious life. Those who wish entrance should be accepted if they are suitable, without a dowry."

The women were eagerly agreeing with the council's decisions. "Drunkenness and sexual license in the clergy will not be tolerated. Guidelines for the proper care of church buildings and tabernacles must be followed."

Francesco paused. The ladies, he knew, would greet the next announcement less enthusiastically. "Lord Pope proclaimed a Fifth Crusade."

He heard a stifled groan. The ladies wanted the Holy Land to be in Christian hands, but they hated the violent wars against the infidels that would bring it about. The brutal Fourth Crusade had never reached the Holy Land. Instead, the crusaders had viciously pillaged Constantinople and violated its inhabitants. There followed the pitiable Children's Crusade, in which huge numbers of unarmed French and German youngsters tried to walk to the Holy Land, believing that the innocent and pure of heart could retake it. All but a few had died of starvation, cold, disease, or drowning—or been captured as slaves. The survivors had returned home in shame.

"The Crusade will begin in 1219 with Egypt the first to be attacked." Behind the curtain came a thin gasp of horror. "During the next four years of preparation, there is to be a Truce of God."

"Four years of peace everywhere," Christiana breathed. "God be praised."

"No one is to trade with Egypt or with any infidel nation."

"Perhaps the Saracens will surrender the Holy Land without a fight," Pacifica suggested.

Francesco doubted it. "Only if the Saracens became Christians."

Christianity reminded him of his gift. From one of his deep pockets, he pulled a small wooden cross in the shape of the capital letter T, the Tau, and poked it through the bottom of the grate.

"Lift the curtain, Christiana, and take this."

The curtain was lifted and the cross plucked from his fingers before the curtain was again lowered.

"Lord Pope said that this is the shape of the cross on which Christ died."

The women gave soft whistles of reverent wonder.

"Pope Innocenzo said that only those marked with the sign of the cross—the Tau—will obtain mercy." Francesco was quoting Lord Pope almost word for word. "Those so marked fall into three groups. The crusaders. Those who combat heresy at home. And those who admit to being sinners, who mortify their flesh, and who conform their lives to that of the crucified Savior, as you ladies and we friars try to do."

Now to reveal his wondrous plan. "We will make the Tau the sign of the Lesser Brothers. And of the Poor Ladies, if you agree, Christiana."

"So perfect. So beautiful. How could we not agree?"

Francesco smiled. "Fra Masseo made that Tau for San Damiano, and others for the Porziuncula and the Carceri."

"Grazie."

Francesco pressed on. "The council condemned the heresies. Strongly. Some heretical groups practice strange penances. You can almost recognize a heresy by its penitential practices."

No word came from behind the curtain.

"Do you still sleep on vine branches, Christiana?" There, that was out.

"Sì, but no one else does."

"From now on you must sleep on a plank."

"I sleep well on the branches."

Francesco shook his head. "It doesn't matter. Get rid of the vine branches. Lord Pope's visitator must not see a bed that resembles a heretic's."

"But, brother, I'm very willful. Penance helps me to yield my will."

Francesco broke into an irrepressible laugh. "The vine branches help you yield your will? Yet you're resisting me."

Agnese burst into a stifled chuckle. Christiana laughed lightly. "You're right. Out of obedience, I'll sleep on a plank."

"And no stone for a pillow."

A moment of hesitation. "No stone, brother."

Francesco heaved a little sigh of relief. "Good. Better to relinquish penances than lose a way of life."

Now a second hurdle. The Poor Ladies, like many enclosed religious, kept a perpetual Lenten fast, eating only one frugal meal daily. On Sundays, during Easter week, and on the Nativity of our Lord, as well as on all non-Friday feasts of the apostles and of the Blessed Virgin, the ladies could take two meals as part of the general rejoicing. Other than during the greater Lent preceding Easter and the lesser Lent preceding the Nativity, each lady chose whether to fast on Thursdays, the day of the Lord's Ascension. Francesco had given the ladies these rules for fasting. But did Christiana herself fast imprudently?

Francesco voiced his concern. "Before I left for Rome, the ladies had sent me a message that you're not eating enough, Christiana."

"I'm eating what the other sisters eat. Bread. Water. Wine on Sundays if we have any."

"The ladies say you're too thin."

"I'm fine."

"Madonna Pacifica, is Christiana eating?" Francesco asked.

"Some days." The voice was very small.

"Which days?"

"Sunday, Tuesday, Thursday, and Saturday."

"And the other days?"

"On the other days, she doesn't eat."

"Or drink?"

"Sì."

"I'm fine," Christiana said. "I sew. I garden. I tend the sick sisters. Don't I, sisters?"

"Sì. Sì, you do, Suor Chiara."

"How much food and drink does she take, Madonna Agnese?"

"Very little." Agnese's voice was very little.

"Even on Sundays, which are days of rejoicing?"

"Sì."

"You ladies eat fruits and vegetables, don't you, Madonna Pacifica?"

"When we have them."

"And you, Christiana?"

"I need only bread and water, brother."

"Christiana," Francesco made his voice firm, "the ladies fear that your fasting will make you ill. They often weep over how little you eat. You must begin to eat more on the days that you do eat. And eat something on the days that you are now eating nothing."

"Fra Francesco," Christiana said, "I've heard that you fast for forty days and eat nothing."

How had she heard about that? Francesco took a deep breath. "I'm healthy, Christiana."

"I've never gone without food for even four days, much less forty."

She knew that she had him cornered. "All right, Christiana. But eat enough to keep up your health."

"Enough to keep up my health."

Francesco shifted on his bench. That confrontation had ended in a draw. Now for the big battle, the one on which the future of the Poor Ladies depended.

"The council said that no new religious groups may be formed in the Church."

"Lord Pope Innocenzo has always been receptive to new religious groups," Christiana noted. "Didn't he welcome back the Waldensians and Humiliati whom some called heretical?"

"Sì, Lord Pope is receptive. But not the council. Pope Innocenzo couldn't sway the abbots. The council has decreed that any new ordine must take an already recognized Rule."

Christiana let out a little gasp of amazement. "It's good Lord Pope approved your Form of Life six years ago when you visited him."

"The approval is oral, not written. Lord Pope told the council that he had approved the *Forma Vita*. But the council won't accept it as a Rule because it wasn't composed by one of the Church Fathers."

"You can still live it, can't you?"

"Because Pope Innocenzo had approved it prior to the council, sì."

For a moment, Christiana said nothing. Then she spoke. "Lord Pope approved the Form of Life that you gave us, didn't he?"

"I showed it to him, Christiana."

"It's so simple. And so beautiful. 'Because by divine inspiration you have made yourselves daughters and handmaids of the most High, most Exalted King, the heavenly Father, and have taken the Holy Spirit as your spouse,'" Christiana was reciting part of the *Form of Life* that Francesco had written, "'choosing to live according to the perfection of the holy Gospel, I resolve and promise for myself and for my brothers always to have the same loving care and special solicitude for you as for them.'" She paused. "Lord Pope must have approved that and the rest of it."

"He approved it," Francesco said, "but he said that it's not specific enough."

"That's because we also follow the Form of Life you wrote for the Lesser Brothers. Did you tell him that?"

"I told him." *Lord, help me.* "Lord Pope said that our Form of Life deals with friars who travel about. It doesn't apply to cloistered ladies."

He heard a sharp rustle behind the curtain, as if Christiana had leaped to her feet. "But we do follow it."

"We had long discussions about it, Christiana. Lord Pope and the council were adamant. Ladies are not permitted to travel and preach, so they may not follow the friars' Form of Life."

"Bishop Guido has allowed us to follow it."

"Bishop Guido has never given you any official document that recognizes your community. Following this council, the Church will now recognize a community as authentic only if it follows an already approved Rule and is subject to Lord Pope."

"What must we do?" The question was almost too sharp.

"Choose a Rule that has been approved, that will give the Poor Ladies canonical status. Either the Augustinian Rule or the Benedictine or Cistercian one."

The silence behind the curtain was unnerving.

Lord, make her understand. "Christiana, the friars and I have been praying and praying about this. We know what you must do. You must accept the Benedictine title of abbess."

"Abbess? I can't believe you would say that."

"Christiana, listen . . ."

"God called me and my sisters into poverty and this way of life." Christiana's voice was shaky. "We wish to serve Christ and all others in poverty. I can't believe that you want me to break that promise of poverty that I made to you, to Messer Bishop, and to God. Do you want to turn this place into another San Paolo delle Abbadesse?"

"No, Christiana. No. Never. Christiana, listen. The abbess has supreme authority in Benedictine convents. If you accept the title of abbess, you can run San Damiano as you please. You will not have to answer to anyone except the Holy See."

"I want to serve, in poverty, as I have been serving." Christiana's voice was still shaky. "I don't want people to serve me. We are not to own anything."

Francesco could feel her anguish. As gently as possible, he advised, "Then be a poor abbess who serves."

"A poor abbess who serves? That's a contradiction."

"Look at the cross that I gave you. God is the Lord of contradiction."

He could see nothing behind the curtain. Hear nothing.

"Christiana, please don't make me put you under obedience. To preserve the Form of Life for the Poor Ladies, you must do this."

Christiana groaned.

"Even Christ was obedient. To death."

"All right. My father used to say, 'One has to know which battles to fight and which to avoid.'" Christiana's words were feeble, wounded. "I want the Church to accept us as an approved *ordine*. And if I must take this title, I will. But as abbess I will not accept possessions, money, or property." Her words were even, firm. "Lord Pope can't make me accept them."

"If Lord Pope commands you to accept them, you must." The words were almost too painful to speak. "Just as I must accept them, if Lord Pope commands me."

"No. He won't make us accept property or possessions. He won't make us own this place or any other."

Francesco didn't want her to own this place or any other. "Lord Pope may argue that the friars live in huts. If someone turns us out of one place, we can build huts elsewhere. Women can't do that. If you lose this place, you'll have nowhere else to go."

"God will provide the place."

"You may have to convince Lord Pope of that."

"God will convince Lord Pope."

The woman's faith was unshakable. "I know what to do!" Christiana's voice was exultant. "I will write to Lord Pope and request from him the privilege of owning nothing."

The privilege of owning nothing! Monasteries and convents were always requesting privileges of owning many things. "You want to request the privilege of having no privileges?"

"He granted it to you, brother."

The answer caught him off guard. "The Lesser Brothers work . . ."

"We work. We make altar linens and vestments."

"You receive no money for them."

"You receive no money for your work."

"But," Francesco pointed out, "we work in exchange for food. You give away your work in exchange for nothing."

"Not for nothing. In exchange for God's blessing."

"Lord Pope will say that you can't eat God's blessing."

Christiana was silent.

"Christiana, we friars aren't enclosed as you are. We can beg if we can't find work, or if we work but aren't given enough food."

"Your friars beg for us. I'll send the friars at once to beg for parchment and ink. Then I'll write to Lord Pope and tell him that you have made me abbess. I will then ask him to approve the privilege of poverty in writing so that no one can say that we haven't received it."

Her confidence was contagious. "May God make you successful," Francesco prayed. "May He convince Lord Pope to grant you the privilege of owning nothing."

NOTES

At this time, through Masseo, Francesco consulted Chiara and Silvestro about his living a hermetical life of prayer. Both told him to preach (FA:ED II 622–23). The primary sources for the life of San Francesco tell us that Masseo was tall, robust, and handsome.

Francesco made the journeys mentioned in this chapter and suffered the illness described.

A meeting such as the one described here must surely have taken place between Francesco and Chiara, probably sometime soon after Francesco returned from the Fourth Lateran Council, which had opened November 11, 1215, in Rome. He was one among fifteen hundred delegates to this council. If Francesco did visit Chiara, he would have taken along another friar as a companion. According to Chiara's *Form of Life*, any sister who spoke in the parlor had to have two other sisters with her. By never meeting alone with anyone, the friars and sisters ensured their own virtue and good reputation. This was especially important because some other religious groups were being accused of scandalous behavior.

In this chapter, Francesco states some of the decisions of the Fourth Lateran Council. He probably adopted the Tau as the symbol of the Lesser Brothers following Innocenzo's praise of it at the council. There is no evidence that Masseo ever carved a Tau or that Francesco ever gave one to Chiara.

Apparently both Francesco and Chiara realized how the council's decisions threatened the existence of the religio of the Poor Ladies, who, at the time, were following a Form of Life that Francesco had written for them. Most likely this Form of Life closely paralleled the friars' Form of Life. When Chiara wrote her own *Form of Life*, she included Francesco's in it. She shares his words in this chapter beginning with "Because by divine inspiration" (CA:ED 118).

Because of the council's decisions, Chiara was required to choose a Rule approved by the Church in order to become canonically established. Francesco had to practically force her to accept the Benedictine title of abbess (CA:ED 146). This would imply that she accepted the Benedictine Rule—at least officially. Also about this time, Chiara exchanged her bed of vine twigs and stone pillow for a plank (CA:ED 156, 171, 179). Chiara shared with the sisters in Prague the fasting regulations that Francesco gave San Damiano (CA:ED 52–53).

Tradition tells us that Chiara thought of petitioning the pope for the privilege of poverty. The current debate about whether the privilege can be found appears in various references listed in the bibliography. Historian David Flood (interview with author, 1997) believes that Chiara went in person to obtain the privilege—if she did attempt to receive it—but this cannot be proven.

PART FIVE

The Abundant Kindness of God

18

Lucia

Via San Petrignano, Assisi (Late Winter 1216)

Lucia was very little and this hill was very steep. She and Papà had walked so many days from Rome that the cloths covering their feet were heavy with caked mud. They'd been sleeping in towns, cities, forests, caves. Under the dismal gray sky, Lucia's head was cold despite the cloths wrapped around it. All along this road, Papà had been asking noblemen and women for something to eat, but all of them had ridden by without stopping. Someplace up this hill, Papà said, lived Madonna Chiara, who would give Lucia some food. A penitent named Francesco—who, in Rome, had given Papà his better tunic and taken Papà's worse one—had said so.

Had Francesco seen Papà's face? Lucia hadn't seen it for months. Papà kept his face hidden in the shadow of his cloak's big hood. He said his face was no longer pretty.

Papà got sick after Mamma had died trying to birth Lucia's baby brother, who had died too. Then Papà took Lucia away from the piazza that she had called home. They had wandered throughout Rome. Maybe they would still be in Rome had they not met Francesco, who had told them about Madonna Chiara.

Lucia imagined Madonna Chiara to be a beautiful woman in a red silk gown sparkly with jewels. A little silk cap would sit like a nest on her head, and she would be aloof and grand as all ladies were.

"Bambina, we're here," Papà said gleefully. Lucia blinked. She had been fantasizing so intensely about the lady that she hadn't noticed that Papà and she had arrived at a church.

Papà scrambled down the stairs entering the church, then turned toward Lucia. "Jump, Bambina!"

Grinning, Lucia jumped into Papà's arms. He put her down before she could kiss him.

"No kisses, Bambina. Papà is sick."

Wasn't Papà ever going to get better?

Taking her tiny hand in his, Papà led Lucia to the altar, where he picked her up and held her close to a rope hanging from the wall. "Pull that, Bambina. Hard."

Lucia pulled. On the other side of the wall, a bell chimed. An unbolting and banging so startled Lucia that she jerked in Papà's arms.

"Don't be afraid. It's only the good lady opening the window."

"Pace e bene."

The high, gentle voice came from behind a grate covered on the inside with a curtain.

"Fra Francesco sent me to speak to Madonna Chiara."

"Wait a moment, please."

Something clunked into place behind the curtain.

"Was that your mother, Papà?"

"No, Bambina. My mother is dead."

"My mamma is dead, too."

"I know, Bambina. I miss her like you do."

The sliding noise came again. "Pace e bene. This is Suor Chiara."

Why didn't the lady move the black curtain aside?

"Madonna, I am a leper from Rome."

A leper? Lucia squirmed in Papà's arms and stared at him. Lepers were ugly and horrible. Nobody liked them. They made you sick. They had to live at the leper hospital. Papà was too good, kind, and handsome to be a leper. And he wasn't at the leper hospital.

"Fra Francesco suggested that I ask you to take my child Lucia and care for her. She has no one else."

As the curtain slipped back from the grate, Lucia looked curiously at the woman behind it. Why, Madonna Chiara was a penitent in a black veil! They had come this far to see a penitent?

"What is your name?" The voice was soft.

"Forte. But I don't feel strong today."

"Are you sure about your leprosy, Messer Forte?"

Messer? People called a *noble* Messer, not Papà.

"Sì, Madonna. Look." Papà threw back his hood. Above his black beard, Papà's forehead and cheeks were red and blotchy. His bushy eyebrows were gone.

"Ugh. Papà!" Lucia grunted.

Papà drew the hood back up over his head. "Ugh is right, Bambina. I'm not a pretty sight for your young eyes." He turned to the window. "Madonna, the leprosy has spread to my arms and legs. The tunic hides it. I can beg while keeping my hand and arm covered, but it's a miracle that no one has discovered that I'm ill. When someone does, I shall be forced into a leper hospital. And that's no place for a child." Papà reached up and patted Lucia's rag-bound head. "Who will want to care for a leper's child if I don't take her with me? What do I do with her? Leave her in the streets to starve? Or have worse befall her?" Papà's voice trembled the way it had when Mamma had died. "She's all I have. And she's a good girl, aren't you, Bambina?"

Lucia nodded.

"For the love of the good God, would you care for her? I have no one else to ask."

The lady's eyes were wet with tears. Was she thinking about Mamma? "Of course we will take her, Messer."

"God be praised. Grazie. Grazie." Papà hugged Lucia fiercely.

"Now, Lucia," Papà said. He always called her Lucia when he had something important to say. "Someday, probably very soon, I'll have to go to the leper hospital. It isn't a good place for you. You can live here with Madonna Chiara and all the ladies. They will be like Mamma to you." Papà's voice began to shake. "Say addio to Papà now."

From behind the window grate came the plaintive mewing of a cat. There it was! Sleek, gray, rubbing against the gown of another penitent standing behind Madonna Chiara.

"They have a cat, Papà!" Lucia wanted to play with the cat. "Addio, Papà," she said.

"Remember, Lucia, that I love you."

"May I bless you, Messer?" Madonna Chiara asked.

"No one," Papà stuttered, "except Fra Francesco has ever blessed me."

"Come closer to the grill, Messer Forte, so I may touch you."

Shakily, Papà approached the grill. Madonna Chiara placed her hands on Papà's shoulders and closed her eyes. Her lips moved but Lucia could hear only an unintelligible whisper. Then Madonna Chiara made a strange motion above Papà's head. "In the name of the Father and of the Son and of the Holy Spirit," she said.

"Amen," Papà answered in his tiniest voice.

"Messer Forte," Madonna Chiara said softly, "will you meet us at the front of the church? We will lower the staircase so Lucia can climb up to us."

Lucia was disappointed. "Can't I see the cat, Papà?"

"I'll bring Suor Gatta with me." The lady smiled.

"Papà, come on!" Lucia tugged Papà's sleeve. "She's going to show me the cat."

"All right, Bambina." Taking Lucia by the hand, Papà started out of the church. They waited by the door. Then Lucia heard a clumping. On the floor above the church, a wooden door was opening. A big penitent was unfastening a chain that held a wooden staircase flush against the outside wall of the building. The chain slipped slowly through the woman's hands as she lowered the staircase to the ground, where it struck with a clump.

Standing in the doorway at the top of the staircase was Madonna Chiara with the sleek gray cat in her arms. "Would you follow Lucia up the staircase, please, so that she doesn't fall?"

Eagerly Lucia started to climb. Partway up, she halted. The ground was far below. There were holes between the steps.

"Papà!"

"I'm here, Bambina." Papà pressed his chest against her back. "Go on."

"Come, Lucia. Come and see Suor Gatta," the lady called encouragingly.

Up she went. One step. Another. Papà pressed against her, protecting her. Finally she scampered into a big room with long, low wooden platforms pushed against the walls. Near the door in a little open compartment sat the big penitent who had lowered the staircase. The woman smiled broadly at Lucia, who smiled back. My, that lady had fat red cheeks.

"Messer Forte, here is some bread for your journey." The red-cheeked lady handed Papà, still on the ladder, a pouch.

Papà slipped the pouch's strap over his head. "Grazie."

"Did Fra Francesco tell you that his friars help care for the lepers at San Lazzaro d'Arce?" Madonna Chiara asked.

"Sì, Madonna. Pray that I may be taken there if I'm discovered. But I'll do all I can not to be discovered. I've heard of those places." Papà's voice was harsh. "I would rather die than go there. Now, Bambina," Papà said, his voice softening, "give Papà a big hug."

Lucia bent down and flung her arms around Papà's head, her hands mashing his hood against his face.

"I love you, Bambina."

Kneeling before the staircase, Madonna Chiara placed one of her hands on Papà's hand. The cat was quiet in her arms. "Go in Christ's peace. We'll take good care of Lucia. You will always be in our prayers."

"Grazie." Papà's voice was hoarse and odd. "Bambina, let me see your little dark eyes one last time." Lucia wrenched her gaze away from the cat and looked at Papà. "Addio, Bambina. Always remember that I love you."

"Can I play with the cat now?" Lucia asked.

"Sì," Papà said. His voice was very deep.

Madonna Chiara turned to Lucia. "Sit down, Lucia, and I'll put Suor Gatta into your arms."

Lucia sat.

Madonna Chiara placed the cat in Lucia's lap. The cat nestled its head under Lucia's stained gray cloak and purred. Lucia scratched, patted, and stroked the animal. The whirring came louder and louder.

"Papà, she likes me," Lucia said.

Papà didn't answer.

"Papà?" Lucia looked up, confused.

Madonna Chiara and the other penitent were fastening the staircase against the outside wall. They closed the door and pushed a big log across it.

"Your Papà is very brave," Madonna Chiara said. "He loves you very much."

She knelt in front of Lucia. "Suor Balbina," Madonna Chiara nodded at the red-cheeked sister, "has brought clean cloths for your feet."

Lucia thrust her feet out in front of her, tumbling the cat out of her lap. Quickly Madonna Chiara unwrapped the muddy cloths and gave them to Suor Balbina. Then Madonna Chiara rubbed each of Lucia's feet vigorously, warming them just like Papà did, before she wrapped them in clean rags.

"Why don't you ladies wear rags?" Lucia asked, noticing Madonna Chiara's bare feet.

"Because we don't wish to." Madonna Chiara smiled as she took Lucia's hand and helped her to her feet. The lady's hand felt warm, like Mamma's or Papà's. They began to walk through the long room.

"Are you going to beg for something to eat?"

"No. We can find something to eat in the kitchen."

"Is a kitchen a pouch?"

"It's a room."

"Do you live here?"

"Sì."

The ladies had a house to live in. Lucia had never been in a house. She pointed to the low wooden platforms against the walls. "What are those?"

"Beds."

"What do you do with them?"

"Sleep on them."

Sleep on them? And not on the ground? How strange!

"Lucia," Madonna Chiara whispered softly at the top of some steps, "we'll go down into the oratory now. God is there. He's greater than any nobleman. We show Him respect by being quiet in the oratory. We kiss the floor before Him because He's so much greater than we are and He loves us so much. The kiss says, 'I love You and honor You, my God. I give myself to You.'"

Madonna Chiara walked down the stairs and kissed the floor. Lucia copied her. Then they walked down more steps and into another room that held long, high platforms with colorful clothes on them, such as nobles wore. Other peni-tents were in the room, too, doing something with the clothes. Madonna Chiara called the women to her.

"Sisters, this is Lucia. She is staying with us. Lucia, these are your sisters. You'll learn our names very quickly." Lucia looked from one smiling face to the next. The ladies seemed very nice. "We'll make you a little tunic and mantle, just like ours, to keep you warm."

Then, still holding Lucia's hand, Madonna Chiara led her into a smaller, narrower room. "This is a kitchen, Lucia. Here we keep things that are used for cooking."

Imagine! A room for cooking. Sometimes beggars cooked over fires in the piazza. Cooked food was good—especially in winter, because cooked food was warm.

"Now as soon as we thank God for our food, you can eat."

Thank God? Lucia had never heard of such a thing.

"Kneel with me." Madonna Chiara knelt and Lucia copied her. "Now put your hands over your chest like this." Madonna Chiara crossed Lucia's two arms over her chest and patted them. "Now you hold them there." Then Madonna Chiara crossed her own arms on her own chest, closed her eyes, and began to speak softly. "Our Father, Who art in heaven."

Who was she speaking to? Her father in some city called heaven?

"Amen." Smiling, Madonna Chiara took a broken roll, a fig, and a slab of cheese from a ledge.

Lucia gazed, wide-eyed, at the food placed in her hands. "All for me, Madonna Chiara?"

"Sì, Lucia. We call each other sister here. Can you say Suor Chiara?"

Lucia nodded vigorously and took a big bite of roll. Then she remembered that she had not done what Mamma had taught her to do. "Grazie, Suor Chiara," she said, her mouth full. "Are you going to eat, too?"

"I will, later. We sisters eat only once a day, for supper."

"Do you eat every day?"

"Sì, unless we don't have anything to eat."

Every day. Imagine that! It must be wonderful to be so rich and live in a big house with beds and kitchens and food every day. How long would Lucia be here before Papà came for her? She hoped it would be a little time. Suor Chiara was nice like Mamma. And the ladies had a cat. And figs. Lucia would like it here, until Papà returned for her.

NOTES

Little is known of Suor Lucia of Rome, who, during the early years at San Damiano, was accepted into the monastery "because of the love of God when she was very little" (CA:ED 173–74). Chiara's *Form of Life* allows for the entry of "young girls who are received into the monastery before the age established by law" (CA:ED 111–12). Lucia founded the monastery of Cortona in 1225 and died in 1253 (CA:ED 173 footnote).

How, in the earliest years, did someone from Rome hear of San Damiano in Assisi? Did Francesco tell Lucia's family when he was in Rome in 1215 for the Lateran Council? If Lucia belonged to a wealthy family, why would they place her in San Damiano, the poorest of monasteries? If Lucia had been of noble stock, why is she listed as Lucia of Rome without mentioning her family background? This chapter is one fictitious possibility that attempts to answer these questions while adhering to the few facts we have.

At this time, a Suor Balbina (also spelled Balvina) was in the San Damiano community. She could be the Balbina who came from the castle of Porziano (Fortini 351), but the date of Balbina of Porziano's entry is not recorded.

19

Suor Felicita

Via San Petrignano, Assisi (Late May 1216)

A huge sack of flour, topped with a napkin of yeast, bumped rosy-cheeked Suor Felicita's side as she fairly skipped down the steep Via San Petrignano on the way back to San Damiano. Dark-eyed Suor Giovanna was practically skipping too, a jug of milk in one hand and a jug of oil in the other. The Perugian shepherdess and the Assisian candlemaker's daughter were bringing back ingredients to make fresh bread! The alms were an unexpected gift from Messer Paolo di Scipione di Offreduccio, whose young son Bonaventura had emerged, about an hour ago, from a life-threatening fever. The best doctors in Assisi could do nothing for the child, so Messer Paolo had asked his cousin Madonna Chiara to send some sisters to pray for the boy. Giovanna and Felicita were the only sisters who served outside the monastery, so they had come to anoint Bonaventura—as they anointed lepers, the wounded, and the diseased—with medicinal ointments the sisters made from herbs and roots grown at San Damiano. Then they had prayed for him as the enclosed sisters were doing back at the monastery. When the fever had broken, an ecstatic Messer Paolo had loaded the sisters with bread ingredients, proclaiming, "No broken loaves tonight! You'll have fresh bread with our deepest gratitude."

Fresh bread! Chiara always instructed the sisters to praise God whenever they left the monastery, but today their praise was an anthem, rising to the sunlit May sky, dancing across the silvery-leafed olive trees, rivaling birdsong. How good was the good God!

As Felicita and Giovanna approached San Damiano, a huge, colorful cortège, so long that they couldn't see its end, was approaching in the distance.

"That must be some fine noble," Giovanna said.

"Indeed, but we're richer," Felicita sang. "Our fine Lord erases fever and gives us bread."

"Our Lord owns all the world!" Giovanna cried.

The sisters pulled the bell cord, then ascended the staircase when Suor Pacifica let it down. At the door to the dormitory, they unfastened their heavy boots while Felicita winked at thin, dark-eyed Lucia, standing like a puppy next to Pacifica. Cleaning the serving sisters' boots was Lucia's job. Proudly she hoisted a boot and trotted to the stairs that led to the enclosed yard. Outdoors, she would use a sturdy twig to scrape mud from the boots. Then she would wipe them with a moist rag and place them in the refectory, ready for the next excursion.

On nimble bare feet, Felicita and Giovanna hurried downstairs to the refectory. Near the door, spreading the makings of a chasuble across a table, stood lean Suor Ortulana, her wide blue eyes smiling at the beaming sisters. About a month earlier, following the wedding of her youngest child, Beatrice, Ortulana, the mother of Suor Chiara, had entered San Damiano. Felicita gave Ortulana a giant hug, then skipped through the refectory, where other sisters were busily working with cloth.

"Sisters! God is so good!" Felicita called as she and Giovanna bounded to a side bench where Chiara always washed the serving sisters' feet when they returned. Brushing aside rapid-fire questions, Felicita and Giovanna explained the gifts of abated fever and bread ingredients while Chiara sloshed a rag in a pail of water to wash their feet.

The bell at the speaking grill rang. Suor Agnese, who was tending the grill today, went to answer the summons.

With a soft rag, Chiara dried the sisters' feet, then kissed them as she always did.

"Before we went to Messer Paolo's, we gave the used tunics to the beggars at the Porta del Sementone. How happy they were!" Giovanna exclaimed.

"One of them had terrible facial ulcers. We washed them and anointed them with the salve you made, Suor Chiara. She was so grateful," Felicita chimed.

Chiara pushed to her feet and picked up the bucket of dirty water by its rope handle to toss its contents outdoors. "God has blessed so many people through you sisters. God be praised!"

"His Holiness, Lord Pope, is at the grill!" Agnese's frantic cry startled Felicita. Her heart leaped. Lord Pope? Here?

"Does he want to come in?" Chiara asked peacefully.

"He wants to speak to you at length, see San Damiano, share our meal, and then proceed to Assisi. I think it's about your request to own nothing."

"Very well." Chiara placed the pail of water on the floor near the bench and, along with Agnese, walked toward the speaking grill.

Dumbfounded, Felicita stared after Chiara.

"How can she be so calm?" Suor Benedetta said, hoisting the pail and heading toward the doorway to empty the water.

"Lord Pope! Here!" Benvenuta exclaimed.

"What are we going to feed him?" Cecilia asked.

Felicita and Giovanna stared at each other. "Bread," Felicita whispered almost reverently. "God has given us fresh bread for Lord Pope."

NOTES

"The sisters who serve outside the monastery" were allowed to wear shoes when they left the enclosure (CA:ED 112). Presumably, these were not the soft-soled, cloth shoes of noblewomen, but heavy boots used by peasants who traveled the roads. Chiara admonished the serving sisters to praise God for His creation and to speak only of heavenly things (CA:ED 189). What were the duties of the "serving sisters"? Historians assume that they served in the manner described in this chapter and perhaps begged alms along with the friars assigned to San Damiano. Since Chiara called them serving sisters and not questing sisters, their main role was, perhaps, service.

Chiara used to wash the feet of the serving sisters (CA:ED 148, 150, 178). We have no details on how she did this.

Messer Paolo and Fra Rufino were both sons of Chiara's uncle, Messer Scipione di Offreduccio. Paolo's son was Messer Bonaventura. The incident involving Bonaventura's fever and an alms of bread ingredients is fictional.

The year that Ortulana entered San Damiano is unknown. Whether Beatrice had ever been married is likewise unclear.

20

Pope Innocenzo III

Church of San Damiano (Late May 1216)

P ope Innocenzo III stood near the speaking grill at San Damiano, an involuntary grin spreading across his beardless cheeks. Baptized Lothario Conti, Innocenzo was descended on his father's side from one of the four oldest and noblest families on the Roman peninsula. Fifty-five years of age, he had been pope for eighteen years and had made decisions regarding emperors and crusades, heresies and schisms, plagues and poverty. His influence was felt throughout the world, which was undoubtedly why the lady at the grill had been so flustered when she heard that he was here.

Innocenzo doubted that he would fluster Madonna Chiara, a woman he already liked, because her name was a variation of his mother's name, Clarissa. A woman who would ask to possess nothing should take everything, including an unannounced papal visit, in stride. Could enclosed women live in the poverty Chiara had requested? Today he would discern the answer.

Chiara's almost laughable request reminded him of the one made by Fra Francesco of this same city, who had come in 1209 with eleven companions to ask his permission to live as evangelizing paupers, obedient to the Holy See and to Christ. Innocenzo had dismissed the small, shabby fanatic, but later had a dream in which the massive Lateran Basilica, the seat of the Church, tottered to the point of collapse until Francesco propped it up by heaving his shoulder against it. Innocenzo interpreted the dream to mean that Francesco would save the Church, so he had approved Francesco's *Form of Life*.

The curtain at the speaking grill rustled, lifted.

"Most Holy Father, I am Suor Chiara." The open, fresh face behind the grill was smiling pleasantly, the deep blue eyes intent on Innocenzo's face. The stately woman bowed. Innocenzo bowed in return.

"I would like to see the monastery, then speak with you over a small meal, if I may."

"Certainly, Most Holy Father." The woman bowed again. "If you exit the church, we'll lower the staircase into the enclosure. Please bring the fewest attendants possible, as men don't enter our living quarters."

Innocenzo scanned the servants, cardinals, and attendants who filled the church. For propriety's sake, at least one ought to accompany him.

A sturdy, gray-bearded cardinal to his left stepped forward. "My uncle, these women and their way of life intrigue me."

Innocenzo smiled at his grandnephew, who was over a decade older than he but who had the stamina of a much younger man. Cardinal Ugolino dei Conti di Segni, cardinal bishop of Ostia, former legate to Germany. Innocenzo nodded. "The others remain here," he said.

Innocenzo inspected every part of the monastery—the dormitory, infirmary, refectory, choir, parlor, gardens, yard, well, hermitages, enclosing walls and hedges. Furnishings were few and scratched. He exchanged pleasantries with young penitential women weeding an ample herb garden. He spoke to others stitching in the refectory. He chatted with penitents shaping a great many loaves of bread in the kitchen. He told a child named Lucia how the golden filigree on his flowing red cape was made.

Then he asked to speak privately to the friars who begged for the women. Innocenzo and Ugolino met the friars in their poor, simple house that abutted the church. The starkness of the plain-walled dwelling struck Innocenzo with its rare, unappreciated beauty.

In contrast to the friars who had come to see Innocenzo with Fra Francesco, these friars were elderly.

"Fra Francesco sent only old men who didn't want to come," a bald friar explained. "He feels it's safer for older, weak men to serve beautiful young ladies."

Innocenzo nodded. It was safer, but the friars soon made him realize the burden of old, weak bodies begging enough food for a growing women's community.

Smelling the baking bread, Innocenzo remarked, "It appears that the women have sufficient food to eat."

"They have had little at times," the bald friar said, "but something always."

A bell rang for Vespers. Innocenzo and Ugolino joined the ladies in the choir while the friars and Lord Pope's entourage chanted the Office in the church.

Upon completing the Office, Innocenzo and Ugolino returned with the women to the refectory for a meal, eaten in silence, as was customary for all religious. The women sat on benches around long, bare wooden tables, while Chiara beckoned Innocenzo to join her at the table closest to the kitchen entrance. An older woman handed Chiara a washbowl, a pitcher of water, and a long towel. Setting the bowl on the table, Chiara poured water over Innocenzo's hands, then offered him the towel. She did the same with Ugolino.

Innocenzo was incredulous. Lowly pages washed the hands of nobles and their most honored guests, while others had to use a common washbowl. He had expected to be handed water to wash his hands, but not by the abbess. Then Chiara did a more amazing thing. She proceeded to bring the wash bowl, towel, and water to each of the women, then washed her own hands before carrying everything back into the kitchen. She then emerged with a refilled pitcher and poured water into Innocenzo's chipped cup, Ugolino's, and then everyone else's, returning again and again to the kitchen to refill the pitcher until all were served.

Now she'll sit down, Innocenzo thought. But no. This time she emerged with a tray of small cheese wedges and slices of peeled orange. On Innocenzo's and Ugolino's napkins, she placed a cheese wedge and two orange slices, then served the same to the seated women. When she returned to her own seat, she placed the final orange slice on her napkin, then disappeared into the kitchen.

This time she emerged with two bowls of steaming greens, one of which she placed on the table before Innocenzo and Ugolino. Impulsively, Innocenzo gently took the other bowl from Chiara and brought it to one of the other tables. When he returned, he and Ugolino took from Chiara two more bowls and brought them to the other two tables. Then Innocenzo, Ugolino, and Chiara passed small, finely shaped loaves to the women until each had a loaf. The novelty of serving pleased Innocenzo as few things did.

"Madonna Chiara," Innocenzo requested softly, "may we allow speaking at this meal?"

"As you wish, Most Holy Father," Chiara bowed.

Innocenzo turned toward the women. "Madonne, you have a most peaceful place here. And oranges, my favorite food."

"A merchant brought them yesterday from the south," Chiara explained.

"So, the good God sent them ahead of me. And you have baked this fresh bread, most tasty with oranges."

The women were smiling at him, nodding.

"Madonne," Innocenzo asked spontaneously, "what is the secret of your joy?"

Apparently startled at being questioned, the women looked from one to the other.

"Jesus."

"Our Lord and His cross."

"Living with others who love as we do."

"I just like it here," Lucia said, smiling.

"I do, too," Innocenzo chuckled. "And, Madonna Chiara, what is your secret?"

"Contempt of the world always brings joy," Chiara answered peacefully. "In the poor, despised Christ, we are made rich."

Innocenzo nodded. "Your humility humbles me." He raised his distinctively arched eyebrows to emphasize his words. "The sanctity of this place is as a sweet odor reaching throughout the world."

Chiara's cheeks reddened. "God be praised for any good you hear of us, Lord Pope."

"Madonne," Innocenzo said, gazing from one table to another, "I was concerned when you asked to own nothing, but God richly provides. Since He blesses you, I shall also bless you. I grant your request to own nothing."

Huge smiles spread across the women's faces. "Grazie. Mille grazie," resounded in the room.

"God be praised!" Chiara bowed deeply.

Innocenzo grinned. "Now, Madonne, shall we eat?"

Chiara smiled back. "Certainly. Most Holy Father, would you kindly bless these loaves?"

"My most faithful Suor Chiara, I want you to bless this bread, and make over it the sign of the most holy Cross, to which you have given your whole self."

Chiara gasped. "Most Holy Father, forgive me, because I would be worthy of the greatest rebuke if in front of the Vicar of Christ I, who am a vile little woman, should presume to give such a blessing."

"So that this may not be attributed to presumption but to the merit of obedience, I command you under holy obedience to make the sign of the most holy Cross over this bread and bless it in the name of God."

Obediently Chiara faced the tables, her eyes downcast. Raising her hand, she made a large sign of the cross over the loaves, pronouncing an inaudible blessing.

"Grazie, Madonna Chiara," Innocenzo said, reaching for his loaf. How clever! The loaf was marked with a small cross cut into the crust. He glanced at the tables. All loaves were so marked. Strange that he hadn't noticed the crosses until now.

"Madonne," Innocenzo remarked, "we must tell our household about your custom of carving crosses into the loaves before baking. These symbols recall the Bread of Life who died upon a cross for us."

Murmurs rippled throughout the room.

"Most Holy Father," Chiara said, "we always make undecorated loaves here."

Undecorated? Innocenzo picked up his loaf and turned it over. It was an ordinary, small loaf of bread with a neatly carved cross baked into its upper crust. If the women had not carved the cross, then who had?

Astonished, Innocenzo bowed his head. "Let us thank God," he called in a tremulous voice, "for granting miraculous signs to strengthen our weak faith."

NOTES

Some historians say that the incident in the *Fioretti* of Chiara making the sign of the cross over the loaves and a cross appearing on each never happened. The story does not give the year or the pope. According to the story, Agnese and Ortulana were in the monastery at the time, and Francesco sent people to them and to Chiara for prayers and cures. Innocenzo's and Chiara's words are taken verbatim from this account (FA:ED III 624).

The relationship between Innocenzo III and Cardinal Ugolino is accurate. Their physical descriptions are taken from paintings.

It was customary at the time for all religious to eat only a single daily meal. Chiara's *Form of Life* stated that silence was to be maintained in the refectory during meals (CA:ED 116). Chiara "made herself less than the other person by serving them, giving them water by hand" (CA:ED 157, see also 147, 150). Was this water to drink or to wash? Or both? Today, visitors to San Damiano are shown Chiara's seat near the entrance to the kitchen.

Currently some scholars are questioning whether the privilege of poverty was granted to Chiara in 1216 or at all. Lezlie Knox (*Creating Clare of Assisi*) summarizes both sides of the debate.

21

Suor Filippa di Leonardo di Gislerio

Hermitage, San Damiano (Summer 1216)

Suor Filippa di Leonardo di Gislerio knelt on the ground, bathed in light streaming through the open doorway of this cramped reed-and-mud hermitage. Instead of fastening shut the thick reed mat that served as a door, Filippa had lifted it off its pegs because the day was warm. The hut was one of several that the sisters had built along the far wall surrounding San Damiano. Sisters could come to these huts any time to pray, but they also took turns staying here for several days in solitude, with a large jug of water and a loaf of bread to sustain them.

Filippa had not intended to come to the hermitages today. With the other sisters, she had been picking raspberries along the enclosure's upper wall when, as sometimes happened without warning, she had been thrown back in time. Suddenly she was no longer a twenty-three-year-old woman, but a fragile child huddled in Mamma's skirt while baby brother Teodimo wailed in his nurse's arms and older brothers Oddo and Monaldo scrambled for their swords. She heard warlike shouts, saw flaming arrows streak through nursery windows, felt the awful pumping of thin, short legs as she ran through smoke, past tumbling walls, down tottering stairs into the flame-bright darkness where leering men surrounded her, grabbed her, jeered at her terror.

She was screaming when the sisters shook her into sensibility. Unsteady, she had watched them carefully pull the thorny canes from her skirt—she had somehow tangled herself in the thicket. Chiara had taken her by the hand and had led her here to pray, then knelt silently beside her, saying only, "May God heal you of these memories, sister." Chiara was beside her now, bowed deep in prayer.

Filippa had entered the community a month ago because Chiara had constantly preached to her about Christ's Passion. Her father, Messer Leonardo di Gislerio, was delighted. Now that Mamma was dead, Teodimo a squire, and Monaldo married, Filippa's joining the Poor Ladies freed him to join the Lesser Brothers.

Teodimo had no memories of Sasso Rosso's destruction. Monaldo didn't let his memories bother him, despite having fought in the war between Perugia and Assisi and seeing their brother Oddo and their uncle Messer Girardo killed. Papà must have buried his memories; six years ago, he, along with Uncle Messer Fortebraccio and many others, had returned to Assisi from Perugia and signed the peace pact drawn up under Emperor Otto IV. The pact officially ended Assisi's ten-year civil war by having nobles and common people pledge to work together for the comune's good. For Papà and Monaldo, the past was past. Why was it still so present to Filippa?

On the way here, she and Chiara had talked about sufferings.

The question was not *would we suffer* but *when*, for sufferings were part of this fallen world as surely as slender gray cat snakes were part of these environs: startling when encountered, yet hardly unexpected.

Or suffering was like the juice of nightshade berries, whose slim vines clambered over the undergrowth and twisted up toward the sun. As one drop of nightshade juice could poison a goblet of water, so did Adam and Eve's disobedience poison creation, causing sufferings that no one deserved.

Or suffering was the result of demons who could attack body, mind, or spirit.

Or it was the result of human choice for evil.

Or suffering was sent by God to bring about a greater good, as when Filippa's father used to punish her for leaning out of the windows of Sasso Rosso. He didn't spank to be mean but to keep her from tumbling out.

Or suffering could make us turn to God when nothing else would.

It was one thing to philosophize about suffering. It was another to experience it.

Filippa opened her eyes and gazed at a large slab of wood leaning against the hut's back wall. Suor Giovanna had used a red-hot nail to burn a finely detailed outline of Christ crucified into the wood. Today one of the lines appeared too light and thick. Filippa smiled in recognition. A fat yellowish-green-striped caterpillar was inching across the belly of Christ. Was Filippa like that caterpillar, touching Christ yet unchanged?

What did Chiara say about Christ? "Your Spouse Who though more beautiful than the children of men became, for your salvation, the lowest of men, was despised, struck, scourged untold times throughout His entire body, and then died amid the suffering of the Cross."

Christ chose suffering to change—not Himself, but us. To do this, He gave up every glory and good of heaven. He gave His all so that we might possess All.

Filippa watched the caterpillar inch toward Christ's shoulder. An idea was forming. To possess the All, one had to relinquish all. "You want everything, don't You?" she whispered to the etching of Jesus. "Even our sufferings, our memories, our regrets, our plans. What will You do with them, Lord? What will You do with my pain and my sin if I give them to You?"

Filippa cocked her head toward the caterpillar creeping along the upper edge of the slab. That was the wrong question, wasn't it? No one would ever suspect that a caterpillar would turn into a butterfly. If the ugly caterpillar of pain and suffering were given to God, He could do what He wished with it.

She gazed at the Crucified, sensing something new. "You know, don't You?" Jesus had experienced the hurts of humanity. Poverty. Betrayal. Abandonment. Homelessness. Exile. Death of loved ones. Torture. Fear. Assault. Degradation. Misunderstanding. Ridicule. Hatred. Murder.

What had Chiara said? "If you suffer with Him, you will reign with Him; weeping with Him, you will rejoice with Him; dying on the cross of tribulation with Him, you will possess heavenly mansions with Him among the splendor of the saints."

Filippa gazed at the Crucified, no longer obstructed by a fat, moving creature. The question was not why she had suffered or why did anyone suffer, but rather: What was she to do with her sufferings?

Her bitter memories were like a big striped caterpillar clinging to her spirit. In her mind, she plucked the caterpillar out of herself and handed it to God. God enclosed the creature in His palm, then opened His hand—and a large, yellow-and-black swallowtail butterfly darted out. It flew directly into Filippa's soul and gave it wings.

NOTES

Four years after Chiara entered San Damiano, Filippa was moved to join her when Chiara "described how our Lord Jesus Christ suffered passion and death on the cross for the salvation of the human race" (CA:ED 155).

Filippa called herself "the third sister" of Madonna Chiara (CA:ED 156). She was not the third to join Chiara in religious life, nor was she a blood sister. However, if Filippa, Balvina, Ginevra, Benvenuta, and Chiara had the sisterly relationship in Perugia that was portrayed in Part Three of this book, then Filippa was indeed the third of those sisters to enter San Damiano, having been preceded by Benvenuta and Ginevra.

The burning of Sasso Rosso (Fortini 124–25) and probable deaths of Messer Oddo and Messer Girardo during the Assisi-Perugia War (Fortini 155) would likely have had a traumatic effect on the child Filippa.

Teodimo and Monaldo were sons of Messer Leonardo (Fortini 124). Their probable ages in this book are postulated from other information Fortini records of them. Filippa and her family returned to Assisi in 1210. On November 10, 1210, Messers Leonardo and Fortebraccio di Gislerio signed the peace pact in Assisi (Fortini 310). Sometime between 1210 and 1219, when he is recorded as accompanying Francesco to Damietta, Filippa's father, Messer Leonardo, became a follower of Francesco (Fortini 396). We have no information on Filippa's mother.

Most likely, the sisters had hermitages, little cells in the woods, for solitary prayer. Suor Giovanna's icon is imaginary.

Part or perhaps all of San Damiano was walled in so that the sisters could work and walk outdoors within the walls. The land within this enclosure was uncultivated except for a garden (CA:ED 119).

The climbing nightshade, European cat snake, and swallowtail butterfly are found throughout this part of Italy and were even more common in Chiara's time.

Chiara's words, remembered by Filippa, are from her *Second Letter to Agnes of Prague* (CA:ED 49).

22

Bellezza

San Damiano, Assisi (Late Afternoon, August 2, 1216)

Bellezza leaned against the outer wall of the Church of San Damiano. She was so tired. Maybe she was pregnant. She had been so tired when she was pregnant with Mattiolo.

Where was Mattiolo? Oh, there, scratching in the dirt with a stick. Maybe if her dark-complexioned husband, Scuro, could watch their lithe, black-haired three-year-old, Bellezza could rest.

Kissing Bellezza quickly on the cheek, Scuro agreed. Bellezza sat against the wall of the church and closed her eyes.

Bellezza's little family were peasants employed by Messer Gualtieri Cacciaguerra of Spoleto. They were here in Assisi because a year ago, Messer Gualtieri's daughter Madonna Cecilia had become an enclosed recluse at this monastery. She had written to her family about a special indulgence that could be received today at a small stone church, the Porziuncula, not too far from here. Messer Gualtieri had brought his family and household—excepting those needed to tend his livestock—to receive the indulgence. Having received it, the nobleman and his wife were visiting their daughter in the monastery. Then the Cacciaguerra household would return to Spoleto.

This morning, at the noble's encampment in the forest, Bellezza had plaited her auburn hair, wrapping it in two spirals on either side of her chubby face. She had donned the russet tunic and perky cap she had made for this special day. With the other peasants, she had stood near the back of an immense crowd surrounding a platform erected near the Porziuncula. She had heard seven bishops—could she remember their cities? Assisi, Perugia, Todi, Norcera, Gubbio, Foligno, and Spoleto. Sì!—they all spoke of the indulgence.

Fra Francesco spoke, too. He said that, a month ago, he had been deep in prayer at the Porziuncula. In a vision, Jesus and His Mother had invited him to request whatever he thought best for the salvation of souls. He had asked if all repentant persons who entered the Porziuncula, confessed their sins, and obtained absolution from a priest could obtain complete remission of all penalty for all sins ever committed. That was a great favor to ask, Bellezza thought, but Jesus had consented! But only if Lord Pope agreed. But there was a new pope then because Pope Innocenzo had died in July. The new pope was Onorio III. Francesco said he went to see him in Perugia, where he still was after his swift election. He had granted the indulgence, but not year-round as Francesco requested. Francesco had seemed disappointed at that.

Bellezza couldn't understand it, but Scuro had tried to explain. "It's the same indulgence granted to crusaders," he said, because he seemed to know everything. "That's why crusaders go to fight to regain the Holy Land from the infidels. If they could have all their sins forgiven by going to a church and saying some prayers, do you think they'd want to risk their lives in battle? Somebody has to fight to regain the Holy Land for Christ's followers."

That did make sense, Bellezza admitted. Lord Pope had limited the indulgence to today, the second of August. The indulgence could be obtained from Vespers last night until Vespers tonight, provided one confessed his or her sins, did appropriate penance, and said required prayers for certain specified intentions.

Bellezza had fulfilled the requirements. Now, if only she would never sin again, she would go straight to heaven if she died.

Bellezza felt her exhausted body relax against the wall. Was it possible not to sin? All her sins, it seemed, involved Mattiolo. Scuro had named him Mattiolo, after Scuro's father, but sometimes he so exasperated Bellezza that she wondered if he really was a "gift from God."

Today when the bishop of this comune had been speaking about purgatory, Mattiolo had been scampering through people's legs, pelting a dog with pebbles, throwing rocks at birds, and shredding ferns with a stick. When Bellezza had picked him up, he had pulled her hat from her head and put it on his own, then wanted Scuro to hold him and put the hat on Scuro. Maintaining patience while parenting Mattiolo was the real "gift from God"! If only Bellezza could have that gift!

What had the bishop said? "Only the perfect can enter paradise. Imperfect souls are perfected in purgatory. In purgatory, souls learn to always say 'Sì' to God, to give Him the glory, thanksgiving, service, and praise that are His due. The soul is then at peace and enters heaven."

Bellezza was feeling a bit peaceful right now. She seemed to have that peace only when Mattiolo was asleep or in someone else's care.

A terrifying shriek rent the air. Mattiolo! Leaping to her feet, Bellezza bolted toward Mattiolo, who was thrashing and grabbing at his grimy face. Scuro swept Mattiolo into his arms while Bellezza pushed aside the boy's flailing limbs and swiftly examined him. He was dirty but not cut.

Maybe he swallowed a pebble! Bellezza shoved her finger into Mattiolo's mouth, but she could feel no foreign object.

Squatting, Scuro threw Mattiolo over his knee, the child's face downward. With two sharp slaps, he struck his son between the shoulder blades, but nothing dislodged from Mattiolo's throat. Mattiolo coughed and cried louder.

Swiftly a crowd gathered. Questions. Advice.

"I don't know what's wrong!" Bellezza screamed.

A gray-haired friar tried to place his hand on Mattiolo's thrashing head, but Mattiolo flung it off.

"Take him to Madonna Chiara," the friar ordered.

Mattiolo was kicking and screaming in Scuro's arms as he carried him into the church to the speaking grill, where the friar frantically pulled the cord that rang a bell. To the sound of a door sliding open, the friar barked, "Get Madonna Chiara!"

Scrambling behind the wall. Mattiolo thrashing. Shrieking.

The black curtain shot up. Behind the grill, a gray-robed woman, her face anxious, beckoned. "Bring the child to the grill."

Bellezza reached out to stroke the child. He kicked her away.

The woman put her hand between the iron bars and tried to caress Mattiolo's head. Violently, he shook off her touch.

"What's his name?"

"Mattiolo, Madonna." Bellezza's voice quavered.

"Mattiolo, shh. Shh, Bambino." The woman reached again for Mattiolo's tossing head. This time he allowed her to stroke it. "Shh, Bambino. Mattiolo, shh." Mattiolo's sobbing cracked and broke into a whimper. He stopped flailing. How dirty and disheveled he looked!

"Shh, Bambino. I am Suor Chiara. I like you, Mattiolo. You're a good boy."

Whimpering, Mattiolo blinked at the woman. "You're a good bambino, Mattiolo." The voice was soothing, gentle. "We're going to ask our good Jesus to bless you." The woman placed her left hand under Mattiolo's chin and tipped his face upward toward her own. At the touch, Mattiolo quieted. With her right hand, Chiara traced the sign of the cross over him. "In the name of the Father, and of the Son, and of the Holy Spirit. Amen."

Mattiolo wriggled.

"Oh!" the lady said suddenly. She slipped her hand away from Mattiolo's chin and closed her fist. With her right hand, she stroked Mattiolo's cheek. "You're a good bambino, good Mattiolo."

Mattiolo sighed. His head drooped in Scuro's arms. Just that swiftly, he fell asleep.

Chiara held her left hand toward Scuro and Bellezza and opened her palm. In it lay a wet, pinkish pebble.

"It fell out of his nose," Chiara said simply.

His nose? Bellezza had never thought to check Mattiolo's nose.

"Madonna, grazie," Scuro said thickly.

"Grazie," Bellezza said. The phrase was so inadequate.

"Thank the good Jesus," Madonna Chiara said. "He has released the pebble."

"But you are the one who prayed," Scuro said.

The lady's smiling eyes were bright. "And so must you pray. Parents must pray a great deal." Chiara placed her left hand on Mattiolo's head. "Take Mattiolo before the crucifix," she said, pointing to the one above the altar, "and dedicate him to our Lord, who was once a little boy. With your prayers, your love, and God's grace, may Mattiolo grow to be a fine man."

Chiara raised her right hand in blessing. "May the Lord give you faith in His Son and in yours. May you know the gift of your child. May God bless you. In the name of the Father, and of the Son, and of the Holy Spirit. Amen."

As Bellezza blessed herself, an idea came to her. Could raising Mattiolo be a purgatory? Might he teach Bellezza patience? Impatience, not Mattiolo, was Bellezza's barrier to peace. Maybe Mattiolo really was a "gift from God."

NOTES

In an unspecified year, an apparently dangerously injured three- or four-year-old Mattiolo from Spoleto was brought to Chiara, who made the sign of the cross over him. A pebble dropped from his nose and he was cured (CA:ED 154).

Messer Gualtieri Cacciaguerra was the father of Madonna Cecilia, who joined the San Damiano community in 1215 (CA:ED 167 and footnote).

The history of the Porziuncula indulgence and the ceremony granting it follow the research of Fortini (381–85). The seven bishops mentioned were present. Tradition accepts the Porziuncula indulgence, but some modern historians question whether it was ever granted.

Father Francesco Bartoli, as quoted by Father Leone Bracaloni in "Storia di San Damiano in Assisi" (pp. 69–77), states that the same seven bishops who granted the Porziuncula indulgence also gave one to San Damiano. Father Mario Bigaroni postulates that the indulgence was granted to the oratory, not to the entire church of San Damiano, because the oratory was the presbytery of the original church. In a letter to the author (May 22, 1997), Father Bigaroni explained that only public churches and not private oratories could be so indulgenced, and that if the indulgence had been granted and was not merely a legend, it would not have happened in the time of Chiara. Historian David Flood (correspondence, April 28, 1997) also doubts that there ever was a San Damiano indulgence.

The Porziuncula indulgence may now be gained in any public or semi-public oratory in the world beginning from noon August 1 until midnight August 2. It cannot be gained in a private chapel. The person wishing to gain the indulgence must fulfill the following requirements: intend to gain the indulgence; be detached from all sin; while in the church pray one Our Father, one Apostles' Creed, and one other prayer of the individual's choice; pray for the intentions of the pope (prayerfully saying an Our Father and a Hail Mary will suffice, although other prayers may be said); and receive the

Sacraments of Reconciliation and Eucharist within twenty days either before or after August 2. The indulgence, if the person gaining it is free from every sin including venial sin, remits all the temporal punishment due to sin and may be applied to the individual or to a soul in purgatory. If there is any adherence to sin in the person gaining the indulgence, the indulgence becomes partial.

PART SIX

To Imitate the Way of
Holy Simplicity, Humility, and Poverty

23

Messer Ugolino di Pietro Girardone

Church of San Damiano, Assisi (Early Autumn 1217)

Dismounting, Messer Ugolino di Pietro Girardone left his gray mount in the shade with his squire and entered the Church of San Damiano. His shoulder-length black hair was windblown beneath the fitted linen coif tied under his chin and the tight-fitting green cap above it. Today was windy, just as it had been three days ago when he had overseen the last of his wheat harvest and returned to his palatial home on the Piazza del San Rufino to find two friars from San Damiano waiting for him. Madonna Chiara, they said, had an urgent, personal message for him. Today had been the earliest he had been able to ride down to the church to receive it.

Ugolino strode through the church and pulled the cord at the speaking grill. His former neighbor, Madonna Chiara, still looked beautiful after five years behind these walls. He hoped she would be quick, because harvest season was the busiest time of year. Plowing and replanting fallow wheat fields. Picking and drying apples and pears. Gathering chestnuts. Plucking grapes and making wine. Grinding flour. Plus the constant chore of hunting meat for the household.

"Messer Ugolino, I'll be brief," Chiara said. "I've had a vision. You must receive your wife, Madonna Guiduzia, back immediately and the two of you must have a son who will give you great joy and consolation." The lady's voice was kind but firm. "Ask Jesus to give you the grace to do what He asks. We sisters here shall be praying for you."

What should he say? "Sì, Madonna," he grumbled.

The curtain dropped back over the grill. The door slid into place. Ugolino stood dumbly, staring at it.

What did God mean, instructing him to take back his wife? Twenty-two years ago he had sent her away, refusing to take her back despite her pleas and those of others. That long-ago day his raven-haired new bride had made him look foolish to his friends when she had refused to sing for them at a banquet, claiming hoarseness from a cold. Ugolino had heard her sing well with a cold, so why the refusal? "Ah, she probably sounds like a frog!" his guests jeered. "Perhaps we need to call her Messer Guiduzia and you Madonna Ugolino!"

The painful memory brought Ugolino to his senses. Why was he stupidly staring at a curtained grill? Today he didn't feel like praying before the gold-rimmed crucifix, so he tromped past it, toward the exit of the church.

It wasn't only Guiduzia's refusal to sing. She was willful. She made her gowns in her favorite colors, not Ugolino's. Sometimes she refused his advances of love, claiming to be tired. Without consulting her husband, she frequently visited her ill mother, leaving the chief servant in charge of the household. Refusing to beat his wife into submission, as many men would have done, Ugolino sent her home.

On the top step leading out of the church, Ugolino paused. He always prayed in front of that crucifix. Disgruntled, he turned on his heels, approached the crucifix, and knelt. *There. I came back.*

The figure on the cross answered not a word.

How would You like to live with somebody who's willful?

I LIVE WITH WILLFUL PEOPLE ALL THE TIME.

The thought caught Ugolino short. Was he being willful by not following Madonna Chiara's request? Had *he* been willful by not giving his bride a chance?

A line from the Our Father nudged Ugolino's mind. "Forgive us our sins as we forgive those who sin against us." If Ugolino wanted God to forgive him, did he have to forgive Madonna Guiduzia? Even more, did he have to ask Guiduzia to forgive him for sending her away?

Ugolino looked intently at the crucifix. Christ's arms were widely spread as if to embrace with loving forgiveness all who approached Him. "Your sins are forgiven." Christ's words to the repentant woman, to the paralyzed man. To Ugolino. To the world.

Ugolino knew the scriptures. His mother had used them to teach him to read, and now, as part of his nightly routine, Ugolino read her precious, worn Bible so that he could fall asleep. Forgiveness was a big theme in the Bible.

FORGIVE, UGOLINO.

But how, Lord, when I do not wish to?

FORGIVE.

The words rolled over on themselves, like a revolving waterwheel. Sì. He was supposed to visit his mill today. Ugolino said a quick Our Father. There. He had prayed.

Accompanied by his squire, Ugolino guided his horse away from San Damiano. Under bright sun they rode north, past laden olive groves and plowed fields ready for next year's wheat. Tilled lands yielded to the wild Tescio River Valley, where maples and aspens bore faint hints of autumn yellow and red.

Like the leaves, Ugolino was still young and fresh, yet the occasional slight lapses of stamina, the barely perceptible sagging of his cheeks, the faint wrinkles in his forehead were unmistakable signs. The autumn of his life had begun. Someday his body, like the leaves, would rest in the dark, insensitive earth. Where would his soul be then?

FORGIVE, UGOLINO.

How, Lord?

While still a good distance from the mill, Ugolino heard the faint yet persistent rumble of the upper millstone grinding grain against the bottom stone. At the mill, where the noise was deafening, the waterwheel turned as the Tescio flowed beneath it, striking its paddles. Inside, flour dusted every cog, peg, and board and danced in sunbeams streaming through the doorway and the chinks in the walls. On a platform above the millstones stood the floury miller, pouring wheat berries into a funnel-shaped bin that led into a hole in the center of the revolving upper stone.

The upper millstone was turning, grinding. From the hole in the stone's center, the wheat berries slid between the upper and lower stones where the rotation pulverized them. The lower stone was sloped downward and outward so that the flour worked its way to the outer edge and spilled out a chute into an empty sack.

Grain was crushed into flour, flour baked into bread, bread eaten to give life. More verses from his mother's Bible leaped to Ugolino's mind.

"He was put to death for our tresspasses."

"I am the bread of life."

Ugolino thrust his hand into an open sack of wheat berries leaning against a nearby wall. Tiny beige grains slipped through his fingers. Ugolino had planted the wheat because he had intended to crush it into flour. Christ had become man to be crushed for our sins and, thus, forgive them.

FORGIVE AS I HAVE FORGIVEN YOU.

Ugolino opened his fingers and the wheat berries trickled between them into the sack.

Teach me how to forgive, Lord.

God didn't teach him how to forgive. God taught him how to love. Within days, he began to long for Guiduzia. He yearned to fondle her luscious black hair, to hear her lilting laughter, to sway to her ballads, to smell her pungent perfume, to share his soul with her. He came to realize that even though he was still angry with Madonna Guiduzia, he missed her—he loved her. Once he loved, he forgave, for love forgives all. He repented of the harsh way he had treated her.

Ugolino sent for his wife.

She had aged. Little wrinkles lined her eyes and age freckles spattered her face. Her thick hair had thinned and was beginning to gray. Her round face had hollowed, making her look her age—close to forty. But her laughter, her song, and the soothing way she listened when he opened his heart were the same. When he asked her forgiveness for sending her away, her wordless kiss gave him his answer.

With time, he noticed other changes. Madonna Guiduzia was not so willful anymore. Or perhaps he was more willing to compromise. Perhaps they both had mellowed as they entered the autumn of their lives.

One year later, Madonna Guiduzia bore him a son. With awe, Ugolino kissed Guiduzia tenderly, then took the swaddled newborn from her as she lay in bed after the marvelous birth.

Ugolino could not take his eyes from the red-skinned boy, so small in his father's massive hands. "We'll name him Pietro," Ugolino declared, "after my father and after San Pietro the apostle whom Christ so graciously forgave." He smiled at his wide-eyed son. "I'll take you to see Madonna Chiara," Ugolino whispered. "We'll bring her woolen cloth to make new habits for the sisters. What do you think, Pietruccio?" Ugolino bounced the boy lightly in his arms. "Will she open the curtain and give you her blessing? Will she, Bambino?"

With dark, unfocused eyes, forgiveness born of love gazed at Ugolino and gurgled in laughter.

NOTES

Chiara had a vision (probably after she entered religious life—no year is specified) in which God instructed Ugolino di Pietro Girardone to take back his wife, Madonna Guiduzia, whom he had dismissed twenty-two years earlier for unexplained reasons. Chiara promised a son from the union. After being initially dismayed, Ugolino began to desire his wife and so followed Chiara's advice. A son was later born (no year specified) who was still alive in 1253 (CA:ED 190–91).

Ugolino's family was part of the San Rufino consortium and neighbor to Chiara's family (CA:ED 190 footnote; Fortini 328). Fortini (*Nova Vita di San Francesco II* 322–24) lists several court cases involving Ugolino and his family. Ugolino's son Pietro was a witness in a court case in 1239. Fortini lists no other children of Ugolino. Assuming that Pietro was the predicted son and that the young man had to be at least fourteen or fifteen years old to be a witness, we can approximate when Pietro may have been born. The arbitrary date of this chapter has been figured from that calculation.

The Scripture passages Ugolino recalls are drawn from Matthew 9:2, Luke 7:48, Romans 4:25, John 6:35, and Colossians 3:13.

24

Cardinal Ugolino dei Conti di Segni

Outside the Church of San Damiano (Holy Week 1220)

Standing beside Fra Cappellano near the façade of the Church of San Damiano, Cardinal Ugolino dei Conti di Segni looked above to the second-floor door. He'd come to consult Madonna Chiara, who was too weak to descend the stairs to the parlor. So he'd climb up to her.

The door swung open. Suor Balvina di Martino di Ugolino di Offreduccio, a woman as large as her name, appeared in the opening. As deftly as if the staircase were a slipper, Balvina lowered the stairs. The thick chain that held the staircase to the monastery swayed as Ugolino began the ascent. Cappellano followed him.

Ugolino's oval face, always pinched and thin, had grown hollow-cheeked with age and fasting. His trimmed gray beard was still full, as was the ring of thick silver hair that fringed his scalp. Having left his silk shoes and rich cape in Cappellano's hut, he seemed not the wealthy cardinal of Ostia and Velletri, but a simple, barefoot man. Ugo.

Ugo had been born the Count of Anagni in the Patrimony of San Pietro. More titles followed. Priest of the church of Anagni. Papal chaplain to his great-uncle, Pope Innocenzo III. Cardinal-deacon of Sant'Eustachio. Chief counselor of Pope Onorio III. One of Lord Pope's many legates. Yet, to him, the most meaningful title was his unofficial one of spiritual father to Fra Francesco's and Madonna Chiara's followers.

Ever since that meal last year at San Damiano, Ugo had been impressed with Chiara, so much younger than he, yet of the same class. Ugo was the son of a count, Chiara the granddaughter of one. He knew what he had relinquished to embrace religious life, but she had surrendered more. Ugo still had fine clothes, good food, servants, and steeds, but Chiara had nothing but God. Ugo could reveal his soul to her—she seemed able to read his heart.

He had come to San Damiano this Holy Week because, upon Pope Onorio's directive, he was visiting all communities of women in this part of the empire—to approve, regulate, correct, or even dismiss them. Last year, Ugo had written a Form of Life for the Damianites, parts of which disturbed Madonna Chiara. Ugo wanted to discuss those sections.

Chiara was propped up on her raised bed at the dormitory's opposite end. Sitting on one of the half-dozen stools surrounding the bed, Ugo took Chiara's thin right hand from the alb she was stitching and kissed it.

"Are you in pain?" he asked as he heard the staircase clunk against the wall and the monastery door swing shut.

"Only when I walk."

"Doesn't my Form of Life state that ill sisters should be in the infirmary?"

Chiara nodded gaily. "Messer Cardinal, as abbess, I must be with my sisters in the dormitory. If you wish to make a healthy sister abbess, I'll gladly recover in the infirmary."

Ugo patted Chiara's hand. "Stay in the dormitory, Madonna Abbess." He lay her hand in her lap. He glanced at Fra Cappellano and Suor Balvina, who were standing nearby. "May we speak privately?"

Fra Cappellano picked up two stools and carried them to the opposite end of the dormitory. Offering one to Balvina, he sat on the other, facing Ugo and Chiara.

Ugo lowered his voice. "Your letter stated that some portions of the Form of Life I gave you last year displease you. I've given that Form of Life to several convents. It contains regulations demanded of enclosed women, but I also attempted to have it reflect how I observed your living."

"Messer Cardinal," Chiara spoke softly, "see the lace on this alb?" Chiara pointed to a row of fine lace embroidered with stags and birds. "It resembles a forest glade. Yet it isn't a glade. Even so, your Form of Life is quite beautiful, but it doesn't fully capture how we live."

Ugo felt for the relic he carried in his silk purse. Some time ago Bishop Jacques de Vitry of Belgium had given Ugo a relic of Marie d'Oignies, a holy, austere recluse favored with mystical gifts. Jacques, Marie's confessor until her death seven years earlier, had advised Ugo, who frequently lost his patience even to the point of swearing, to seek patience through Marie's intercession. Ugo fingered the relic and kept his voice down. "What's wrong with my Form of Life?"

"Messer, we fast daily. Yet you have asked that we also abstain from fruit, vegetables, and wine on Wednesdays and Fridays outside of Lent and that we fast on bread and water four days a week during Lent and three days during the Lent of Saint Martin. Messer, you have mercifully dispensed the young, old, and weak sisters from fasting but have overlooked those who serve outside the monastery. They expend a great deal of energy walking and have been growing faint on such a severe diet, so I have dispensed them as well."

Ugo could see her point. "Very wise, Madonna Chiara. Continue to dispense the serving sisters."

"Grazie, Messer. Now regarding silence. Here, Messer, we have always spoken of spiritual things. But your Form of Life allows speaking only out of duty. It doesn't permit encouraging the ill sisters nor talking about God's graces. The serving sisters may not speak, except out of duty, to those they meet in the world. What are we permitted to say to those who approach our grills? Some sisters were forgetting how to talk! We can teach each other much about our Lord. Therefore, I've permitted the sisters to speak, in quiet tones, of the things of God and of whatever is necessary or helpful to one another."

Ugo rubbed the relic. "I trust your experience, Madonna Chiara."

"And one other matter, Messer. Enclosure isn't a prison. It's a gift. It enables us to commune with our Lord in solitude so that we may share His graces with the needy. While the parlor is a place of privacy sealed by a curtain, we raise the curtain in the choir when God's Word is preached. We also raise the curtain at the speaking grill if we wish to bless someone. We've continued these practices even though they aren't mentioned in your Form of Life."

"Perhaps I didn't observe your practices well enough," Ugo admitted. "Have you anything else?" His lack of irritation surprised him.

"No, Messer Cardinal. God has been good to us."

Ugo released the relic. "Madonna, many things are troubling me. May I share them?"

"Of course." Chiara's gaze focused on him, encouraging him to speak.

Ugo knew every important person in the Church. Last year he had inspired the crusaders by his eloquent preaching. He had memorized the Bible and was zealous for the faith. But since January, when five followers of Francesco had died for their faith in Morocco, Ugo had had no spiritual peace. The martyrs' blood had seared his soul. Last spring, Francesco told Ugo that he was planning to sail to Egypt, hoping to help bring peace between crusaders and Muslims. Ugo suspected that he may have thought he'd be martyred if he tried. Despite her sisters' pleading and prayers, Chiara, too, had wanted to go to the Holy Land where martyrdom beckoned. Francesco? Ugo had heard nothing more. Chiara? Bedfast, she was going nowhere. Ugo? Was his desire for martyrdom from God? Or from himself? He asked Chiara about it. She closed her eyes in silent prayer.

"Messer, I believe that you are to remain alive and that your martyrdom is to do God's will. You're doing His will now. Time will reveal more."

"Madonna, I've been consecrated to God for decades. Yet the life of the friars appeals to me. Ought I to become a Poor Brother?"

"God knows the answer to that, not I."

"My soul is disquieted."

"Messer, look." Chiara plucked from the floor a wooden frame holding a length of bleached linen, deftly embroidered with a recurring, unfinished pattern of block-shaped crosses. "Your disquiet may be a cross that is preparing you for another cross. Crosses, you know, conform us to Christ."

"How have you created these?" Ugo asked admiringly.

"Like this." Chiara drew out a threaded needle thrust into the pattern and plunged it through the cloth, bringing it up to create a tiny, perfect stitch.

"Thus, you embroider the stitches," Chiara explained. "To create the tiny spaces around the designs and to make lace, you pull out the width-wise threads." With the tip of the needle, Chiara drew a width-wise thread away from the fabric. Picking a minuscule blade from the floor, she nimbly cut the thread where it joined two of the crosses. Then she pulled out the cut thread with the tip of the needle so that tiny open spaces appeared where the cut thread had been, one space between each crosswise thread.

"Clever," Ugo said. "If only we could pluck out our bad qualities as swiftly as you plucked out that thread."

Chiara smiled. "God is good at drawing threads if we ask."

"Sometimes He draws them very slowly."

Chiara laughed. "True, Messer. And look." Chiara pointed at the slender crosswise threads with the tip of the needle. "When all the width-wise threads are pulled out and only the crosswise ones remain, you gather a few crosswise threads together with a tiny stitch here and there, and it looks like lace. Do you think father Francesco will like this deacon's alb? Every stitch has been a prayer for him."

"He will greatly appreciate it, I'm sure. Have you a few prayers for me?"

"We pray for you daily, Messer Cardinal," Chiara said.

Ugo nodded. "Grazie. I fear my office may endanger my soul."

"God has used your office to bless us and many others. A few days from now, you'll give us the Body of Christ on Easter!"

Ugolino nodded, recalling Chiara kneeling on the simple wooden kneeler at the window in the choir grill behind San Damiano's altar, tears streaming, her face aglow, as she received on her tongue the Body of Christ. Like Chiara, Francesco, too, wept and trembled upon receiving the Lord.

"As God uses simple bread to come to us bodily, so He uses you to come to us bodily. We are most blessed in you, Messer Cardinal."

Chiara turned the crosses toward Ugo. "Your cross, Messer, is to accept God's way. In time may you see His wisdom."

Ugo gazed at the cloth and Chiara's hands resting so peacefully on it. He took one of her hands and kissed it. "Madonna Chiara, I am a wretched and sinful man," Ugo whispered. "I entrust my soul and commend my spirit to you, just as Jesus on the Cross commended His spirit to the Father, so that on the day of judgment you may answer for me, if you have not been concerned for and intent on my salvation. For I have a certain belief that you will obtain from the most high Judge whatever the insistence of so great a devotion and abundance of tears implores." He bowed his head to her. "Therefore, promise that you will pray fervently for my salvation."

Chiara placed her hand over Ugo's. "Messer," her voice quivered, "I am a sinner, too. But of course I will pray for you. Do you pray for me."

NOTES

Papal histories list Cardinal Ugolino's birth as anywhere from the mid-1140s to 1170. Many sources (but not all) say that Cardinal Ugolino was eighty years old when he was elected pope on March 19, 1227. He was known, at least to some, by the shortened form of his name, (H)ugo (FA:ED I 245).

The primary sources mention Ugolino's habit of visiting the friars barefoot. His physical description is based on paintings. His titles and activities are accurately described. Ugo's bad temper, swearing, and his reliance on Marie d'Oignies' relic are mentioned in a footnote to page 175 in Englebert's *Saint Francis of Assisi*.

Balvina di Martino di Ugolino di Offreduccio joined the San Damiano community in 1217.

Before Chiara became so ill, she desired martyrdom after hearing of the slaughter of five friars in Morocco (CA:ED 168–69, 171). In Marco Bartoli's biography of her, he assumes that Chiara didn't go to Morocco precisely because she became ill. We don't know Ugo's response to the friars' martyrdom.

During her illnesses, Chiara seems to have stayed in the dormitory, not the infirmary. Visitors were not permitted in the dormitory, but an exception would have been made for a papal legate or friar (CA:ED 124).

Chiara's *Form of Life*, approved in 1253, and Ugolino's of 1219 differ from each other in the ways described in this chapter. In addition, Chiara's *Form of Life* states that the sisters were to keep silence continually in the dormitory. Yet Chiara spoke frequently from her sickbed (CA:ED 159–60, 166, 177, 180, 181, 188). It seems that the continual dormitory silence would apply not to her but to the other sisters who wanted to talk among themselves. They were to speak elsewhere. However, those who came to Chiara for counsel and who worked about her bed while she sat and stitched or spun could have conversed with her: a section of the *Form of Life* permitted speaking "with discernment in the infirmary for the recreation and service of the sick" (CA:ED 116). Chiara's *Form of Life* adds that the sisters "may always and everywhere communicate whatever is necessary, briefly and in a quiet voice" (CA:ED 116).

The Basilica di Santa Chiara in Assisi possesses the alb, accurately described in this chapter, that Chiara made, at some point, for Francesco. No one is sure of her embroidery techniques. According to *The Dictionary of Needlework*, the method described in this chapter was common for the period.

Ugo visited Chiara often and exchanged several letters with her. Only two are preserved, one written after celebrating Holy Week (presumably in 1220) and another in 1228. Ugo's conversation with Chiara, "a wretched and sinful man," is taken from his 1220 letter to her (CA:ED 129–30).

Chiara's sisters noticed her tearful, trembling reception of the Eucharist (CA:ED 152, 156).

On August 27, 1218, Pope Onorio III authorized Cardinal Ugolino to investigate and regulate the lifestyles of women religious. In 1219, Ugo gave women's communities the *Rule of Saint Benedict* to observe, in an "attempt to maintain the juridical legality of each foundation, thus positioning the papacy to protect its members from accusations of heresy" (CA:ED 335). Chiara's community tried to live the Rule but found it too severe and were thus given permission to live as they had been.

In 1220, presumably at Francesco's request, Pope Onorio III made Ugo cardinal protector of both the Lesser Brothers and the Poor Ladies.

25

Fra Stefano the Simple

Porziuncula, Assisi (November 1220)

ra Stefano screamed in his sleep because Fra Leone's dream was coming true in his own dream. A few nights ago, at Francesco's bedside, Leone had recounted his dream of many friars crossing a great, flooded river. Those bearing heavy loads drowned, while those carrying nothing crossed safely. Fra Francesco had explained that the river was the world and the heavy loads carnal goods and desires. Only friars free of worldly attachment safely crossed the river to eternity.

In Stefano's dream, he was drowning in a raging river, pulled down by a heavy keg on his back. He awoke screaming, choking for air. He slept no more that night.

Over the weeks, Stefano's chubby, innocent face grew hollow and tense with worry. Leone's dream and his own became an obsession, for Stefano knew his sins.

Stefano had been defiant. He had sneaked away from the convent to find Francesco in the Holy Land and tell him that the two vicars he had appointed to take his place had changed the Rule.

He was guilty of presumption. He had left Assisi without Francesco's permission, then begged Francesco's forgiveness when he found him.

He had secretly taken a copy of the new, stricter regulations and given them to Francesco as proof that Francesco must return home.

He had been disobedient to the new rule. When Stefano found Fra Francesco and Fra Pietro di Catanio on an abstinence day after the new regulations were in effect, they had just been served meat. Francesco had decided that they should follow the Gospel and eat what was set before them. But that wasn't what the new rule said.

He was slothful. Since he couldn't remember all his prayers, he sometimes didn't say them.

He was untrustworthy. Whenever he shared food that he had begged, he always managed to forget someone.

He was stupid because he frequently forgot to do errands.

He should have been named Fra Stefano the Sinful instead of the Simple.

How could God accept him? Stefano's sins oppressed him. Previously happy and carefree, he became despondent, withdrawn. He was going to hell.

Fra Pietro di Catanio, whom Francesco had appointed minister, couldn't lighten his fears. Francesco, so gaunt, wan, and feverish, his red-rimmed eyes watery with an inexplicable disease contracted in Egypt, couldn't cure him. The doctor's medicines did no good. Stefano's depression deepened until he could no longer eat or work. Nor did he care if he died. He was going to hell.

Francesco said that he must see Madonna Chiara. The friars half-carried, half-dragged him to San Damiano. He was so totally exhausted when they arrived that he crumpled into a whimpering heap at the speaking grill. Too drained to look into Chiara's face, he felt her hand firmly pressing his head, his shoulder. As he heard her speaking the words of the sign of the cross, exhaustion overcame him. His heavy eyes closed. He felt his body drowning in welcome sleep.

The dream came again. The river, Stefano crossing it. This time he was bearing on his back a white dove that lifted him in its talons and carried him across the flood to the opposite bank, where he floated above a plain of colorful, fragrant flowers that filled him with joy.

Muddled, Stefano awoke. He pushed himself erect. How had he gotten here, to the speaking grill in San Damiano?

"Brother, are you all right?"

Stefano smiled shyly at the woman behind the grill. "Of course, Madonna Chiara. Why wouldn't I be?"

"God be praised!" Chiara gasped, reaching through the grill to clasp Stefano's hand.

Why did she do that? Had he been sick? He didn't remember. He was terribly thirsty, however. Sheepishly, he looked at Chiara. "Madonna Chiara, could you bring me a cup of water, please? And . . ." Dare he ask? "And perhaps a little bread, unless I am to be fasting."

"Brother," Chiara said, her voice a bit breathless, "no one whom our Lord has just healed is to be fasting."

NOTES

Fra Leone's dream of the drowning friars is recounted in the *Fioretti* (chap. 36). Fortini places this dream in autumn 1220 (Fortini 459). Fra Stefano suffered from "madness." No details about the ailment are given. Francesco sent Stefano to Chiara to make the sign of the cross over him. He then fell asleep "in the place where the holy mother usually prayed" (wherever that was) and awoke cured (CA:ED 153). A Fra Stefano from Narni traveled to Egypt to bring Francesco news of the troubles in the order. There he met Francesco and Pietro as they were about to eat meat, as this chapter describes. Was this the Fra Stefano cured by Chiara's prayers? We don't know.

When Francesco returned from the Holy Land, he dismissed the rebel vicars and appointed Pietro di Catanio in their place. The generally accepted year is 1220, but dates as early as 1217 and as late as 1221 are also postulated.

26

Brontolone

Via San Petrignano, Assisi (Christmas Eve 1220)

Brontolone hobbled down the steep hill of San Petrignano toward San Damiano. A chill December wind lashed his torn mantle and the ripped sleeves of his tunic. Stupid ruffian children! They'd pounded him yesterday because he wouldn't share the fowl some noble had tossed at him. Despite his age and skinny limbs, he'd fought them off, but the scuffle had ripped his garments and injured his back. The Lesser Brothers who saw the fight told him that the Poor Ladies would mend his garments and that Madonna Chiara would pray over his back. They'd better mend them. She'd better pray.

Finally. The church. Brontolone hobbled down five steps leading into the nave, his cloth-wrapped feet slipping on the third step. Damn step!

In the apse on the left side of the altar was that speaking grill the friars told him about. He pulled the bell cord. He pulled again. Again. Again.

Sliding. Unbolting. Through the grill's black curtain, a harried voice. "Pace e bene. May I help you?"

"Friars said ya'd mend my tunic 'n mantle."

"Put them on the turn, please."

Near the grill was a barrel, its rounded end facing Brontolone. "The turn ain't turned."

The barrel swiveled. It was cut in half lengthwise. Brontolone whipped off his mantle and slipped out of his torn tunic. Throwing the tunic on the floor of the barrel, he pulled his mantle tight around his shoulders. Brr!

The turn swiveled inward. "Where's your mantle?"

"I'd be here in my breeches if I give it to ya."

"I'll send out my mantle. Put yours on the turn."

The turn swiveled again. Brontolone tossed his torn, threadbare mantle on the turn and wrapped himself in the newer, warmer one.

The turn swiveled inward. "Please wait."

Bolting. Sliding. Why'd they lock everything? Brontolone pressed his face against the grill and shouted, "Hurry up! It's freezin'."

Brr. He stomped his feet to keep warm. Ow! Daggers of pain shot up his back. Damn, stupid kids!

Unbolting. Sliding. So soon?

"My good man, we have a better tunic for you and a fur cape."

The turn swiveled. If these were Poor Ladies, how'd they have fur capes? Brontolone dressed himself in the garments, throwing the fur cape over the mantle he'd been given before.

"What about my blessin'?"

The curtain over the speaking grill drew upward. Brontolone jutted his pointy chin at the tall penitent who was dressed in a poor gray tunic and black veil. She wasn't much to see, rubbing her upper arms vigorously as if trying to warm up.

The lady raised her right hand. "May God bless you." The woman's teeth were chattering. If she was so cold, why'd she not put on one of them fur capes? "May He give you more than you can imagine. In the name of the Father and of the Son and of the Holy Spirit. Amen."

"Nothin' about my sore back?"

"May Christ heal your sore back. Amen."

Brontolone arched his shoulders. Ow! "Didn't do no good. You that holy nun?"

The penitent was rubbing her upper arms again. "You mean Madonna Chiara?"

"Yeah. You her?"

"Do you want Madonna Chiara to pray for you?"

"Well, sure. Don't ya' know nothin'?"

"I'll call her."

The curtain dropped. Women. Only dogs was dumber.

Within a few moments the curtain rose. Madonna Chiara, with her oval face and full lips, was a bit more attractive. She was wearing a patched gray lazzo tunic and a black veil. The taller, shivering penitent stood behind her, now wrapped in a shabby mantle.

"Yer prayers better than hers?"

"Would you let me touch you?"

Brontolone pushed against the grill. Madonna Chiara placed her hands firmly on Brontolone's shoulders. She closed her eyes and began to whisper.

"Can't hear ya."

"Shh. Listen to God speak within you."

"Never talks to me."

"Shh."

Why'd she not pray louder? He wanted to know what was said. Moments later, she released her grip. "In the name of the Father and of the Son and of the Holy Spirit," she said. Awkwardly, he signed himself.

Brontolone wriggled his back. Ow! "Still's sore."

"We'll pray for you daily," the woman said.

"Little good that'll do." Pulling the fur cape about himself, Brontolone hobbled out of the church. He had to climb all the way to Assisi with his sore back.

Friars. Holy ladies. Rubbish.

NOTES

The fictitious character Brontolone represents the poor and needy whom the friars referred to San Damiano for counsel and help but who didn't receive a cure from Chiara's prayers.

27

Suor Benvenuta di Peroscia

San Damiano (Christmas 1220)

D rawing Chiara's mantle around her, Suor Benvenuta di Peroscia closed the refectory door and stepped into the courtyard. The first of the two meals allowed on Christmas and on Sundays had been eaten. With the dishes washed and the refectory tidied, the sisters were laughing and chatting. When the friars arrived, they would gather in the parlor, the friars on the church side and the sisters on the monastery side, to talk about the infant Christ. Since coming here eight years ago Benvenuta had loved this Christmas gathering, but today she was somber.

Benvenuta walked across the courtyard matted with dried weeds and grass. She passed the vegetable garden with its green but wilted parsley. Despite the raw air, she wanted to be alone at the hermitages, to ask what she must now do.

In the leafless forest, Benvenuta followed the path quickly, dried leaves crackling under her bare feet. At the first hut, she pushed aside the leather flap that served as a door and entered, bumping into someone who was kneeling inside. Madonna Chiara.

Benvenuta sputtered an apology. She would use another hermitage.

"Wait, sister," Chiara said, turning to her with a gentle smile. "You seemed distracted yesterday and today. Is something troubling you?"

"You." The word burst out. "Not you. A vision. Remember when you prayed for that old beggar yesterday? The one whose tunic and mantle were so rotted that we gave him a fur cape and new tunic? After you left, the whole alcove by the speaking grill seemed to be on fire with the fire of God."

"The beggar must have brought it," Chiara mused.

"Him? The fire came because of you."

"Me? You prayed there, too."

"There wasn't any fire when I prayed."

"There wasn't any fire when I prayed, either. You saw it after I left."

"That's true. But it had to be because you prayed there. You even gave me your mantle when the beggar took mine."

"You gave the beggar your mantle first."

"Only to borrow," Benvenuta pointed out. "I didn't think he'd keep it."

"You're only borrowing mine," Chiara said, "until the friars can beg wool to make you a new one. And I'm warm in this scrap of wool." Chiara hugged the ragged piece about her.

The whole conversation was totally confusing.

Benvenuta dropped to her knees and sat on her heels. "I wish I were like you."

"Whatever for?"

"You're holy."

Chiara's rich laughter echoed through the little hut. "Oh, sister, if I'm holy, then you're a saint."

"I can't do what you do. I can't pray all night, wear hairshirts, or live on a bit of bread. Or even wash the mattresses of the sick sisters without feeling sick myself. Today at Mass you were weeping to receive our Lord in the Eucharist."

"I always cry. I can't help it."

"It's the gift of tears. I don't have that gift."

"Oh, sister, you have other, more useful gifts." Chiara sat back on her heels and patted Benvenuta's hand. "Dear Suor Benvenuta, you must imitate Jesus, not me. Poverty and enclosure have value if we are poor in spirit and enclosed in the will of God. This doesn't happen when we imitate others, because then we may be doing God's will for them instead of God's will for us." Chiara threw her arms around Benvenuta and gave her a quick, hearty hug. "Don't look so sad at my little scolding. I, too, have mistakenly tried to be like someone else. First, Mamma. Then Suor Pacifica. Then Fra Francesco. But we must be like Jesus."

Chiara took Benvenuta's hand again. "Do you remember the parable of the wineskins?"

"New wine, new skins," Benvenuta said.

"Sì, because new skins are flexible. They expand as the new wine ripens. Our lives must be like new wineskins, not rigid old ones that can't expand to hold what God is fermenting in us. Our Rule is like new skins, sister, confining yet flexible. Within our Rule's constraints, God calls one sister to greater mortification, another to greater prayer, a third to greater service. One sister can read hearts; another, heal; a third listens with the heart." Chiara smiled. "God gives the gifts and the call. At times God may change the call or the gift. True poverty is relinquishing our own ideas of how we may be sanctified and following God's plan."

Benvenuta hugged Chiara's mantle about her. "God's plan. If only I knew it!"

"But you do know it. 'Love one another; even as I have loved you,' Jesus said." Chiara embraced Benvenuta again. "Sister, all you do speaks of love. Your tending the grill, your painstaking embroidery, your willingness to serve, your fervent prayers."

"They're duties, sister."

"To do one's duty well is an act of love. But you go beyond duty. You give a beggar your mantle when you know you will be cold without it. You come to the hermitage when the others are laughing in the refectory. You listen patiently to my little lecture while you wish to pray instead. You do another's will rather than your own. That's love, sister. When you act with love, you're in God's will, you're holy, you're imitating Christ. Your soul is full of love."

Benvenuta thought about the fire. It had been at the place where Chiara and Benvenuta had prayed, where they had shown love to a disgruntled, rude beggar. Scripture said that God is love and God is a consuming fire. The fire Benvenuta saw must have been God, must have been love. Benvenuta nodded slowly as she understood. "Sister, to become holy, I think we must become Love—the One who was born this day." A grin spread across her face. "Can we share that with the friars and sisters today?"

Chiara laughed. "I think that is just what we're about to do."

NOTES

Before Chiara fell ill, Benvenuta alone saw above Chiara's usual place of prayer a great brilliance that she thought were real flames (CA:ED 153–54).

The sisters seem to have eaten only one meal daily but could eat twice on Christmas (CA:ED 113) and presumably also on Sundays, as Sunday was never a day of fast or abstinence. It seems reasonable that the friars would make a Christmas visit, but we have no proof.

This chapter is an attempt to show how Chiara may have consoled and admonished her sisters. Some of Chiara's thoughts expressed in this chapter are in her writings.

The quote "Love one another as I have loved you" is Chiara's remembrance of John 13:34.

Part Seven

Given Up Their Own Wills

28

Fra Francesco Bernardone

Parlor, San Damiano (May 1221)

Fra Francesco Bernardone and the newest brother, youthful, eager-eyed Fra Giacomo, sat facing the black-curtained grill in the parlor at San Damiano.

"Pace e bene, Fra Francesco, Fra Giacomo." The pleasant voice was Christiana's.

"Pace e bene." Suor Cecilia's deep, throaty tone.

Francesco was not feeling very pleasant. "Christiana, we must discuss this privately." He nodded at Fra Giacomo, who moved to the far end of the parlor. He heard a gentle shuffling on the other side of the grill, which meant that Suor Cecilia had likewise moved out of earshot.

Francesco drew close to the grill and tried to keep his voice calm and low. "Christiana, two days ago I sent you five women to be accepted into the community. Why have you sent me word that you will accept all but Madonna Gasdia?"

The firm whisper came through the curtain. "Madonna Gasdia will not persist."

Francesco took a deep breath. He and Christiana had an eternal, spiritual bond. A pure and holy love existed between them. Each prayed daily for the other. Each understood this way of life as no one else, and each could see and rejoice in the other's faith and efforts for holiness. So firmly was each committed to poverty, chastity, and obedience, so fully did each understand the other, that one seemed to be half of the other's soul. They even lived in much the same way, often praying through the night, fasting severely, and trading their tunics for poorer ones worn by others.

But sometimes, like now, Christiana exasperated him.

"Madonna Gasdia di Taccolo di Aregnato is a holy widow," Francesco said in a measured tone. "Her son is married and she is free. She wishes to serve God more totally and believes God is calling her to live here. Her family approves."

"Sì. She told me these things."

"Why do you disapprove?"

"Madonna Gasdia has a burning desire to follow the poor crucified Christ. She wishes to possess the kingdom of heaven as do the other four women you sent. When I questioned each one privately, Madonna Gasdia was most eager to enter here."

Sì, most eager. Madonna Gasdia had been cured of a violent fever at the tomb of Saint Rufinus, and, ever since, had felt that her spiritual life had been lax. She wished to do penance, to grow sanctified, before she died. Several times she had spoken to Francesco about giving herself completely to Christ.

"Madonna Gasdia is a pious woman," Christiana was affirming, "with a most loving family. She has been following Christ closely for many years. But, as you know, penance and sanctity are quite possible outside a monastery. Our life here is one of holy poverty and destitution. Those the Lord calls to this life will rejoice always in Him, but others will find only bitterness here."

"Do you think she won't persist because she's so eager?"

"As you have experienced with your friars, often those most eager to enter fall away, while those who struggle intensely with the decision persist. Unless I'm deceived, she won't persist, even should she stay here three years."

Francesco grunted. "Did God tell you to reject her?"

"He told me to discuss it with you and obey your decision."

Francesco took a deep breath. She would be obedient to the minister general. "Fra Elia agreed with me that you are to accept her."

Christiana's voice was crisp. "So be it. I disagree. But I'll do as you say."

NOTES

Francesco sent five women to Chiara to be received. "Lifting herself up" (from praying prostrate? from her bed where she was lying ill?), Chiara said she would receive four of them but not Madonna Gasdia di Taccolo, because she wouldn't persist should she stay at San Damiano for three years. Only under great pressure from an unnamed source (or sources) did Chiara accept Gasdia (CA:ED 170).

Fortini mentions a Pietro di Gasdia as being a witness in a legal matter in 1201 (vol. 3, p. 201). Madonna Gasdia's brother Messer Andrea was an important person in Assisi in 1235 (Fortini, vol. 2, p. 417). A Gasdia (no surname) was cured of fever at the tomb of Saint Rufinus (vol. 1, part 2, p. 9). Madonna Gasdia's approximate age is calculated from Fortini's supposition that Pietro was her son, who would have to have been at least fourteen or fifteen to be a witness. Since Pietro was listed as "di Gasdia," his father may have been dead.

Pietro Catanio died in March 1221. By the chapter meeting held in May 1221, Francesco, who had suffered illness and eye disease in the Holy Land, was weak and ill. With Cardinal Ugolino's approval, Francesco made Fra Elia of Cortona the minister general of the friars.

29

Suor Agnese

Woods at San Damiano (September 1221)

Suor Agnese was stumbling through the sun-dappled woods behind San Damiano, her soft blue eyes brimming with tears, her slender form a shadow among the tree trunks. After prayer at the hour of Terce, she had obtained Chiara's permission to come to the hermitages to plead for courage. But she had been so bursting with emotion that she couldn't stay on her knees. So, on her small bare feet, she had run into the forest to cry out her prayers.

Oh, God! Agnese had been named after martyrs—Catherine of Alexandria, whose tomb Mamma had visited on Mount Sinai and who had been tortured on a spiked wheel before being beheaded, and Agnes, a twelve-year-old virgin who had also been beheaded. They hadn't run from their martyrdom, but she was running from hers.

How could she leave San Damiano? Leaving was a martyrdom.

Nine years ago, at the age of fourteen, Agnese had come here. She had prayed to die here. Now she was being sent to Florence. Oh, the bitterness!

With small, delicate fingers, Agnese pulled aside a bramble that snagged her skirt. Love was a bramble, snagging her. She loved too much. San Damiano. Mamma. Beatrice. Chiara. All her sister Damianites. The valley of Spoleto, sprawled beyond the dormitory windows.

Could she love an unknown group of sisters the way she loved these?

Like mushrooms, monasteries of Poor Ladies were springing up all over. Vallegloria in Spello. Santa Maria della Carita near the fountain of Carpello outside Foligno. Monticello in Florence. Monte Luce in Perugia. Santa Maria in Siena. Santa Maria di Gattaiolo in Lucca. Santo Spirito in Arezzo. Some of the sisters had traveled to this place and that to establish monasteries. Pious women, in touch with Chiara through letters, had founded others.

The sisters in the new monasteries wanted to live like the sisters at San Damiano. So they wrote letters, full of questions, to Chiara. But letters couldn't answer everything. Some things had to be experienced. So Francesco, with Chiara's approval, had sent Suor Benedetta to Siena and Suor Balvina di Martino to Arezzo. And now they were sending Agnese to Florence.

Why not Benvenuta or Pacifica, Cecilia or Filippa, Marsebilia or Cristiana or Balbina? Why Agnese?

How could Agnese leave Chiara? After Christ, Chiara was Agnese's support. Chiara had taught her nearly everything she knew about religious life. How was Agnese to teach the Monticello sisters without Chiara? Without Chiara, could her faith maintain any depth?

Chiara. Chiara. Chiara could read Agnese's soul. One night months ago, after praying Matins at midnight with the friars and helping Chiara extinguish the lamps, Agnese had joined Chiara and a few other sisters in the oratory to continue in prayer. As always, Agnese prayed gazing at the shadowy nook to the left of the altar in which the Eucharistic Lord rested in a small silver box.

The Lord had drawn Agnese deeply into His being. Her prayer had become a silent, internal song notated with tears.

My Father, how good, how patient You are! We constantly offend You, yet You mercifully continue to love and call us. Oh, compassionate Lord, luring the most stubborn sinners to Your side!

My Jesus, You have left nothing undone. Your hands and feet, pierced with nails, Your side with a lance. Your wounds spurted the blood of love. What agony to have loved so!

Oh, suffering souls in purgatory, what agony must you feel away from God! May God mercifully grant you the grace to give your wills totally to Him so that you may unite totally with Him!

When the intensity had faded, she had returned to the well-lit dormitory, curled up on her bare plank bed, and fallen swiftly asleep.

The next morning, she had just thrust five loaves of bread into the outdoor oven when Chiara came by. Smiling curiously, Chiara had casually stated, "Last night, after the others had gone to bed, I saw you praying."

Agnese nodded. "I saw you praying as well."

"I saw you rise above the ground," Chiara had said.

Agnese turned from the oven in utter disbelief.

"Then I saw a vivid brilliance, an angel, take shape next to you."

Agnese stared at Chiara in incredulous silence.

"The angel put a crown upon your head. Later a second crown. Then a third."

Unbelievable.

"Did the devil deceive me, sister, or did the crowns correspond to your prayers?"

Chiara deceived? Impossible. Yet Agnese had seen no angel or crowns. Nor had she any idea that she'd been floating. She only knew that she had meditated thrice, on the Father, Son, and suffering souls.

Now, in the woods, Agnese thought of her prayers that night. Had they been mere words? Or did she trust God enough to give Him all her will? In obedience, she had to leave San Damiano.

Agnese reached the monastery as the bell was ringing for Sext.

In the choir, Agnese tried to pray, to praise. But unbidden tears were streaming down her cheeks and she could barely speak. This was the last time that she would pray here, with her sisters.

The prayers ended as the bell rang. Agnese's heart leaped.

Suor Gasdia, who was tending the grill, peeked into the choir. "Suor Giacoma and Suor Forina have arrived from Monticello."

Agnese grit her teeth. "I will get my traveling pouch."

As Gasdia left, Chiara rose from prayer. With the slightest tremor in her legs, weakened with a strange, recurring illness, she approached Agnese and caught her hand. "I'll go with you to the door, sister."

Dazed, Agnese plucked the pouch packed with her mantle from the foot of her bed, flinging it over her shoulder. She reached for the hand-sized cross resting on the wooden block that served as her pillow. Every night she fell asleep clasping in prayer those two dark sticks tied together at right angles. She pressed the cross into Chiara's hand.

"Pray for me, dear sister." Agnese's voice cracked.

Chiara hobbled to her bed and took from beneath her own pillow the lighter-toned twig cross she had made and slept with. She gave it to Agnese. "And you for me."

Wordlessly the sisters looked at each other, then threw themselves into each other's arms. The hug between them was fierce. It might have to last until heaven.

NOTES

The year 1221 is traditionally accepted as when Francesco sent Agnese to Monticello in Florence, although some scholars place the event in 1219 or 1228–1230. We have no details on Agnese's parting. In *Without Turning Back: Life of Saint Agnes of Assisi*, Sister Chiara Lucia Garzonio mentions that Suor Giacoma from Monticello accompanied Agnese to Florence, along with the brothers. Since the friars traveled in pairs, it seems likely that the sisters did also. Suor Forina may or may not have been Suor Giacoma's traveling companion. According to Sister Chiara Lucia, Forina was sent in 1222 to found a Damianite monastery in Milan, along with Giacoma and two other sisters.

Chiara's visions during Agnese's ecstasy are in biographies of Agnese.

It is difficult to determine the exact years of Balvina's and Benedetta's transferals. It seems likely that they could have taken place when the monasteries were founded, both prior to 1221.

Ugolino's Rule allowed each sister two tunics—most likely the outer tunic and inner chemise, which was the style for all women at that time—a mantle, and a scapular that covered and protected a sister's tunic while she worked. Not all communities used the scapular. Chiara's *Form of Life* allows "three tunics and a mantle" (CA:ED 111).

30

Suor Gasdia di Taccolo di Aregnato

Dormitory, San Damiano (November 1221)

Half asleep, Suor Gasdia heard sleet pinging the shutters of the dormitory windows at San Damiano. Curled into a tight ball on her wooden pallet, her tunic pulled over her bare feet, she shivered. Groggily, she tried to pull up her blanket. Had she kicked it off?

She should arise and find her blanket. But she was half dreaming, walking through the small garden behind her palatial Assisi home. She could see herself clearly. Her shoulder-length auburn hair threaded with silver caught up in a lace cripinette at her neck, the red velvet cap on her head fastened snugly beneath her chin with a black velvet strap. In her oval face, her deep brown eyes were bright as she watched two grandchildren darting among red poppies.

Gently a woolen blanket dropped over her shoulders. Sighing, Gasdia pulled it around her neck. She tried to mumble, "Grazie, Suor Chiara," but she was too groggy. She drifted into a dream where Chiara, as she always did, was covering the sisters who had kicked off their blankets, while Gasdia was back home covering her son Pietro and her grandchildren, who had all become youngsters again.

Six months ago, Gasdia, hopeful and zealous, had entered San Damiano. For three months she had lived in bliss, relishing the prayers, silence, and love. Then nagging longings surfaced. She longed again to see those she had counseled, advised, served, and loved. Her family. Servants. Neighbors.

Yet she loved the sisters, too. She had shared their concerns, offered her insights, helped many.

Still, the pull to leave was strong and had grown stronger. When she spoke to Chiara about it, Chiara had told her that she must discern.

So she had prayed, and words had come from deep within. YOU CANNOT STAY.

Today she was leaving San Damiano.

Gasdia felt a gentle shaking and heard a soft, cheery ringing—Suor Chiara waking the sisters with a small silver bell. Time for Lauds and Prime. Before becoming a Poor Lady, she had hardly been aware of these second and third offices of the day.

Gasdia pushed back her blanket and nodded to Chiara, who was smiling brightly at her. Chiara smiled often, even during this penitential season of the Lent of Saint Martin.

Gasdia straightened her veil, awry from sleeping in it, and smoothed the skirt of her tunic. Then, wrapping herself in her mantle, she proceeded downstairs to the dimly lit choir.

Several silent minutes later, Chiara, bundled in her patched lazzo mantle, unlocked the small doors that covered the grill in the apse of the church. Drawing back the curtain, she took her place among the sisters. In the church, Fra Cappellano began to chant Lauds. "In the name of the Father and of the Son and of the Holy Spirit." As Gasdia blessed herself, she bit her lip to hold back her tears.

Back and forth the stanzas alternated, the friars praying one verse and the sisters the next. A friar in the church read the readings; Suor Filippa read today's prayers. The pace was measured, devout.

In the church, Fra Cappellano began today's Mass. The sound of sleet pelting San Damiano waned as a raging wind blew up, snaking frosty fingers through cracks in the shutter over the choir window. The light pressing through those cracks was sickly gray. Gasdia began to shiver. Standing beside her, Suor Pacifica took her large mantle and draped one end of it over Gasdia's shoulders, drawing Gasdia close to her side. The gentle gesture was sweet. Gasdia could no longer restrain her tears.

When Mass ended, Chiara drew the curtain over the grill and bolted the doors. Turning, she raised her hand over the women to give them her usual morning blessing. Making the sign of the cross, Chiara prayed, "May the Lord bless you and keep you. May He show His face to you and be merciful to you. May He turn His countenance to you and give you peace. May the Lord always be with you, and may you always be with Him."

One by one, the sisters embraced Gasdia before filing out to their day's work.

"We will pray for you, sister. Do pray for us."

"Your family will be glad for your return."

"We'll miss you."

"Come and visit."

The words did little to assuage Gasdia's pain. Unlike these other women, she had failed in this life. Like them, she could fast, pray, mend, live in poverty. Yet she wanted to be home.

She didn't want to leave. And yet she did.

Finally, Gasdia was alone with Chiara. "We had asked your brother and your son to meet us at the speaking grill following Mass," Chiara softly reminded her. "Shall we see if they're here?"

Messer Andrea and Messer Pietro were, indeed, at the speaking grill, not in the parlor as they had been when Gasdia entered San Damiano. During the Lent of Saint Martin, except in special and needful circumstances, the parlor remained in penitential silence.

"Mamma, it will be good to have you home," Pietro said, his voice joyful. "The children have missed you. Bringing them here to visit has only made them miss you more."

"The house hasn't been the same without you," Andrea confided. "The servants seem more quarrelsome and discourteous. I can't bring out the best in them as you can."

Struggling with her anguish, Gasdia murmured to the black-curtained grill, "Have you brought my clothes?"

They had. They sent them in on the turn. A new plum-colored gown and cap and a deep-chestnut mantle. Accompanied by Chiara, Gasdia carried the garments to the dormitory, where she removed her religious garb and clothed herself in worldly clothes. Then, like a wooden puppet, she approached the doorway at the dormitory's far end.

"Madonna Gasdia," Chiara said tenderly, touching her arm. She held out to Gasdia the wooden cross that Gasdia had kept beside her pallet, two sticks bound together with thread.

Gasdia took the simple sacramental. "Pray for me, sister," she begged, her voice husky.

"And you pray for us. Always remember that God has the right to call us into whatever He wishes. Our duty is to follow His footsteps wherever they lead. God's vision is better than ours."

The two women embraced quickly. Then Gasdia opened the door to the enclosure and saw Pietro and Andrea at the bottom of the staircase, their horses' heads bowed into the whipping wind. Between them stood a third, riderless palfrey, waiting for her.

"Grazie, Suor Chiara," Gasdia said. "Mille grazie for everything."

Chiara smiled. "You haven't failed, Madonna Gasdia. You've grown here. Nourish that growth and continue in it."

"Grazie," Gasdia said again. She stepped out into the bitter, driving wind and began the descent. Suddenly she knew that the Gasdia leaving was not the Gasdia who had entered. What she had learned here about prayer, penance, and love, she could take home. It felt right to be going back.

NOTES

Gasdia remained at San Damiano for six months. History did not record why she left nor the details of her departure (CA:ED 170).

No sources tell how the friars and sisters at San Damiano prayed the Divine Office, which was either chanted or sung.

The dossal of Saint Clare, which shows scenes from Chiara's life, depicts her in bed fully clothed. In medieval times, people wore hats to bed, so the sisters most likely wore their veils while sleeping. Even though medieval people slept nude, the dossal indicates that Chiara's sisters slept clothed.

Chiara covered her sisters at night, called them to prayer with a handheld bell, and lit and extinguished the lamps (CA:ED 152, 178). The bell can still be seen at San Damiano.

Chiara's blessing is based on Numbers 6:24–26, but whether she actually used this blessing, we do not know.

PART EIGHT

What Is Painful and Bitter

31

Fra Francesco Bernardone

Hermitage within Chaplain's House, San Damiano (April 1225)

On a chilly April night, Fra Francesco Bernardone was lying on a straw bed in a little hut inside the chaplain's house at San Damiano. The house abutted the church so that, through its walls, Francesco could hear and join in the Office. Matins had concluded, but Francesco hadn't fallen asleep. Mice that bred in the walls of this cell clambered over him like thoughts that troubled his mind. Too weak to flick off mice or thoughts, he offered the torment to God as another penance.

Weeks ago, his concerns had grown so intense that he knew he must be alone to pray. The friars wouldn't allow him to stay at the Porziuncula because the March humidity and fog worsened his health. So he had come here, to the friary closest to the beloved center of his ordine, intending to stay in one of the sisters' hermitages. The friars had refused, constructing for him instead this indoor hermitage, using reed mats that the sisters had woven.

Days and nights had merged while Francesco lay weakly in the dark, praying, exhausted, depressed. Suffering so much himself, he could hardly meditate on Christ's sufferings. On Monte La Verna, he had asked God to allow him to feel all the physical and spiritual pain that Christ had suffered. God was answering his prayer.

Were demons spawning the questions that beat his soul more severely than demons ever beat his body? Or did the questions result from his own sinfulness? How could he be sure of God's grace? Had he founded a burgeoning ordine on mist? Had his willfulness spawned the tensions dividing the friars? What would happen to the ordine? Did it matter?

Due to illness, carelessness, or ignorance, he hadn't always kept the Rule exactly nor prayed every hour of the Office. This he had confessed in a recent general letter to all the brothers, in which he had urged them to follow the Rule with perfect humility and obedience, as he would do from now on.

His sin was as black as the darkness into which an eye disease had plunged him. The thought of going blind terrified him. However, his eye pain was mild compared to the throbbing in his hands, feet, and side. The wounds had appeared in September on Monte La Verna during his forty-day fast before the feast of Saint Michael. He had no idea what they were. However, the brothers who cleansed and bandaged them were convinced that they were like the wounds of Christ. That conjecture was more agonizing than the wounds. How could he, a sinner, merit to bear the Lord's pain?

He poorly endured the intermittent fevers, persistent abdominal cramps, worsening eye pain, and constant headaches that the brothers now said were reminiscent of the crown of thorns. Worse, people who heard him preaching throughout Umbria and the Marches were proclaiming him a saint. No! He was an arrogant, vain sinner.

He couldn't even govern the ordine. Certain brothers had expressed reluctance to beg for the Poor Ladies. His vicars had attempted to change the Rule while he was in the Holy Land. His friend Fra Elia was becoming domineering in his new role as minister general. Elia knew the Rule called for poverty, so why had he allowed Francesco's brother, Angelo, to construct, at the Porziuncula, a sumptuous building to house the friars for their 1221 chapter meeting? When Francesco had tried to demolish it, Angelo reprimanded him with, "It's not yours. It belongs to the comune." The building had escalated the division among the brothers. It stirred in some of them a desire for property, houses, and possessions. The squabbling about his Rule was increasing.

The only one he felt sure of was Christiana. And now she was ill. He couldn't go to visit her, though she asked for him, nor could she come to him.

Maybe he'd been wrong to visit Christiana so infrequently, despite her begging. He'd always been concerned about purity, even refusing to look at women—except for Christiana and Madonna Jacopa dei Settesoli, the holy penitent. He hadn't been so concerned about carnality before his conversion. Now he understood how insidiously unchaste thoughts could pop up and warp a vocation. He used as excuses his trips, illnesses, prayer vigils, and fasts: they left him little time and energy to visit San Damiano. He'd obtained Cardinal Ugolino's permission to add to the Rule a provision that friars weren't to visit nuns without permission of the Apostolic See.

Yet Christiana was a model of chaste love. She made ointments for his wounds. She had asked to mend his tunic and wished to sew new slippers for his feet. Many times, he'd worn the pale deacon's alb of fine lace, tiny gathers, and delicate embroidery that she had made for him from the cast-off clothing of the nobility.

Oh, Lord, help me. Give me strength.

TELL ME, BROTHER, a voice within his soul said, WHAT IF, IN EXCHANGE FOR YOUR ILLNESSES AND TROUBLE, SOMEONE WERE TO GIVE YOU A TREASURE. AND IT WOULD BE SO GREAT AND PRECIOUS THAT, EVEN IF THE WHOLE EARTH WERE CHANGED TO PURE GOLD, ALL STONES TO PRECIOUS STONES, AND ALL WATER TO BALSAM, YOU WOULD STILL HOLD THESE THINGS AS NOTHING, COMPARED TO THIS GREAT TREASURE WHICH WAS GIVEN YOU. WOULDN'T YOU GREATLY REJOICE?

The inner voice startled him. *Lord, this treasure would indeed be great, very precious, greatly loveable, and desirable.*

THEN, BROTHER, BE GLAD AND REJOICE IN YOUR ILLNESSES AND TROUBLES, AND, AS OF NOW, YOU ARE AS SECURE AS IF YOU WERE ALREADY IN MY KINGDOM.

An indescribable joy swept Francesco's soul, thrusting aside his depression. Surely God was blessing him in these trials, preparing him for eternity! Though too feeble to sing with his lips, Francesco sensed a hymn bubbling in his soul. Oh, if only he listened, he could catch the words!

NOTES

Francesco went to San Damiano in March 1225, where his eye disease rapidly worsened. All the details concerning Francesco in this chapter and the next are in the primary sources. God's words to him during his depression are in *The Mirror of Perfection* (FA:ED III 347).

Francesco claimed to recognize only two women by sight, presumably Chiara and Madonna Jacopa (FA:ED II 322). He behaved this way because he thought that looking at a woman could enkindle flames of passion or stain purity of heart (FA:ED II 563). Not looking at women was considered a sign of sanctity.

Chiara patched Francesco's tunic and made him slippers and ointment. Most likely she did this while he was at San Damiano. Some time earlier, she had made him a deacon's alb. The alb and slippers can be seen in the Basilica di Santa Chiara in Assisi. The tunic is on display at the Basilica di San Francesco in Assisi.

At San Damiano, Francesco stayed in a hut constructed of reed mats "in one part of the house," presumably the chaplain's house, which would have been outside the walls around the sisters' enclosure. This house was eventually overrun with mice who made their homes in the reed walls (FA:ED III 347).

32

Suor Filippa di Leonardo di Gislerio

Chaplain's House, San Damiano (April 1225)

Suor Filippa followed Pacifica and Chiara into the reed hut where Fra Francesco lay. By the light of a candle in Fra Leone's hand, Filippa could see that Francesco was a living shell. Tears welled in her eyes as she backed against the hut wall so that Chiara could draw near to this saint.

Chiara touched Francesco's thin fingers with her own bony ones. "Pace e bene, Father," she said softly. "Here is your mended tunic and some new buckskin slippers."

Chiara had made the slippers and mended the tunic, cutting a piece from her own mantle to patch it.

Francesco feebly reached toward the bundle Chiara had placed across his chest. "Grazie for these and for coming to me."

"You're so ill." Chiara's voice was beginning to quake. "You couldn't come to me . . . I was too ill to come to you. Thanks be to God that I can see you now."

A feeble smile crept across Francesco's lips. "But I can't see you." Indeed, he couldn't. His eyes were tightly bandaged. "Yet I do remember your face. It was thinner than when we first met."

Chiara was smiling. "I fear I looked better when we first met than now."

"Christiana, what's your illness?" Francesco's voice was fatherly.

"A weakness that comes and goes."

"Are you eating?"

"Every day I eat at least half a roll, as Bishop Guido commanded—at your request."

"Do you sleep?"

"Well enough. The discreets wish me to use straw bedding and a pillow as allowed the sick."

"*Buono.* Your prayer vigils?"

Filippa marveled at Chiara's prayer vigils. She'd been remaining in prayer from Compline at the day's end until midnight when she'd rouse the sisters for Matins. Only then, as far as Filippa could tell, did she go to bed. However, after praying the Office of Terce at midmorning, she'd been keeping another prayer vigil until Sext at noon.

"The vigils are sweetness, brother."

He smiled. "Continue to keep them. One can keep vigil when sick."

"Grazie. We brought warm water, new bandages, and ointments to cleanse your wounds."

"Fra Leone cleanses my wounds." His crisp words had a sharpness about them. Then, in a softer tone, "But would you wash my face, Christiana?"

"Gladly."

As Chiara tenderly bathed his face, tears trickled down her cheeks and splashed against Francesco.

"You wished to speak to me?"

"Sì. Brother, if the devil has been tormenting you, you must oppose him bravely and pay him no heed."

Francesco drew in his breath in a low whistle. "What makes you share this?"

Chiara sat back on her heels. "The friars say that doctors believe your eye disease occurred because of your excessive weeping over our Lord's sufferings. I fear the devil may use it to dissuade you from these fruitful meditations."

Francesco nodded. "The devil has tried to dissuade me."

Chiara dried Francesco's face. "I feared so. For he tried to dissuade me. One night shortly after you arrived here, I awoke. By my bed stood a child as black as night. 'You should not cry so much because you will become blind,' the child said. 'Whoever sees God will not be blind,' I told him. And the child disappeared in confusion."

Francesco nodded thoughtfully. "So you have seen the devil."

Francesco had seen him, too, the friars said.

Chiara's voice was shaky. "Later that night, after Matins, I remained as usual to pray and weep over my Lord. Again, the child appeared. 'You should not cry so much. Otherwise your brain will dissolve and flow through your nose because you will have a crooked nose.' 'Whoever knows the Lord suffers nothing that is crooked,' I told him. Again, he scampered off and vanished."

"These frightened you." Francesco's tone was soothing.

"He returned." Chiara's voice grew lower, quieter. "Last week, while still unable to rise from bed, I was praying at None and thinking of the hour in which Christ breathed His last. I could feel His sufferings as if I were below the cross. Quite suddenly the devil child appeared and struck me on the cheek so hard that my eye filled with blood and my cheek was badly bruised."

Feebly, Francesco reached toward Chiara. She caught his fingers in hers. "Does it still hurt, Christiana?"

"Not much now." Chiara paused. "Bravely oppose the demon's onslaughts, for the subtle prince of darkness will attempt to reduce your soul to nothing."

"This is what I needed to hear. Grazie." His voice cracked. He seemed unable to speak. Finally Francesco managed to ask, "Anything else?"

"No."

"Do you remember my sermon here last year when I was on my way from Foligno to Monte La Verna to keep the Lent of Saint Michael?"

Remember? How could any one of the sisters forget? Chiara had been begging Francesco to preach to them, but he never came. Then, one day, he appeared. Fra Elia, he said, had ordered him to come. Eagerly the sisters had gathered behind the grill while Francesco stood before it as usual. And he stood there. And stood there. Arms raised to heaven. Wordlessly. Finally, after what seemed an interminable, awkward silence, he beckoned a companion friar whom Filippa didn't recognize and whispered something to him. The friar had dashed to the hearth, scooped up a handful of ashes, and brought them to Francesco, who sprinkled them around himself in a circle and then flung a few on his head. Kneeling in the circle, he had bowed to the floor and prayerfully chanted the great psalm of repentance and misery, Psalm 51. "Have mercy on me, God, in Your kindness. In Your compassion blot out my offense." Upon completing the psalm, he had left.

"Did you understand the sermon, Christiana?"

"I understood that we are all sinners."

"The sermon had a deeper meaning. In Foligno, a holy, white-haired priest, perhaps Saint Felician, the city's patron saint, appeared to Fra Elia in a vision. The holy priest told Fra Elia that I would live two more years, making twenty the total number of the years since my conversion. Next year will be the twentieth year."

Chiara shuddered. "No! You began the ordine." Her voice was shaking, her tears swift. "You begot us. You are our father. Don't leave us orphans!"

"Christiana, when I die, the brothers and sisters will look to you as mother." Strong, forceful words. "You must take care of your health and get well."

"How can we continue without you?" Filippa heard fear in Chiara's voice. "I am but your little plant. Who will feed and water me if not you?"

"God has always fed and watered you. You have always been His. He is all you need."

"God is good, trustworthy, powerful, and great. But I'm weak."

"No. Your body is weak. You are strong because you love our Lord. Much love makes much strength. When I die, you must always follow the poor Christ as the head of the ordine."

"You know I will," Chiara's voice quaked. "It's all I ever wanted. Pray for me. Wherever you are, pray for me."

"I will pray for you until you reach heaven." Francesco's voice was catching. "Continue to pray for me and for the ordine as I do."

"I shall pray for you until you reach heaven and for the ordine forever." Their fingers, still touching, were trembling.

"Be brave, Christiana. God is with you. Now let us bless each other."

NOTES

Doctors told Francesco that excessive weeping caused his eye disease. Modern doctors speculate that the disease was either inflammatory glaucoma, tuberculosis of the eyes, conjunctivitis, iritis, cataracts, trachoma, or ophthalmitis (Father Octavian Schmucki, "The Illnesses of Saint Francis of Assisi before His Stigmatization"). Sister Joanne Schatzlein and Father Daniel P. Sulmasy believe that Francesco suffered from a borderline or tuberculoid type of leprosy that would affect his eyes ("The Diagnosis of St. Francis: Evidence for Leprosy"). The primary sources mention that the friars made him an oversized hood and blindfold to block the light. Fra Leone's care of Francesco is also in the primary sources.

Many have proposed theories regarding the illness that kept Chiara bedridden and her sisters deeply concerned for her health. Most likely Chiara suffered loss of bone mass and other ailments resulting from many years of severe fasting (interview with Linda A. Hughes, Remuda Ranch Center for Anorexia and Bulimia, February 1995). At some point, Francesco ordered Chiara to sleep on a straw mattress (CA:ED 179), and, with Bishop Guido's command, to eat, at least, half a roll a day (CA:ED 146, 151, 163). By that time, her health had already been broken. Despite her illness, she continued to keep her daily prayer vigils (CA:ED 178).

Chiara's *Form of Life* calls for "discreets," who are discerning sisters who advise the abbess and vicaress and assist in making community decisions (CA:ED 116). The sources don't reveal who served as discreets under Chiara.

In her article "The Refining of the Light," Sister Mary Francis Hone suggests that Chiara's spiritual battles, described in this chapter, may have come in the wake of a doctor telling Francesco that weeping was causing his blindness (FA:ED II 565).

The "silent ashes" sermon is in the historical record (FA:ED II 379–80).

Mechtild Flury-Lemburg ("The Cowl of St. Francis of Assisi" in *Textile Conservation and Research*) details in words, diagrams, and photos how Chiara cut a large piece from the back of her mantle to patch Francesco's tunic.

Did Chiara ever speak to Francesco or act as his nurse while he was at San Damiano? After his death, she had a vivid dream in which she was bringing a towel and warm water to him to tend his wounds (CA:ED 161). Did she actually do so or just yearn to do it? Would Francesco have wanted to speak to Chiara about the order before he died? History doesn't answer these questions.

33

Suor Agnese di Oportulo di Bernardo

Oratory, San Damiano (Late July 1225)

Sixteen-year-old Suor Agnese di Oportulo prayed, her lank face bowed to the brick floor of the oratory at San Damiano, her Eucharistic Lord before her. *Oh, God! Papà, do you know what you've done?*

Papà, Messer Oportulo di Bernardo, was podestà of Assisi. Stubborn, strong, intimidating, Oportulo ran the comune like an army, meting out unrelenting justice to thieves, bribers, heretics, army deserters, and the sacrilegious, and maintaining fierce loyalty to his friends. But he could not embrace Francesco's ideal that all people were equal. Thus Oportulo had become entangled in Perugia's bitter civil war.

As had happened in Assisi—in a civil war that had officially ended the year after Agnese was born—the Perugian commoners had ejected the nobility in a bloody struggle to establish a communal government. When the Perugian knights had asked Assisi for help, the knights of both cities had created an alliance that was prolonging the Perugian class struggle. Desiring peace, Lord Pope had dissolved the alliance, only to have representatives of both cities defiantly meet in Deruta to renew it. When Messer Oportulo swore to observe the agreement, Bishop Guido had excommunicated him. So Fra Leone had told the sisters.

Excommunicated? Slender Agnese could hardly breathe. Papà—cast outside the Church? He couldn't receive the sacraments nor have public prayers said for him. No indulgences could be applied to his soul, nor could he receive Christian burial.

With her high, broad forehead wrinkled in misery, Agnese had sent Papà a tearful message via Fra Leone—"Papà, I'm praying for you. Repent. Do what Lord Pope asked."

Suddenly, strong arms embraced her. A face pressed between her bony shoulder blades, radiating strength, sorrow, empathy. The bottom edge of a habit, patched with a zigzag remnant, caught her eye. Chiara. In the grip of her spiritual mother, Agnese pleaded for her father. *Oh, God! Oh, God!*

Other sisters entered the oratory, falling to their knees. Agnese heard their whispered pleas, their quiet sobs.

Oh, God!

Agnese had been a skinny, curly-haired, eager-eyed ten-year-old when she had begged Papà to let her join the sisters at San Damiano. After a year of pleading, Papà had relented. Chiara had cut her hair around her head and made her a sackcloth tunic and coarse chemise. Pacifica had taught her about the saints, and Filippa, stitching. Cecilia had taught her to cook and Giovanna to garden. Chiara had instructed her on care of the sick, and her sister Agnese had taught her how to pray. Lucia, a dancing-eyed girl three years older than herself, had become her best friend.

A year later, Agnese had been clothed as a sister. She had sold her family inheritance to her family and given the money to the poor. When Papà sent her something, she kept it if she needed it, or gave it to another sister or the poor if she didn't. She was happy.

Now ladies closer to her own age were entering—this year, worrywart Suor Angeluccia of Spoleto, and last year, eager Suor Benvenuta of Madonna Diambre, whom everyone called Suor Venuta. Since Chiara had sent Lucia to Cortona to found a monastery, Angeluccia and Venuta had become Agnese's best friends.

The bell rang for the prayers at Sext. Chiara gave Agnese's shoulders a firm, loving squeeze. With a sad smile, Agnese caught Chiara's hand in gratitude and held it as they silently descended the stairs to the choir.

The Office was that for the hour of Jesus' death. Chiara often wept during this Office. Today Agnese wept as well.

When the Office was completed, Agnese lingered while Chiara dropped the curtain over the grill and bolted the shutter. As Chiara left the choir, Agnese caught up with her. "Sister, may I wear one of your hairshirts as a penance for Papà?"

Chiara's finely shaped eyebrows arched as a thin smile traced her full lips. She motioned for Agnese to follow her upstairs.

In the dormitory, Chiara lifted her straw-filled pillow. Beneath it lay a horsehair shirt laced with knots.

"Say nothing about wearing it," Chiara cautioned, her finger to her lips.

"Grazie, sister." Stripping off her tunic and chemise, Agnese slipped on the horsehair shirt, tied it to her body, and immediately questioned her idea. Each hair seemed an iron filament. Her clothing worn over the shirt pressed the hairs into Agnese's flesh. *This is penance*, she thought, as she and Chiara proceeded to the infirmary to tend the ill sisters.

Agnese struggled through the day, trying not to squirm or scratch. That night, as Chiara was washing the feet of the sisters in the refectory, Agnese had an idea. When Agnese's feet had been washed and Chiara was about to discard the gray water in the washbasin, Agnese impulsively asked, "Sister, allow me to drink that water as a penance for Papà."

Chiara shook her head. "Sister, pray instead."

"Please, sister. For Papà."

"These penances can become extreme."

"Please. For Papà. This one time."

Chiara glanced from the filthy water to Agnese's pleading face and nodded. "Just this once."

Taking the basin but refusing to look long at it, Agnese swallowed her courage along with a small mouthful of water. The honey sweetness of the water startled and almost gagged her as Chiara quickly took the basin away before Agnese could drink more.

"Your sincerity and desire for penance please God," Chiara said, "but never again drink anything foul."

Was God pleased? Agnese had wanted to drink the entire basin for Papà's return to the Church, yet she had trouble swallowing a little mouthful. Nevertheless, she still wore the hairshirt. But, oh, it was bothering her.

For three days, Agnese wore the shirt, so distracted by it that she could hardly pray or sleep, until she returned the garment to Chiara. How could Chiara wear it?

That morning, while Agnese was drawing water at the well, Pacifica approached her. "Sister, are you still wearing the hairshirt?"

Agnese felt her face grow red. "How did you know?"

"Your bed is next to mine. We stand together in choir. You've been itching, squirming."

Agnese hung her head as she picked up her full bucket. "I couldn't stand it any longer."

"Whose was it?"

Should she tell?

"Whose, my child?" Above her aristocratic Roman nose, Pacifica's dark eyes were gently encouraging.

"Suor Chiara's." Agnese's voice was very small.

"Was it the horsehair shirt or the boar's hair one?"

"Horsehair. But it feels like needles."

Pacifica nodded thoughtfully. "The boar's hair shirt is worse. She doesn't require any of us to wear a hairshirt, yet she, who is often ill, wears one."

"Why don't you take them away from her?" Agnese asked.

"We've been trying to for years. I'm going to call the discreets together and discuss this again."

That evening, as the sisters were retiring, Suor Pacifica and the other discreets gathered about Chiara's bed. Agnese heard whispers, some quite agitated. When the discreets finally left Chiara's bedside, Pacifica was carrying Chiara's two hairshirts.

Early the next morning, Fra Leone called for Agnese. "Your father has ordered that no one in the comune may sell anything to Lord Bishop or contract in any way with him or his household. The hatred between Lord Bishop and your father is very great."

Papà! You haven't repented nor made peace. You've struck back. Papà! Hatred isn't of God. Is it you and the comune against our Lord?

"Brother," Agnese said, her voice quaking, "would you tell Papà that our Lord Jesus Christ begs forgiveness and peace? Ask Papà if he wants to go to hell."

Oh, Agnese had to do more penance for Papà! She began to barely eat. But then she grew so ravenous that she could neither sleep nor pray nor tend the ill sisters. So she ate again. She wanted to drink the water she used to cleanse the sick women, but Chiara had told her never again to drink anything foul. So she thought of cinching her cord, tight, tighter. Chiara spotted it and told her to loosen the knot. When she begged Chiara to allow that penance, Chiara told her that joyful obedience and great love in doing daily tasks can win more for God's kingdom than self-chosen penances. Agnese wanted desperately to believe that.

Muggy July slipped onward. The prayers of the sisters continued. One day, very late in the month, Angeluccia, Venuta, and Cristiana di Bernardo da Suppo lay in the infirmary, weak and wan.

"Sisters," Chiara said tenderly, kneeling between Venuta's and Cristiana's beds, "patiently bear these sufferings because you are following in the footprints of the suffering Christ. These trials bring an eternal reward." Daily she gave similar encouragement to the ill sisters. Then, as usual, she traced the sign of the cross over each ill woman.

"I bear suffering so poorly," Angeluccia said, her large eyes brimming with innocence. "Even the little scratchings in my mattress keep me awake."

"Scratchings?" Chiara asked abruptly. "How long have you heard these scratchings?"

"They started last night. I shouldn't mind them."

"Sì, you should," Chiara said. "There are vermin in your mattress, sister. But we shall get rid of them."

"I've heard scratchings, too," Venuta said weakly.

"And I, too," Cristiana added.

"Come, Suor Agnese." Chiara pointed to fresh mattresses leaning against the opposite wall. She and Agnese dragged the bulky mattresses across the floor and helped the three sisters onto them.

"Oh! The moving made me sick," Angeluccia grunted.

In an instant Agnese had thrust a bowl under Angeluccia's chin while Chiara tenderly rubbed her back. When Angeluccia's thin little body sank back onto her fresh mattress, Chiara dipped a cloth into a bucket of water and bathed her forehead. Agnese picked up the bowl to dump its contents outdoors.

"When will we get well?" Venuta asked. "We pray up here when we hear the prayers in the choir, but it's not the same as being with the others."

"It's better," Chiara said, "because your prayer is joined with suffering as was Christ's prayer."

Carrying the bowl, Agnese descended the ladder leading to the yard. As she approached scrubby bushes at the edge of the enclosure, she heard a mattress splat on the grass. Turning, she saw a second and then a third mattress tumble out the open doorway. Then Chiara started down the ladder.

Agnese chucked the bowl's contents into the bushes as Chiara unstuffed the mattresses and tossed the straw into the outdoor oven several feet from the infirmary stairs. Agnese rinsed the bowl and carried it upstairs, then carried a bucket down to fetch cool, fresh water for the ill sisters.

The smell near the well stopped her. Chiara was scrubbing the mattress covers. How could they smell so bad wet when they hadn't smelled so bad dry?

Agnese wrinkled her nose as she drew the water to fill the bucket. "Oh, that smell!"

"It's sweet and delectable, isn't it?"

Agnese was dumbfounded. Why did wet mattresses and chamber pots that Chiara voluntarily emptied smell sweet to Chiara and foul to everyone else? As Chiara draped a mattress cover over shrubs to dry, Agnese lugged the bucket upstairs while offering this duty for Papà.

In the infirmary, Angeluccia was beaded with sweat. Agnese bathed her burning face, struggling to bring down the young woman's temperature. What if Angeluccia died? Now?

As she ran the moist cloth over Angeluccia's bony arms, Agnese bumped into a truth. She could care for the ill sisters and pray for them, but she couldn't heal them. Nor could they heal themselves. God effected physical healing. Spiritual healing was different. Anyone who wished to be spiritually healthy would be. All one had to do was ask and believe.

But one had to ask for oneself.

Agnese could send Papà a message. She could plead with him, love him, pray, and do penance for him. In answer, God might rain graces on Papà, but God wouldn't force him to repent. Papà would have to decide for himself to return to God, Who desperately wanted him back. If Papà repented, God would forgive him, because love could do nothing else.

The hours crept on, shadows lengthened, night came. Agnese was doing all she could for Papà. Papà had to do the rest. Sleep came for Agnese, and with it, peace.

NOTES

The history of the Perugian civil war and the family history concerning Agnese are accurate (Fortini 148–55, 574–75). Agnese entered San Damiano as "a very young girl" (CA:ED 177). Chiara's *Form of Life* tells how children were received (CA:ED 111–12).

Lucia was sent to found a monastery in Cortona in 1225 (CA:ED 173 footnote). Cristiana di Bernardo da Suppo entered San Damiano in 1220 (CA:ED 167) and Angeluccia in 1225 (CA:ED 187). Benvenuta di Madonna Diambre (nicknamed Venuta in this book to distinguish her from Benvenuta from Perugia) entered in 1224 (CA:ED 180 footnote). Their ages are not recorded.

The incident concerning Messer Oportulo's excommunication and subsequent reconciliation is in the histories (FA:ED II 187–88). The exact date of this reconciliation is debatable. This book uses the date proposed by Fortini (574–80).

Agnese requested to wear Chiara's hairshirt (CA:ED 151, 178) and to drink the water that Chiara used to wash her feet (CA:ED 180). At an unspecified time, when Chiara was ill, the sisters took away her hairshirts (CA:ED 151), one of which is on display in the Basilica di Santa Chiara in Assisi.

Chiara cared for the ill sisters (CA:ED 146–89). The sisters marveled that rank mattresses smelled sweet to Chiara and that she didn't mind washing even chamber pots and vermin-infested bedding (CA:ED 157, 169, 172). History doesn't record the names of the other sisters who also worked in the infirmary.

34

Messer Oportulo di Bernardo

Vescovado, Assisi (End of July 1225)

Dressed in armor as the captain of Assisi's army, Messer Oportulo di Bernardo stood straight as a pillar in the enclosed courtyard of the bishop's palace. He hadn't had trouble with the previous Bishop Guido, but this one! Talk about high-handed stubbornness! Aging must have made this Bishop Guido cantankerous.

Oportulo tried to appear calm, but he was seething within. He had no desire to see, much less speak with, that devious enemy of the comune, the supposed man of God. Oportulo was here to meet the bishop only because Fra Francesco, who was suffering unbearable illness at San Damiano, had asked it. Francesco's friars were here, standing between the podestà and the bishop, all of them surrounded by a thick crowd that had assembled to watch the confrontation.

From his chair at the foot of the stairs leading into his palace, the bishop rose. His long pallium, scrolled with gold, dropped to his feet. Murmuring ceased.

In the silence, a stately, good-looking friar called out, "Fra Francesco has composed 'The Praises of the Lord,' to which he asks your full attention." Just that quickly, the friars began to sing a haunting melody.

Oportulo was stunned. He came to hear a song?

Most High, all-powerful, good Lord!
Yours are the praises, the glory, the honor, and all blessing,
To You alone, Most High, do they belong,
and no one is worthy to mention Your name.

The friars were singing, their eyes raised to heaven, their arms elevated in prayer. The stately friar's deep, sonorous voice was carrying the others. One of the friars, it was rumored, had been a ballad singer and poet whom the emperor had honored. Maybe that was him.

Praised be You, my Lord, with all Your creatures,
especially Sir Brother Sun,
Who is the day and through whom You give us light.
And he is beautiful and radiant with great splendor;
and bears a likeness of You, Most High One.

Oportulo felt his soul lifting, its coldness melting. The words sent shivers along his spine. He had heard that Fra Francesco's diseased eyes couldn't bear light, yet he was praising the sun?

The friars went on singing—slowly, plaintively, prayerfully—of all of God's creation. The words and melody were soothing and beautiful, putting all things into perspective.

Sisters Moon and Stars
Brothers Wind and Air
Sister Water
Brother Fire
Sister Mother Earth.

Francesco was dying, yet he was praising God. Oportulo had much to live for, yet he had turned his back on God. He had made no effort to return to the Church, despite the many pleading messages that had come from his dear Agnese. What prayers had she been praying, what sacrifices had she been making—for him? How much suffering had Agnese borne because of his stubbornness?

Praised be You, my Lord, through those who give pardon for Your love
and bear infirmity and tribulation.
Blessed are those who endure in peace
for by You, Most High, they shall be crowned.

The words that drifted like incense into silence became lances in Oportulo's
soul. The friars had sung, "Praised be You . . . through those who give pardon for
Your love."

Tears sprang to Oportulo's eyes as remorse shook his huge frame.

"Truthfully, I tell you all," he called out, "not only do I forgive Messer
Bishop, whom I ought to recognize as my master, but I would even pardon my
brother's and my own son's murderer!" He knelt at Guido's feet, his head bowed
but his voice strong. "For the love of Christ and of Fra Francesco, I will make any
atonement you wish."

He felt big hands, strong hands, on his shoulders, and looked up into the
bishop's sagging face. "Rise, Messer."

Oportulo obeyed.

"As bishop, I ought to be humble yet am quick to grow angry. You must
forgive me." The bishop opened his arms and Oportulo fell into them. The two
men embraced, kissing each other on one cheek and then the other.

NOTES

Most Franciscan scholars agree that Francesco wrote the "Praises of the Lord" while
at San Damiano (FA:ED III 337). Today this is also known as the "Canticle of the
Creatures," the "Canticle of Creation," and the "Canticle of Brother Sun."

Assisi had two bishops named Guido. The first one died in 1212. He was succeeded
by Bishop Guido II (D'Acunto, Nicolangelo. "Il Vescovo Guido Oppure I Vescovi
Guido?" *Mélanges de l'Ecole française de Rome. Moyen âge.* vol. 108, no. 2 [1996]:
479–524).

The reconciliation between Bishop Guido and Messer Oportulo follows the histories (FA:ED II 187–88).

35

Suor Angeluccia

Choir, San Damiano (Early August 1225)

S uor Angeluccia had been thrust toward the front of the sisters clustered around the choir grill at San Damiano. Thin and weak after her recent illness, she hoped she wouldn't faint. Fra Leone and Fra Pacifico were at the grill.

Leone was speaking. "Madonne, Cardinal Ugolino has obtained the consent of papal court physicians to give Fra Francesco the best possible treatment for his eye illness."

Angeluccia nodded. He had been treated unsuccessfully in May.

"So within a day or two, Fra Elia will take Fra Francesco to Rieti." Rieti? Wasn't that where the papal court had fled to escape a rebellion in Rome? She remembered Fra Leone saying something about that last month.

"To bid farewell, Fra Francesco has composed a song for you, so that you might trust in the Lord always."

Fra Francesco was leaving? Angeluccia hadn't seen him once since he'd been here. But still she felt an emptiness to think that he, so near, was going.

Fra Pacifico began to sing a gentle, cadenced melody.

Listen, little poor ones called by the Lord,
who have come together from many parts and provinces.

Live always in truth,
that you may die in obedience.
Do not look at the life outside,
for that of the Spirit is better.
I beg you through great love
to use with discretion
the alms which the Lord gives you.
Those who are weighed down by sickness
and the others who are wearied because of them,
all of you: bear it in peace.
For you will sell this fatigue at a very high price
and each one of you will be crowned queen
in heaven with the Virgin Mary.

As the friars' voices faded into stillness, the words struck Angeluccia. How the sisters had cared for her in her illness! Would they all be crowned queen partly because of that?

"Sing it to us again, brothers." The trembling voice was Chiara's. She appeared almost stricken, her face streaked with tears. "Perhaps . . ." It seemed as if she could not go on. "Perhaps these are the last words," her speech quaked, "that Fra Francesco will ever speak to us."

NOTES

In late summer or early autumn 1225, Fra Elia took Francesco from San Damiano to Rieti for treatment of his eyes. Presumably papal court physicians, or others in Rieti whom they recommended, offered this treatment.

We don't know if the friars sang Francesco's exhortation to the sisters, but this chapter exactly reproduces his words (CA:ED 394).

36

Suor Ortulana di Favarone

Church of San Damiano (Sunday, October 4, 1226)

Suor Ortulana di Favarone was sitting at Chiara's bedside with several other sisters, chatting softly about Fra Francesco, when she heard trumpets blaring and countless men singing exultantly. Curious, the sisters rushed to the windows that opened in the direction of Rivo Torto. In the October sun, up the Via San Petrignano, behind two friars carrying huge lighted candles and six friars carrying a simple wooden coffin, paraded a massive cortège of knights, horses, nobles, priests, merchants, and friars, the bright banners of Assisi's many guilds waving over the crowd.

"What is it?" Chiara asked from her bed.

"A funeral." Ortulana turned from the window, her voice flat. "Fra Francesco must have died."

"He said we would see him again! He's a saint. He can't have been wrong."

Ortulana threw her arms around Chiara's shaky body. "Even saints can make mistakes, Chiara."

"No! Fra Francesco wouldn't make a mistake!" She squirmed out of Ortulana's grip and reached for a loosely rolled parchment on a small stool by her bedside. Ortulana recognized the little scroll as the one Fra Cappellano had brought yesterday from the Porziuncula. When he had arrived, Balvina, Pacifica, and Ortulana were scrubbing the church on their Saturday cleanup day. He had handed Ortulana the parchment, saying that Francesco had dictated it to reassure Chiara.

Reassure? Chiara had been frantic that either she or Francesco, both deathly ill, would die before seeing each other again.

Now, almost savagely, Chiara unrolled the parchment and, in trembling voice, read Latin words that Francesco must have dictated to one of his friars: "I, little brother Francis, wish to follow the life and poverty of our most high Lord Jesus Christ and of His most holy Mother and to persevere in this until the end; and I ask you, my ladies, and I give you my advice that you live always in this most holy life and poverty." Chiara pressed her fingers into her eyes and wiped her tears. "And keep careful watch that you never depart from this by reason of the teaching or advice of anyone."

Heaving a huge sigh as if to bolster her courage, Chiara slowly rolled up the parchment and pressed it to her chest.

Ortulana rubbed Chiara's hands as they clung to the letter. "Fra Francesco has come to you through this message. He told you through Fra Cappellano that he absolved you from any failings, if you have any, regarding his commands and wishes or those of our Lord. He asked you to put aside your grief."

"Sì, because he said I would see him before I die and so would all the sisters. And this would be great comfort for us."

Francesco had left San Damiano over a year ago. The sisters hadn't seen him since.

"God," Chiara said fiercely, "wouldn't take our father away from us. After God, Fra Francesco has always been our one consolation and support. If our father has died . . ."

Clang! Clang! Clang! The bell at the speaking grill.

"Do you think they would bring Fra Francesco here?" Pacifica asked.

"We must go down." Chiara was struggling to push herself out of bed.

Clustering around Chiara, the sisters supported her as they descended to the choir. From the church came vibrant song, exalting God, praising Francesco. With shaky fingers, Chiara unbolted the wooden doors locked across the communion grill and tugged aside the curtain.

Near the grill stood brothers Elia, Leone, Angelo di Tancredi, Egidio, Bernardo di Quintavalle, and others, their faces strained. They were clustered around a simple, closed coffin. With her hand resting lightly on the coffin there stood an obviously wealthy woman, beautiful in her pale linen gown, her finely featured face wet with tears. Behind them the church was filled with mounted knights and men of every class, singing, carrying candles, waving olive branches and silken flags.

"Pace e bene." Fra Elia's voice was oddly husky. Today his black beard made him look grim. "Fra Francesco died at dusk as a flock of singing larks flew over the Porziuncula." Larks? Francesco's favorite birds sang at dawn, not dusk. Did larks singing at dusk mean that Francesco was in glory?

"He promised to come to you," Elia said quietly as the friars placed the coffin on the floor and lifted the lid. He slipped from Francesco's face a white silk veil with the word "Love" embroidered across it in gold silk thread. Francesco's body was clothed in a new tunic.

Tenderly, six of the brothers lifted the gaunt body, the floppy arms and legs, the sagging, hollow-cheeked head. Francesco's skin was pale, his beard trimmed. Across his face, from each ear to each eye, was a nasty red scar. Ortulana shuddered. She had heard that his eyes had been cauterized in a vain attempt to prevent him becoming totally blind.

Shaking, Chiara opened the little window through which the sisters received the Eucharist. Taking Francesco's left hand in hers, she drew his hand through the window and kissed its wound. "Fra Elia, could I have just a fingernail?"

Elia stammered. "Madonna Chiara, we don't want to desecrate his body by taking relics from it."

Chiara nodded, her face pained.

"Madonna Chiara," Leone offered, "with Fra Elia's permission, I'll write some memories of Fra Francesco and some of his prayers, to console you."

Elia agreed. "Grazie, Fra Leone."

"Grazie," Chiara said weakly. Kissing the wound again, she silently turned to Ortulana, who took Francesco's chilled hand in her own. Years ago, she had clung to her dead husband's hand, wondering how she would go on—yet, for the sake of her daughters, she had been strong.

Reverently Ortulana kissed the nail of iron-black, hardened flesh, then offered the hand to Benvenuta, who stroked the palm tenderly, pressed it to her cheek, and kissed it. Then Ortulana, Benvenuta, and Chiara backed away so that the other sisters could venerate Francesco's remains.

"Madonne," Angelo said, his deep voice faltering, "Fra Francesco asked, before he died, that we again sing for you the 'Praises of the Lord,' along with the final verse that he composed at the Porziuncula just a few days ago."

The friars began, their voices weak.

Most High, all-powerful, good Lord
Yours are the praises, the glory, the honor, and all blessing . . .

The voices strengthened and swelled.

Blessed are those who endure in peace
for by You, Most High, they shall be crowned.
Praised be You, my Lord, through our Sister Bodily Death,
from whom no one living can escape.

Death. The new verse. On his deathbed, he was composing verses about dying.

Woe to those who die in mortal sin.
Blessed are those whom death will find in Your most holy will,
for the second death shall do them no harm.
Praise and bless my Lord and give Him thanks
and serve Him with great humility.

As the friars' song ended, the cries of the sisters rose. Sobbing strangled the words.

". . . what shall we do?"

"Why are you abandoning . . . ?"

"To whom are you entrusting us?"

"Who will comfort us . . . ?"

"What would you have us do . . . ?"

". . . without your usual visits . . ."

Chiara was struggling to return to the window. Ortulana supported her under her right arm, Benvenuta on the left.

Gently, the friars eased Francesco's body into the coffin. The elegantly dressed woman slipped the funeral veil over his face, then extended her hand to

Chiara, who clasped it. The woman gazed sorrowfully at the sisters. "I'm so sorry. I'll pray for you, and, if you remember, please pray for me and for my two sons."

Chiara's voice was thick. "You are . . . ?"

"Madonna Jacopa."

"We will pray for you."

Elia's rough, grief-stricken voice broke into the conversation. "We must go."

Only when the coffin had left the church did Chiara close the window. Then she turned to face her sisters, her face streaked with tears. "We are filled with grief because our father is gone. Yet let us express our deepest thanks to our glorious God for our vocation." She paused as her voice cracked. "The Son of God has become for us the Way that our blessed father Francesco . . ." She stuttered, then continued, ". . . that our blessed father Francesco, His true lover and imitator, has shown and taught us by word and example." She looked from one sorrowful face to the next. "Our blessed father, while he was living, was always solicitous in word and in deed to cherish and care for us, his plant. So may his successor always help us to progress in better serving God and, above all, in observing most holy poverty."

Her words were quavering but intense as she knelt. Ortulana and the others dropped to their knees. "May the Lord Himself, Who has given a good beginning, give the increase, and may He also give final perseverance. Amen."

The sisters echoed their agreement. So be it. "Amen."

NOTES

As in many convents, Saturday may have been the cleaning day at San Damiano.

Larks, which sing at dawn, were heard singing for a long time over the Porziuncula at dusk at the time of Francesco's death (FA:ED II 129, III 229–30).

At the time of Francesco's final illness, Chiara believed that she was dying and feared that she wouldn't see him again (FA:ED II 128). In her *Form of Life*, Chiara recorded his final letter to her, dictated in Latin, as recorded in this chapter (CA:ED 118). Whether in the letter itself or via the unnamed messenger bearing it, Francesco assured Chiara that he absolved her from any transgressions and that she should stop grieving because she would see him before she died (FA:ED II 128–29).

Although many friars and men of Assisi were with Francesco in his final hours, only Elia, Egidio, Leone, Bernardo di Quintavalle, and Angelo (presumably Angelo di Tancredi) are named in the primary sources.

Francesco wrote the final stanza of his "Praises of the Lord" (FA:ED I 113–14) in his last days at the Porziuncula. Whether the brothers sang this for Chiara and her sisters is not recorded.

The veil covering Francesco's face was brought by Madonna Jacopa dei Settesoli from Rome (FA:ED II 121–23). It seems likely that she was part of the funeral procession, although the histories don't record it.

Accompanied by a multitude of friars and men of Assisi, Francesco's body, on the way to its interment in the Church of San Giorgio, was joyfully carried to San Damiano, where the sisters could touch it and mourn (FA:ED I 284–86). The eye treatments Francesco received would have left the scars mentioned. By the time his body reached San Damiano, rigor mortis, which stiffens corpses shortly after death, would have reversed itself and the body would have been pliable. Rosalind Brooke, in *Early Franciscan Government* (p. 142), states that Chiara requested a fingernail. There is no evidence that she received it.

After Francesco's death, Chiara, in words that she speaks at the end of this chapter, frequently had the community renew its commitment to poverty (CA:ED 60, 63, 65).

PART NINE

Grow in the Love of God
and in Mutual Charity

37

Suor Egidia

Refectory, San Damiano (Holy Thursday Evening 1228)

I n the soft glow of two hanging oil lamps, young, pallid Suor Egidia sat facing the refectory center. Second in a long line of seated sisters, she watched her ill abbess, supported by sturdy Benvenuta, emerge from the kitchen. Alongside her, Pacifica lugged a pail of water and Filippa carried towels.

Like Egidia's, Chiara's face looked hollow and gray. For the first time in the two weeks since Egidia had entered San Damiano, Chiara had come downstairs. Now she knelt by Agnese, first in line, and began to wash her feet. Every Holy Thursday night after Mass, so the other sisters said, Chiara washed the sisters' feet as Christ had washed his disciples' feet.

The room began to whirl.

God, don't let me faint.

In this unrelenting famine, which Fra Francesco had predicted shortly before his death, Egidia was dying of hunger. She had been a strong enough peasant to survive the fever that had claimed her mother and siblings, but when she had begun to give nearly all her food to Papà, who had died nevertheless, she had weakened. Then, giving her life to God, she had come to San Damiano. Here she continued to eat little so that weaker sisters could have more.

After kissing Agnese's feet, Chiara began to cleanse Egidia's, washing, wiping, drying. Chiara lifted Egidia's left foot toward her lips. A noblewoman, kissing her foot! Unthinkable!

Egidia pulled her foot back. Clumsy in her weakness, she saw, felt, her foot kick Chiara's mouth. Startled but smiling tenderly, Chiara bent again to kiss each foot, the upper then lower side, then wordlessly moved down the row to Angeluccia.

Stunned, Egidia watched Chiara wash and kiss Angeluccia's feet. Cristiana's. Venuta's. Then dizziness slapped her. She crumpled against Angeluccia as everything went black.

Egidia woke to rain lashing the monastery. She was lying in the infirmary next to Suor Giovanna, oil lamps gently brightening the night. Kneeling between the two sisters, Chiara was bathing Egidia's face with a moist cloth.

"God be praised!" Chiara exclaimed. "This is the first you've opened your eyes in five days! You're burning with fever, sister."

Five days? Egidia felt so feeble that a dog could have dragged her anywhere.

"Suor Chiara," Egidia said weakly, "care for others who may get well. I don't think I will."

Chiara dipped the cloth into a washbasin and wrung out the water. "You're stronger than on Easter when Fra Cappellano anointed you and recited the prayers for the dying."

Smiling kindly, Chiara turned to Giovanna and began to bathe her face.

"We're all going to die!" The anguished words came from once-sturdy Suor Illuminata, now wan and thin-faced. She was standing near Chiara, holding an open jar that emitted a pungent medicinal scent. "In Pisa we always had food. Here we starve!"

"Hush, sister." Impulsively Chiara threw herself at Illuminata's feet and embraced them. "God will care for us."

"God has forgotten us!" Illuminata cried.

"No, God is trying us."

"You have told us to follow in the footprints of Jesus. Where is He taking us?"

"It's raining," a thin voice said from the mattress to Egidia's right. Pacifica. When had she fallen ill? "Perhaps the famine is over."

Giovanna spoke softly. "At least we have these." With a shaky hand, she lifted a plate of shriveled turnips and held it, wobbling, toward Egidia. "Sister, eat something."

The turnips were jiggling in Giovanna's unsteady grip. The sick sisters always received the choicest foods, so what did the other sisters have? Nothing?

Egidia's stomach somersaulted. "I have no taste for food."

"Surely you would like something," Chiara cajoled, turning from Illuminata to Egidia. "We shall ask the friars to beg it for you."

Egidia wanted nothing. Nothing except . . . it was Easter. If it weren't for this famine, the people of Norcera, a full day's walk away, would be eating . . . "If only I had a bit of Easter bread baked on a hearth in Norcera and some fish from the Topino River, baked and tender."

"We'll pray for them." Clasping Egidia's hands, Chiara bent her head. As Egidia closed her eyes, she realized that she, who had always served others, was now being cared for by others. The situation was uncomfortable.

IT IS A SERVICE TO BE SERVED.

The thought startled her.

OTHERS SERVED ME.

You, Lord? Always You served others.

NO, EGIDIA. THINK.

Sì, He was correct. Hadn't Simon helped Jesus carry the cross? Didn't women try to console Him on the trek to Calvary? Didn't a bystander offer Him a drink on the cross?

Does following Christ sometimes mean allowing others to serve us?

Egidia heard an urgent, distant knocking.

"The church door," Pacifica offered.

"Why don't the friars answer?" Illuminata asked, moving to answer the door.

"Maybe it is the friars," Egidia suggested.

Chiara shook her head. "The friars know that we bolt the doors at night."

Illuminata returned quickly. "A young man at the door said to give this to you." She handed a plump towel to Chiara.

Kneeling backwards, Chiara placed the towel on her lap and untied its ends. On the towel lay two small loaves of crusty bread, dotted with dried fruits, and a large fish, baked and tender.

Egidia stared. "That is Norcera bread, sister, and Topino River fish."

"God be praised!" Chiara said. "The Lord has done this." She placed the loaves and fish on the platter next to the shriveled turnips, then handed the napkin to Illuminata. "Return this to the young man with our deepest thanks. Ask the friars if he might stay the night with them. The weather sounds harsh."

Illuminata hurried out.

"Will you have a bit of this?" Chiara asked, breaking off a section of Norcera bread.

Egidia looked about the half-full infirmary. "If we all have some."

Chiara smiled. "We'll all have some."

Egidia was nibbling the delicious bread when Illuminata reentered. "Sister, the young man didn't wish to stay with the friars. He took the towel and left."

"In this storm?" Pacifica asked.

"Maybe he was an angel," Giovanna breathed.

Illuminata nodded thoughtfully. "Maybe. He had the kindest, gentlest eyes I've ever seen."

NOTES

Chiara sometimes threw herself at the feet of her sisters to console them, as she did for Illuminata of Pisa (CA:ED 178). We know nothing else about her or Egidia (Aegidia), whose names appear on a 1238 list of San Damiano sisters (CA:ED 429).

In an unspecified year, when Chiara was washing the feet of the sisters on Holy Thursday, an unnamed serving sister accidentally kicked Chiara's mouth (CA:ED 147, 178).

A "frightful famine" followed Francesco's death (FA:ED II 282–83).

The undated incident of an unnamed, infirm serving sister asking Chiara for bread from Norcera and fish from the Topino River and receiving them, as this chapter describes, is recorded in codex 442 in the library of the Comune of Assisi, according to Father Benvenuto Bughetti, OFM. Some historians accept this story as only a legend.

38

All the Sisters

Dormitory, San Damiano (Early July 1228)

"I've had a dream," Chiara said to the sisters clustered about her bed. "It holds a message for us all, I believe."

The sisters nodded at Chiara, who was more mother than abbess. Deeply prayerful, Chiara must have had many visions and dreams, although she rarely shared them. Now, in this light-flooded, airy room, the sisters felt buoyed by joy and expectation. Dreams were windows into the soul, and Chiara was opening that window.

Chiara's blue eyes flashed. "In my dream, I was caring for our holy father Francesco. I was bringing him a bowl of hot water and a towel for washing and drying his hands. He was high above me, so I was climbing a very high stairway to reach him, but I was going very quickly as if on level ground. When I reached Fra Francesco, he opened his tunic, bared his breast, and said, 'Come, take, and drink.' I drank fully without surprise. Again he asked me to drink and I did. What I tasted was so sweet and delightful that I cannot describe it."

"Certainly you have drunk in Fra Francesco's sweet counsels," Benvenuta offered.

All the sisters murmured their assent.

"Indeed, I have, sister," Chiara smiled. "The second time, the nipple, through which the milk came, remained between my lips. I plucked the nipple from my mouth, and it seemed to be gold so clear and bright that I could see everything in it as if in a mirror. And then I awoke."

What a strange vision!

"My sisters, our holy father Francesco is far above us in his faith, knowledge, and love, but when he was ill here, we were permitted to care for him as a mother would. Yet he was our mother who nourished us, his daughters in Christ."

The sisters nodded, knowing this was true.

"In my dream, Fra Francesco said, 'Come, take, and drink.'"

"Like Christ's words at the Last Supper," Ortulana offered.

"Christ gave His life to feed us," Pacifica said. "In a different way, so did Fra Francesco."

"Your dream reminds me of the prophet Isaiah writing about nursing from the breast of the holy city," Cecilia said thoughtfully. "'That you may suck and be satisfied with her consoling breasts; that you may drink deeply with delight from the abundance of her glory. . . . As one whom his mother comforts, so I will comfort you; you shall be comforted in Jerusalem.'"

Illuminata looked intently at Cecilia. "Jerusalem is the city of God, the heavenly city, the Book of Revelation tells us. To nurse from the city is to nurse from heaven."

"Our holy father Francesco is high up, already in the heavenly city," Angeluccia noted. It was true. On the ninth Sunday after Pentecost, less than two weeks away, Lord Pope was going to canonize Francesco.

"And you went up to him as easily as an angel floating up and down the ladder that Jacob saw going up to God," Venuta chuckled.

Chiara smiled, her blue eyes bright. "When we love intensely, we ascend quickly and easily to Christ. As he draws us in love, we swiftly run to Him. Fra Francesco was a living image of Christ. When he nourished us, Christ nourished us. In my dream, Fra Francesco was, I believe, both himself and Christ."

Giovanna's voice quivered. "Death pulled us too soon from Fra Francesco. But a mother brings again to her breast a nursling who has pulled away. So God brought us back to Fra Francesco in your dream."

Chiara nodded. "So we must continue to suck of his faith and strength, which came from Christ, to suckle Christ's hidden sweetness that God has reserved for those who love Him."

"Our Lord Jesus Christ wishes us to always experience His sweet nurture," Filippa mused.

"Our holy father Francesco left us Christ's poor and humble way of life so that, like a precious nipple, it will always nourish us," Chiara reasoned.

She smiled at her sisters. "An infant is totally poor because it is totally dependent on its nurse. Just so, Christ became totally poor for us. Imitating Him, we make ourselves poor and dependent on God, who nourishes us. Poverty looks dark as a nipple to those in the world. But it is gold."

Chiara paused as if to let the thought settle.

"Voluntary poverty promises eternal glory to those who possess it. Like a clear mirror, it reflects Christ's poverty and is the gold given us by Fra Francesco, which nourishes us still."

"Fra Elia needs reminders about poverty, not you," Benvenuta said a bit harshly.

Agreement rippled through the sisters, for they had often discussed the friars' mitigation regarding holy poverty. At Lord Pope's request, Elia had drawn up plans for a massive basilica to be built in Assisi in Francesco's honor. He had set a huge marble vase on the site to collect alms. Fra Leone had purposely smashed it.

"Sisters, let us embrace our own poverty and not concern ourselves with anyone else's," Chiara advised. "We go to heaven on our own merits, not on theirs."

NOTES

Chiara shared her dream, as described in this chapter, with her sisters (CA:ED 161). The interpretations of it are taken from the writings of various scholars of Clare.

The quote "That you may suck and be satisfied" is from Isaiah 66:11, 13.

39

Pope Gregorio IX

San Damiano (July 13, 1228)

·

With Pope Gregorio IX at its head, a pompous entourage wended its way up the steep road from Spoleto toward San Damiano. The July day was pleasant, a good day for travel.

Before becoming pope in March of the previous year, the silver-haired vicar of Christ had been Cardinal Ugolino dei Conti di Segni, cardinal protector of Francesco Bernardone's followers. Having seen how the papacy had consumed his uncle, Lord Pope Innocenzo III, he had resisted his own election. But the other cardinals wouldn't let him refuse, and God had interiorly told him to submit. Yet he thought of himself as he always had: Ugo, servant of God's servants.

Now, like peevish dogs, innumerable concerns, petty disagreements, endless arbitrations, and impossible requests snapped at him. The most dangerous involved the scarlet-haired, scarlet-sinned Emperor Federico II, whom Ugo had excommunicated last year for yet again reneging on his promise to retake the Holy Land from the Turks. Unapologetic, unrepentant, Federico claimed he was too ill to begin the crusade.

Federico's Holy Roman Empire covered much of the continent and extended down the peninsula through Lombardy and Tuscany to the papal states. He also ruled the Kingdom of Sicily, which included the island of Sicily as well as the lower portion of the peninsula including Naples. Squeezed between these two halves of Federico's kingdom were the pope's narrow territories—the March of Ancona, the Duchy of Spoleto, and the Patrimony of Saint Peter—with Rome as its key city. Wanting the Pope's lands, Federico had made Rome so unsafe that Ugo had fled in April.

In May, Federico's second wife, Madonna Yolanda, had died. A month later, with a force too small to fight a crusade, he had sailed for Palestine, where Madonna Yolanda's father, Jean de Brienne, was king of Jerusalem. Rumor had it that Federico wasn't grieving too deeply. He was already considering whom to wed next.

Ugo reined his steed to a standstill and, with the help of an aide, dismounted. At San Damiano, he could momentarily forget his office and be poor and humble. Handing his soft shoes and blue silk cape to an attendant, Ugo beckoned his brother Count Filippo's son to join him. This nephew—Cardinal Rinaldo dei Conti di Segni, young, dark-eyed, and virile—had replaced Ugo as cardinal protector of the Lesser Brothers and the Damianites.

Barefoot Ugo and silken-dressed Rinaldo knocked at the weathered door of a little house thrust against the right side of the church of San Damiano. After the friars' initial surprise and acts of obeisance, Ugo got down to business. He wanted to know how the friars fared in caring for the Poor Ladies. He hadn't expected Fra Cappellano's complaints.

"Lord Pope, the number of ladies is growing, and we must provide food for them. And only poor food. If someone gives us whole loaves, Madonna Chiara scolds us. 'Who gave you these?' she asks. She wants broken loaves, the trenchers people use under their foods."

"It would be difficult to reject generosity," Ugo conceded.

Cappellano arched his thick eyebrows. "The ladies like to hear sermons daily, but we're simple men. If I could preach, which I can't do well, I would preach to the unconverted, not to holy ladies. Moreover, the ladies wish to confess monthly, sometimes more frequently, and receive the Eucharist on all solemnities. They wish us to say Mass within the enclosure for the ill ladies, visit the ill often, and give individual spiritual direction." Cappellano shrugged. "Fra Francesco wanted this, but it's time-consuming. Friars at other Damianite monasteries feel the same."

Last year, Ugo had committed the care of the Damianites to the minister
general of the Lesser Brothers. At least four friars were assigned to each of the
nearly forty Damianite monasteries. The ladies were delighted to have friars as
their visitators and supporters. Ugo would ask Rinaldo to check with the friars at other monasteries to see if Cappellano's assessment was accurate.

When he had completed his interview with the friars, Ugo, accompanied
by Rinaldo, approached the speaking grill in the church and asked to visit
Madonna Chiara. "Don't tell her who's visiting," Ugo admonished the lady
who answered his bell. "I want to surprise her." In his Rule for the Damianites,
Ugo had allowed the pope and cardinal visitator within the enclosure, if
necessity required.

Thus, Ugo and Rinaldo ascended the staircase to the dormitory, where
Chiara lay bedridden.

With her back toward Ugo, Chiara was propped in a high bed, rolls of cloth
behind her back. Above her head was a four-pronged tree branch thrust into a
narrow wooden post affixed securely to a sturdy wooden base. Bound together
with twine, the tips of the branches formed a cone around which was loosely
tied a pale, golden cloud of flax. As Ugo stepped into the dormitory, Chiara
swiftly rolled a spindle against her thigh and let it fall to the floor, twirling rapidly. As the spindle spun downward, Chiara quickly moistened her fingers at her
lips and rolled them upward along a thin line of flaxen fibers that led from the
distaff down through a notched post at her side, and to the spindle. The fibers
twisted together tightly, making a fine, sturdy thread. Seated around Chiara on
stools were three other women, stitching, hemming, or embroidering. Ugo recognized Madonna Ortulana but not the two younger ones.

"Always busy!" Ugo said in honest appreciation.

"Lord Pope!" Chiara turned her head, delight in her voice. "Messer
Cardinal! How are we privileged to have you visit?" Chiara grabbed the twirling
spindle and, quickly wrapping it with the length of thread she had just spun,
placed it in her lap, then bowed low. "Let me kiss the feet of my Lord."

Obligingly, Ugo raised one foot and then the other to Chiara, who kissed
each, right above the instep. To the other three bowing women, he offered his
hand to kiss.

Ugo tapped the spindle in Chiara's lap. "Exquisitely fine thread, Madonna Chiara."

Chiara smiled. "Grazie. The fewer the fibers, the faster the spin, the finer the thread."

"What do you make with this wondrous thread?"

"Corporals, Holy Father. Suor Angeluccia is hemming one now."

One of the young sisters held up a small square of unbleached linen. The consecrated bread and wine would rest on it during Mass.

"You must receive fine alms for such fine work," Ugo reasoned.

"Oh, no. We take no alms for anything," Chiara said. "The corporals are gifts for the churches."

"Your Holiness," Rinaldo broke in, "your dinner meeting with the bishop?"

"Sì, sì." Ugo pulled up one of the empty stools and sat on it. He glanced at Rinaldo and patted a stool next to him. Rinaldo shrugged and sat.

"We heard that you fared ill during the famine."

"God sustained us, and now it is over, Lord Pope."

"True, but we have heard that the Damianites are frequently sick, here and elsewhere. You yourself are ill."

"Illness is a fact of life. Through it, we unite ourselves more closely to the suffering Christ."

"Perhaps your severe life contributes to these illnesses," Rinaldo offered. His strong, highly featured face and direct, pointed gaze commanded respect.

"We aren't afraid of illness or austerity," Chiara noted.

"Madonna Chiara, suppose famine returns. Or hostile armies invade Umbria. How will you eat? The friars may beg and work for food, or they may leave an area as my court and I had to leave Rome. But you're here as in a prison. I wish to permit you to own property on which you may grow crops to use and sell. Then you won't be at the mercy of others."

Chiara's eyes were wider than Ugo had ever seen them. Her voice came with a deep firmness. "Lord Pope Innocenzo granted us the privilege of owning nothing."

"This was fine while San Francesco was alive," Rinaldo offered. Rinaldo was calling Francesco "saint" although he was still three days from being canonized.

"His charm may fade and you may be forgotten. You must grow more secure, Madonna."

Chiara looked from Rinaldo to Ugo, lifting her solid chin as she spoke. "Before he died, Fra—San—Francesco instructed his brothers to lovingly care for us always."

"Fra Giovanni Parenti is the minister general of the Lesser Brothers now," Ugo pointed out. "He will determine how they serve you. God doesn't want you to starve. Therefore, I permit you to own whatever property and possessions you need to grant you a measure of security."

Chiara's gaze pierced him. "Messer, we have taken a vow of poverty here."

"The Damianites in Spoleto and Perugia have accepted Lord Pope's offer of maintaining some useful possessions," Rinaldo said. "It's the safer choice."

"The other Damianite monasteries may do as they wish," Chiara said evenly. "They're not bound to follow our life here."

"On the contrary," Ugo said. "They're following the very Rule that I gave you."

"This is Assisi, Lord Pope. Here we live in poverty."

"If you fear for your vow, I can absolve you from it."

"Absolve me from my sins, Holy Father," Chiara said sweetly but firmly, "but never from following in the footprints of my Lord Jesus Christ."

"Christ would ask you to be obedient to His vicar on earth," Rinaldo said.

"I will be obedient," Chiara answered, bowing low, "but I will ask Lord Pope a question. Did God speak falsehood when He told us neither to sow nor reap nor gather into barns but to trust Him as do the birds? Didn't He promise to take care of us if we put our faith in Him?"

Ugo felt cornered by the very argument that Francesco had always used whenever Ugo tried to force possessions on the friars. He couldn't counter the argument without denying the Gospel.

"All right," Ugo conceded. "As you wish. But merely ask and I will rescind the privilege of poverty."

"Holy Father, I ask you to reinstate for us, in writing, the privilege of poverty."

The request surprised Ugo. He glanced at Rinaldo, who appeared equally startled.

Ugo struggled to put his feelings into words. "Madonna Chiara, I am afflicted by innumerable, bitter, and endless trials. We are surrounded by many dangers and are so human and frail that we cannot possibly conquer these without God's help. Yet we have but a single hope—to bring glory to the Lord and salvation to ourselves and those entrusted to us." Reverently he took Chiara's thin hand in his own. "Your faith consoles me, Madonna Chiara. You are one spirit with Christ. Pray that God will strengthen us and enable us to worthily fulfill the duties He has given us."

Bringing Ugo's hand to her lips, Chiara kissed it tenderly. "Lord Pope and the Church are always in our prayers."

"Then we shall be strengthened," Ugo said hopefully. "You shall receive your privilege of poverty. In writing. And may God grant you the grace to live it."

NOTES

Physical descriptions of Rinaldo and Gregorio are based on paintings.

The titles Gregorio IX held and the political problems he faced are accurately described. From this time on, the friars often tried to relinquish their care of the sisters.

Gregorio IX regularly corresponded with Chiara and greatly admired her. He seems to have visited her whenever possible. Early in his pontificate, she asked him to reinstate the privilege of poverty. It was granted on September 17, 1228.

Chiara used to spin very fine thread to make corporals given to area churches (CA:ED 147, 177). The manner of spinning that she probably used was demonstrated for the author by Heather Minto, an expert on medieval spinning and weaving.

40

Fra Cappellano

Chaplain's House, San Damiano (Early October 1230)

F ra Cappellano sat at the small rustic table in the chaplain's house, staring at the parchments before him. He had read this bull from Pope Gregorio three times. What should he make of it?

Since San Francesco's death four years ago, Cappellano had seen the friars go from grief to discord to disobedience. In May, three days before the official ceremony, Fra Elia had secretly orchestrated the burial of Francesco's body in the new Basilica di San Francesco, which Elia had designed. His excuse, that he was trying to protect the body from relic hunters, did nothing to appease Lord Pope, who had immediately issued sanctions against both the basilica and the friars. In the meantime, Elia's supporters had proclaimed him the new minister general in opposition to duly elected Fra Giovanni Parenti. Only after shameful discord was harmony restored and Fra Giovanni accepted. Then Elia and his supporters went to Rome as summoned by Lord Pope, who lifted the ban on the basilica but dispersed the disruptive friars and banished Elia to Cortona to do penance.

Nevertheless, peace was elusive. The brothers squabbled on the relationship of Francesco's Testament to their Rule, so they sent a delegation to Lord Pope for his direction. His decision was in the bull that Cappellano now held. Copies were circulating throughout the provinces. The guardian of each convent was to read the bull, implement its decisions, and then send it to the next-closest convent.

The bull stated that Francesco's Testament, with its paragraph on absolute poverty and non-ownership of property, couldn't bind the friars, because Francesco had written it without consulting others when he no longer held authority in the ordine. The friars were bound to obey only the papally approved Rule.

Cappellano pursed his lips. He knew Francesco's Rule and Testament well. "The brothers shall not acquire anything as their own, neither a house nor a place nor anything at all," Francesco had written in the Rule. And, in the Testament, "Let the brothers beware that they by no means receive churches or poor dwellings or anything which is built for them, unless it is in harmony with that holy poverty which we have promised in the Rule, and let them always be guests there as pilgrims and strangers." The bull in Cappellano's hand permitted the friars to use property and buildings if they were owned by others, such as Lord Pope or Cardinal Protector. It said nothing about the poverty of such dwellings nor made mention of the friars' living in them as "pilgrims." The friars might live in comfortable convents for decades and be in accord with what Pope Gregorio allowed.

Cappellano had read the Rule so often that he practically had it memorized. Francesco had written, "I firmly command all the brothers that they in no way receive coins or money, either personally or through an intermediary." This bull said that the friars could accept money and have an intermediary hold it for future use.

Francesco's Rule allowed the ministers and custodians to "alone take special care to provide for the needs of the sick and the clothing of the other brothers through spiritual friends." For all their other needs, "as pilgrims and strangers in this world who serve the Lord in poverty and humility, let them go begging for alms with full trust." Lord Pope wrote that, if the friars needed anything, benefactors might purchase it for them. Thus, some communities of friars might do no begging, since benefactors could supply all their needs.

"Finally," the bull went on, "it is written in the Rule that 'the brothers should not enter the monasteries of nuns, except those to whom special permission has

been granted by the Apostolic See.' Up to now the brothers have interpreted
this passage as referring to the monasteries of the Poor Cloistered Nuns for
whom the Apostolic See exercises a special concern. This interpretation is
believed to have been handed down by the provincial ministers in general chapter through a statute at the time when the Rule was approved and blessed Francis
was still alive."

Sì, this was true. San Francesco had promised the Poor Ladies that his
brothers would always care for them. Lord Pope knew that, didn't he? Surely, he
also knew that the ministers were assigning brothers to each women's monastery
as it sprung up. He must have known that friars begged food for the women.
Didn't he realize that priestly friars did more? They said Mass for the Poor
Ladies, preached, offered the Eucharist, shared spiritual direction, heard confessions, anointed their sick, and buried their dead. Cappellano had complained
about this heavy spiritual burden. *I must not have been the only grumbler*, he
thought.

The bull continued: "Nevertheless, you have asked for a clarification. Does
this mean all monasteries without exception, since the Rule excepts none, or
does it refer only to the monasteries of the aforesaid Nuns? We respond: the
prohibition affects communities of nuns of every description."

Goodness.

Cappellano could understand the restrictions for convents outside the
ordine. To them, the brothers were guests or visitors. But to the Poor Ladies,
they were spiritual fathers. Was Lord Pope saying that the brothers now needed
his permission to continue to minister to the women as they'd done for over
fifteen years?

"And by the term monastery we mean the cloister, the living quarters, and
the inner shops."

Really?

The cloister? That's where Cappellano heard confessions so the ladies
wouldn't violate the cloister by having to confess in the church, where they
could easily meet visitors.

The living quarters. That included the infirmary, where he gave spiritual
counsel to the ill sisters, heard their confessions, anointed them when they were

dying. The cemetery was also inside the enclosure. Brothers had dug graves for deceased nuns. Cappellano had assisted spiritually at their burials.

The inner shops. Didn't Lord Pope know that sometimes things broke that women couldn't repair? That sometimes massive objects too heavy for women needed to be moved? In these situations, Madonna Chiara sent for the brothers to help.

> "Those brothers to whom the superiors have granted permission by virtue of their maturity and suitability may go into the other areas to which laypeople also have access in order to preach or beg alms, with the exception always of the monasteries of the aforesaid Cloistered Nuns. No one has any access to them without the express permission of the Apostolic See."

Whew!

Cappellano had read that over and over. Was Lord Pope saying that superiors could give brothers permission to enter public places in other convents, yet couldn't grant permission for the same brothers to go into even the public places of the Poor Ladies? For that, the brothers needed not only the superior's permission but also "express permission of the Apostolic See." That was what he was reading.

How could the brothers help the women as Fra Francesco had promised?

Goodness, Cappellano thought, *without Lord Pope's "express permission," we can no longer speak to the ladies or minister to them.*

Madonna Chiara needed to know. Clutching the bull, Cappellano strode into the church, rang the bell cord, and sent the parchment into the monastery on the turn.

He spoke into the black-curtained grill. "Ask Madonna Chiara to read the bull carefully, especially the passage stating that friars must have explicit permission of Lord Pope to enter the monastery. When she has finished, ring the bell into the chaplain's house and I'll pick up the parchment."

Cappellano was poring over a passage from the Gospel of Mark when the bell rang. He put down the manuscript and went to fetch the bull.

The parchment was lying on the turn. As Cappellano reached for it, he heard Madonna Angeluccia's delicate voice from behind the grill.

"Fra Cappellano, Suor Chiara thanks you for sharing the bull with us. She thanks you for the many years that you and the other friars have assisted us. She wishes you well and bids all the friars God's blessing as you leave."

Cappellano started at the words. "Madonna, the begging friars will continue to beg for you and leave the food at the turn."

"Suor Chiara is sending away the begging friars also. She says, 'Let him now take away from us all the brothers since he has taken away those who provide us with the food that is vital.'"

Incredulous, Cappellano asked, "How will you live?"

"We will send for alms. God will take care of us. Pace e bene, Fra Cappellano."

"Pace e bene," Cappellano said hesitantly. Taking the bull in his hand, he walked slowly out of the church.

Was this what he had wanted? Was this what Lord Pope had foreseen?

NOTES

This chapter is based on what happened in the Franciscan Order from late May 1230, when Elia secretly buried Francesco's body, to early October of the same year, when friaries would have been receiving notice of what Pope Gregorio IX determined in his bull *Quo Elongati*.

When Chiara learned that Gregorio IX forbade the friars to enter the monastery without express permission of the Apostolic See, she reacted with the words and decisions in this chapter (CA:ED 311–12).

Most scholars believe that Chiara sent away the friars in the wake of *Quo Elongati*.

In *The Legend and Writings of Saint Clare of Assisi*, Ignatius Brady says that Chiara sent away the friars either following *Quo Elongati* or following *Etsi Omnium*, a 1236 bull of Gregorio that told "all the Christian faithful who read these letters" that the Poor Ladies must follow Ugolino's Rule of 1219 regarding permission to enter the enclosure of nuns. Ugolino's Rule of 1219 permitted no entry other than by manifest necessity. Outsiders could enter to dig a grave or repair the monastery. A chaplain could enter only to hear confessions and administer the Eucharist to dying nuns and, if the abbess permitted, to conduct prayers at a deceased nun's burial. *Etsi Omnium* excommunicates those who disobey. If directives regarding the chaplain had been settled in 1230, then *Etsi Omnium* would refer to entry by other parties.

41

Suor Amata di Martino

Oratory, San Damiano (October 1230)

With the other well sisters, petite Suor Amata knelt in the oratory, her harsh garments in stark contrast to her delicate, young face. Jumbled distractions were interrupting her prayer.

To Amata's left knelt Suor Beatrice, Chiara's blood sister and Amata's cousin. When childless Beatrice's husband had died last year, Beatrice had entered San Damiano to be with Chiara and Ortulana. Beatrice was kneeling, her head to the floor so that she resembled a plump, gray biscuit. Obviously, Beatrice was thinking about only Jesus.

Why couldn't Amata keep her mind fixed on Christ?

Amata concentrated on the little silver box in the wall niche to the altar's left. In that box reposed Christ, truly present in the consecrated Host. Amata pictured Jesus smiling lovingly at her. Then the silver box reminded her of a larger silver box she had left behind at Correggiano, a gift on her twelfth birthday from her father, Messer Martino di Ugolino di Offreduccio . . .

Poor Papà! How Amata had distressed him two years ago by abandoning her wedding plans and coming here to join her cousin Chiara and blood sister Balvina! Chiara had asked God for a special grace so that Amata would neither be deceived by the world nor remain in it. Her husband-to-be was now courting another lady . . .

Oh! She was trying to imagine Jesus! Why couldn't Amata pray without distractions?

The silver box. Jesus enclosed there as in the womb of His Mother. How did birth cramps feel? Were they like hunger pains? With the friars gone, the sisters had less food. Amata's flat little stomach was pinched.

What was she thinking of? Sì, the Blessed Mother, pregnant. Amata's mother had died. How long ago was that?

The bell rang in the bell tower, ending the period of silent morning prayer. Amata was grateful to begin work.

In the dormitory, Chiara was propped up in bed, spinning. Near her sat Suor Venuta, her eyes intent on the handheld loom in her lap. The loom was a simple wooden frame with nails at the top and bottom, over which was looped the fine linen thread that Chiara had spun. Deftly, Venuta was weaving a weft thread of linen, threaded through a needle, over and under the warp threads. After each pass, she used a wire comb to push each weft row compactly against the row beneath it. When the corporal was napkin-sized, Venuta would remove it from the loom to hem it on all four sides. The rhythmic, measured swish of the comb and the whir of the spindle were the only sounds in the quiet dormitory.

On a wooden stool near Chiara's bed, Amata found the sturdy sheet of heavy paper, about a foot-and-a-half square, and the swath of white silk that she had cut yesterday to fit its outline. With fine, delicate stitches, Amata began to stitch the silk to the paper. When she completed the stitching, she would fold and stitch the paper to make a flat box to hold Venuta's corporal. Before sending the corporals to area churches, the friars used to take them to the Bishop of Assisi to bless. Now the serving sisters would do so.

Ringing broke the silence. Amata went to see who was at the speaking grill.

"We have come from Perugia," an agitated female voice said. "Our son has a film over his eye. We have heard that Madonna Chiara sometimes cures the ill. Could she pray over our boy?"

Touched by the pleading, Amata slipped back the curtain. The wide-eyed, dark-skinned mother was neat and clean, dressed in lazzo, the cloth of the poor. The black-haired child playing with her toes could have been two or three years old. When the child cocked his head toward the grill, Amata was startled at the pale sheath covering his left eye.

"I'll see if Suor Chiara can come downstairs," Amata said to the woman.

But Chiara's legs had been weak and wobbly for years. She asked a serving sister to bring the child to her. So Giovanna did. Chiara blessed the child and touched his eyes, signing him with the sign of the cross. Smiling, the child took from his mouth a half-eaten chestnut and offered it to Chiara. "For you. Eat it."

"Grazie!" Chiara took the piece and lay it beside her. "Chestnuts are very tasty."

Amata smiled at the smiling child, his eye still clouded.

"Ask my mother to pray over him," Chiara instructed Giovanna. "Mamma's prayers are powerful."

Ortulana would be sewing in the refectory. Giovanna carried the boy out as Amata resumed stitching, Chiara returned to spinning, and Venuta removed the corporal from the loom. Long minutes later, Giovanna returned, breathless, with the child.

"Look, sisters! Suor Ortulana blessed the boy, but nothing happened. But on my way back here . . . look!"

The child's eyes were both perfectly clear.

"Mamma's prayers have done this!" Chiara proclaimed.

"When I saw the miracle, I hurried to show Suor Ortulana. She said your prayers healed him."

"God be praised in either case!" Chiara sang.

With a dull thud, the half-eaten chestnut dropped from Chiara's bed and bumped the floor. As the boy struggled in Giovanna's arms, she let him down. He popped the chestnut into his mouth as the sisters burst into laughter.

"Come, time to return to your mamma," Giovanna beckoned. Carrying the child, Giovanna approached the monastery door and the staircase leading to the world outside. Spontaneously, she waved to someone outside. Amata could hear a deep male voice. Fra Cappellano?

Grinning widely, Giovanna turned toward the sisters. "The friars have returned! When Lord Pope heard how you sent the friars away, he changed his mind and told the minister general to have the friars serve us as they had been doing."

"God has answered our prayers!" Chiara breathed.

Amata's insides were tingling at the dual miracles of the child's healing and the friars' return. Both the little boy and the pope had suffered from clouded vision, but prayers had healed both. God could heal Amata's clouded spiritual vision, too, if she . . .

A thought pushed into Amata's consciousness. Turn and become like children. Amata's distractions were as unsavory as half-eaten chestnuts, but maybe if she offered them to God with the candor of a child, God would accept them. Because right now, they were all she had to give.

NOTES

In 1228, Chiara persuaded Amata, daughter of Messer Martino di Ugolino di Offreduccio, to enter San Damiano. Amata looked on Chiara as her mother (CA:ED 162–63). She had been engaged before she joined Chiara (Fortini 352).

Chiara's sister Beatrice entered San Damiano in 1229 (CA:ED 183 footnote). We don't know if she had ever married.

Over fifty sets of corporals were made from thread that Chiara spun (CA:ED 177). To weave them, the sisters most likely used a simple hand loom, affordable for the poor, as opposed to a large, free-standing, expensive floor loom. After the sisters had folded the corporals into silk-lined paper boxes, the friars took them to the bishop to be blessed and then to the churches around Assisi (CA:ED 305).

Although the sisters remembered the cure of a Perugian boy's eye, a miracle involving both Chiara and Ortulana (CA:ED 165), they couldn't remember the year. Amata, who witnessed this incident, entered San Damiano in 1228 (CA:ED 162), so it happened sometime thereafter. By this time, Chiara's health was failing.

When Gregorio IX heard that Chiara had sent away the friars, he immediately rescinded his directive and told the minister general of the friars to have the brothers continue to serve the sisters as before.

The quote "Turn and become like children" is found in Matthew 18:3.

PART TEN

A Mirror and Example to Others

42

Suor Agnese di Oportulo di Bernardo

Choir, San Damiano (Sunday, April 25, 1232)

On the far left of the stark choir behind the altar at San Damiano, Suor Agnese sat between Suor Angeluccia and Suor Francesca, her dark eyes closed, her thin face lowered. *Who are You, Lord? And who am I?*

"We are called to be spouses and mothers and sisters of our Lord Jesus Christ," Chiara often told the sisters. Until midway through Lent, the words had flown by Agnese. Then a nagging question had emerged. If she was supposed to be spouse, mother, and sister to Christ, she needed to know who He was. She didn't doubt His divinity. She knew His virtues. But did she know *Him?*

During the Easter celebration, she had spoken to Chiara about her dilemma. "When our holy father San Francesco was still in the world," Chiara advised from her sickbed, "he used to pray before the crucifix here. 'Who are You, Lord?' he used to pray. 'And who am I?'" Chiara had patted Agnese's hand. "Pray those questions, and God will answer."

Who are You, Lord? And who am I? She had received no answer. Would it come today, on this Good Shepherd Sunday, the Second Sunday after Easter? The church would be full because Assisi's own son, Fra Filippo di Lungo, was preaching.

Filippo's natural poetic eloquence rivaled that of the famous poet Fra
Pacifico, now dead, who had been visitator of the Poor Ladies until resigning
four years previously. Cardinal Rinaldo had appointed Filippo to take his place.
It was his second appointment, because when Francesco had been in the Holy
Land, Filippo had asked Pope Onorio III to be appointed visitator when the
Cistercian visitator Ambrogio had died. That appointment, plus Filippo's
obtaining certain privileges for the sisters, had angered Francesco, who then
appointed another friar to take Filippo's place.

Out in the church, the friars' voices rose. Within the choir, the sisters stood
and sang with them. "I saw water flowing from the right side of the temple, alleluia; and all to whom that water came were saved . . ."

Through the curtain-covered communion grill, Agnese could see nothing.
But she could imagine Fra Filippo dipping a laurel branch into a deep vessel of
water, then sprinkling, like a rain of grace, the altar, himself, his Mass assistants,
the people in the church, the choir grill, and, by extension, the sisters behind it.

"Glory to the Father and to the Son and to the Holy Spirit . . ."

Last Sunday after Compline, Suor Chiara had kept the sisters in the choir.
She had asked Fra Cappellano to give her, through the communion grill, a small
vessel of the holy water used in the sprinkling. Tenderly she had said, "My sisters
and daughters, you must always remember this most blessed water that flowed
from the right side of our Lord Jesus Christ as He hung upon the cross."
Reverently she had blessed herself with the water, then had passed it to the other
sisters to do the same.

Agnese had blessed herself and had felt a little shiver of joy. But today she
felt herself standing beneath the cross on Calvary, gazing at her crucified Lord,
seeing the blood and water from His side covering the world with grace.

She prayed, *Who are You, Lord?*

THE SAVIOR. THE LIVING WATER.

Who am I?

THE REDEEMED. THE ONE WHO LIVES BECAUSE OF THE LIVING WATER.

Singing voices edged into her meditation. "I am the Good Shepherd of the
sheep. I am the Way, the Truth, the Life. I am the Good Shepherd and I know
My sheep, and they know Me. Alleluia."

Shepherd. Way. Truth. Life. *How do the images mesh, Lord?*

Filippo's sturdy, clear voice interrupted her musing. She could see the back of his tonsured head through the communion grill. When had Suor Chiara moved back the curtain? When had the Gospel been read? When had Agnese sat on the wooden plank that formed her choir seat?

"Who is the Good Shepherd?" Filippo asked. "None other but our Lord. 'Come,' He invites His sheep. 'Follow me.'" His words rang out, sparking faith.

What was that indescribable sweetness? The blended scent of flowers, baking bread, spice and incense. A flash drew her gaze down the row of seated sisters. Around Chiara gleamed a scintillating light in which stood a sandy-haired boy, perhaps three years old. His simple tunic aglow, His head rested on Chiara's knee. Chiara's right arm encircled the Child; her hand gently patted His shoulder. The Child's eyes were focused on Filippo, His attitude attentive.

Oh, God, do not let me be deceived, Agnese prayed.

I AM IN THEIR MIDST.

Who are You, Lord?

I AM MADE PRESENT WHEN A PREACHER'S WORDS UNITE WITH A LISTENER'S SOUL.

"I am the Good Shepherd," Filippo was saying of Christ. "I bandage the wounded, heal the sick, feed the hungry, carry the weak."

Agnese's mind was swirling with images. Christ the Good Shepherd. The Child. The Crucified. The Living Water.

As the sermon ended, the Child turned and gazed at Agnese, then disappeared.

Agnese felt a nudge. She glanced at Angeluccia, who silently mouthed the words: "I know you have seen something."

Agnese nodded and, unable to speak of it, bowed her head.

The Mass continued through the consecration of bread and wine into the Body and Blood of Christ.

I AM THE BREAD OF LIFE. I AM THE WINE OF THE NEW COVENANT. YOU ARE THE HUNGRY, THIRSTY SOUL.

Suddenly the choir was filled with a fiery brilliance that coalesced in flame on Chiara's bowed head.

THE HOLY SPIRIT WILL COME UPON YOU. The words of the Archangel Gabriel to Mary, the Mother of Christ.

I am the Voice from the burning bush. The Unquenchable
Fire. True Light. Holy Spirit. I am your Spouse. And you are My
bride.

The flame over Chiara remained throughout the Communion rite before
fading.

Mass ended. The hubbub in the church died as worshipers dispersed. In the
church, the friar cantor began to pray the hour of Terce. The sisters joined in.
The prayers continued, ended.

Who are You, Lord?

Crucified One. Good Shepherd. Holy Child. Living Water.
Bread of Life. True Light. Flame of Love.

Who am I?

One who tries to understand.

How could she understand? There were too many images and now more
came. I am the True Vine. The Beginning and the End. The Eternal
High Priest. God.

Could He not give one simple answer that would sum up all the others?

I am the Creator. All things speak of Me.

Agnese was sitting quietly, her head bowed, her eyes closed. She could see
only darkness. I am Light in darkness.

At the thought, her eyes sprang open and her glance fell on her clasped
hands. I am Molder of all. All rests in My hands.

Her hands were folded on her gray, woolen tunic. I clothe My people
with righteousness.

Agnese had no time to reflect on her racing thoughts. Her glance caught the
zigzagging pink bricks on the choir floor. I am the Sure Foundation. I am
the Rock. Across the floor stabbed a sunbeam from the single choir window
behind her. I am the Light that enlightens every person. In the sunbeam, flecks of dust cavorted. I am the Spirit dancing in the soul.

I am the Creator. All things speak of Me.

There were no simple answers to who God is. There were simply answers.
They were all around her. She need only look.

NOTES

Around 1232, Agnese experienced the vision of the Christ Child and the flaming brilliance around Chiara while Filippo di Lungo was preaching on Good Shepherd Sunday, then celebrated on the second Sunday after Easter (CA:ED 179). Filippo's words aren't recorded, nor did Agnese disclose what her visions meant to her.

Customarily after Compline, Chiara had holy water used in the Easter sprinkling rite brought to her. She then advised the sisters to always keep it in mind (CA:ED 188).

The Vidi Aquam text "I saw water flowing..." is based on Ezekiel 47:1 and has been used since the twelfth century as part of the sprinkling rite during the Easter season. The phrase also recalls the blood and water flowing from the side of Christ. The rite ends with the doxology "Glory to the Father..."

The imagined singing about the Good Shepherd combines verses from John 10:11, 14 and John 14:6. Other parts of Agnese's prayer experience are based on various images and titles of God found throughout Scripture.

43

Sestra Anežka

Speaking Grill of the Damianite Convent, Prague, Bohemia
(Early Summer 1235)

At the grill of the Damianite convent in Prague, Bohemia, thirty-year-old abbess Sestra Anežka was deep in prayer. Above her straight and perfectly shaped nose, Anežka's delicately arched eyebrows pursed together with intense concentration.

Lord, what shall I do? Prayers had helped her deal with an emperor. But how should she pray to deal with Lord Pope?

Anežka had been princess of Prague, betrothed at the age of three to Bolesław, young son of Prince Henryk Brodaty from Silesia and his holy wife, Jadwiga. In preparation, she had been educated in the monastery at Trzebnicy, where God had drawn her to himself. Bolesław had died when Anežka was six, so she had returned to Bohemia to be educated at the monastery in Doksan, where her faith had grown stronger. At age nine, she had been betrothed to Emperor Federico II's son Enrico. After she had fasted, prayed, and done bodily penance to escape this marriage, Enrico had jilted her to marry Margarethe, daughter of Duke Leopold of Austria. This had so angered Anežka's father, the now deceased Premysl Ottokar, that he would have destroyed Austria had Anežka not begged his mercy. Three years ago, she had received two more marriage proposals, one from King Henry III of England, the other from recently widowed Emperor Federico II. If anyone could convert the deceitful, licentious, superstitious, excommunicated emperor, Anežka could! Her brother, King Václav I of Bohemia, had urged her to accept Federico's offer, citing Bolesław's mother, Jadwiga, and their cousin Queen Elisabeth of Hungary as holy married women.

But, hearing from friars about Chiara and the holy ladies of Assisi, Anežka longed to live as they did. Again, to avoid marriage, Anežka prayed and did penance. Under her jeweled robes, she wore a hairshirt and girdle studded with iron points. Before dawn, dressed in rough, rude clothes, she had walked barefoot to the churches in Prague to beg God's intervention, then returned to the palace to bandage her bleeding feet and begin a day at court. When the emperor's ambassador arrived to escort Anežka to Germany for the royal wedding, she had sent her own ambassador to Lord Pope to beg his mediation. His legate returned with the message that Anežka did not have to marry.

But Federico and Lord Pope were at war. So King Václav had allowed the emperor to make a decision. Miraculously he had responded, "How can I take offense if she prefers the King of Heaven to me?"

Thus, with Anežka vowing to pray for Federico until she died, she had become a Damianite. With Václav's cooperation, she had built a grand hospice for the poor and then this massive monastery for herself and dozens of other noblewomen who wished to become Damianites. When she requested some sisters to instruct the women in living a consecrated life, Chiara had sent five Damianites from Trent, whose Germanic language was common in Prague. Then, in a grand, public celebration on Pentecost last year, Anežka had left everything to embrace religious life.

For Anežka, that meant living in poverty. So she had asked Lord Pope to separate the hospice—so generously endowed by her mother, Queen Konstancie—from the monastery, so that the sisters might live without hospital revenue. Many days ago, she had received Lord Pope's letter, which had denied her request while allowing the hospice to support the monastery. Ever since, she had been praying.

Oh, Lord, what shall I do? He's Your pope, Lord. Should I object to his decision?

At the ringing of the bell at the speaking grill, Anežka's eyes shot open. Through the curtain, she spoke San Francesco's traditional greeting. *"Pokoj a pozehnani."*

"*Pax et bonum*," a male voice responded. Only someone who was not Czech would use the Latin for "Peace and blessings." The next words came in Latin, too. "We are two friars sent by Madonna Chiara of Assisi."

Anežka's heart fluttered. "Madonna Chiara has sent a letter to the princess and a few items that she used at San Damiano."

Anežka's soul swelled. "Put the goods on the turn," she replied in Latin. "Please return tomorrow, because the princess will wish to send a letter to Madonna Chiara." A letter asking what to do about the papal decree.

When Chiara had written to Anežka last year upon her entrance into religious life, Anežka had written back, requesting some small tokens to link the two monasteries. These gifts had to be the tokens. A rough wooden cross. An earthenware bowl. A string of wooden prayer beads. A black veil, clean but used. Anežka kissed each as she plucked it from the turn. Poor relics used by a saintly woman. She placed them on the wooden bench near the turn.

Then, giddy with joy and reverence, Anežka broke the wax seal on the parchment letter.

Her eyes devoured Chiara's fine, gracefully penned words. "To the daughter of the King of kings . . . you have despised the splendor of an earthly kingdom . . . one thing is necessary . . . that you always be mindful of your commitment like another Rachel, always seeing your beginning."

Rachel? Anežka remembered her from Scripture. She was the one whom Jacob loved, who had to wait fourteen years before they could finally be married.

How odd that Chiara mentioned Rachel! Was she telling Anežka to be patient, indefinitely if necessary? While human plans marched forward, God's plans would still unfold. If Rachel had not remained true to Jacob, she would not have become the mother of Joseph, who saved the Israelites from death during famine. Jesus would not have been born from Jacob's line. Anežka would not be here, in the peace and joy and faith of this house.

Whew! She had to think about this. She moved the gifts to one end of the bench and sat on the other. Rachel. All the questions she must have had. All the anxiety she had to subdue. All the prayers she must have said. Anežka had heard a sermon once about Rachel. One of the Church Fathers had said that "Rachel" meant "seeing the beginning." Was Chiara telling Anežka to recall the poverty she had vowed at the beginning of her religious life?

Anežka read more slowly. "What you hold, may you hold. What you do, may you do and not stop." Why was Chiara telling her this?

"But with swift pace, light step, unswerving feet, so that even your steps stir up no dust, may you go forward securely, joyfully, and swiftly, on the path of prudent happiness, believing nothing, agreeing with nothing that would dissuade you from this commitment or would place a stumbling block for you on the way . . ."

Stumbling block? Was she referring to the papal decree?

". . . so that nothing prevents you from offering your vows to the Most High in the perfection to which the Spirit of the Lord has called you."

She read on as Chiara told her to follow the counsel of Minister General Elia. He had done penance as Lord Pope had instructed. He had been reinstated into the Church. The friars had elected him minister general. The latest news was that Elia was in Assisi, working on the upper level of the Basilica di San Francesco. He must have discussed with Chiara Lord Pope's desire to grant possessions and income to the Damianites in Assisi and elsewhere.

"If anyone has said anything else to you or suggested any other thing to you that might hinder your perfection or that would seem contrary to your divine vocation, even though you must respect him, do not follow his counsel. But as a poor virgin, embrace the poor Christ."

Hmm. Chiara must have suspected that Lord Pope would attempt to grant possessions and income to Anežka's monastery, too. Poor, misguided Holy Father! If only he trusted God's providence as the sisters did!

Anežka pressed the letter to her chest. Oh, how her sisters would rejoice as she read Chiara's words to them! She wouldn't scrape the ink off this expensive parchment and reply on the same sheet. No, she would save this letter as she had saved Chiara's letter written upon her entry into religious life. She had read that letter so often that certain words from it came to mind.

> O blessed poverty, who bestows eternal riches on those who love and embrace her! O holy poverty, God promises the kingdom of heaven and, beyond any doubt, reveals eternal glory and blessed life to those who have and desire her! O God-centered poverty, whom the Lord Jesus Christ . . . came down to embrace before all else! . . . The kingdom of heaven is promised and given by the Lord only to the poor, because she who loves what is temporal loses the fruit of love.

God had answered Anežka's prayers. Begging God for the proper words, she would write to Lord Pope, telling him that she couldn't accept his kind offer of stability and again pleading with him to separate the monastery from the hospice so that the sisters could possess nothing but God.

NOTES

Princess Anežka of Premysl (known in English as Agnes of Prague—the Premysl family was the only native dynasty that ruled the Czechs) successfully petitioned Pope Gregorio IX to grant her permission to refuse marriage to Emperor Federico II, who was courting her, and then to enter religious life. Federico's agreement is in the historical record.

Anežka built a Damianite monastery in Prague and entered it as a Poor Lady in 1234. The remarkable woman earned widespread admiration.

Some discrepancy exists in various historical sources concerning certain dates in the life of Saint Agnes of Prague. This book follows the chronology given by Regis Armstrong, OFM Cap., in his article "Starting Points."

In an undated year, in response to Anežka's request, Chiara sent the gifts mentioned in this chapter. The five sisters from Trent arrived in Prague prior to Anežka's entry into religious life. Father Celsus O'Brien, OFM, in his booklet *Clare of Assisi in Her Writings*, speculates that Chiara chose these sisters because Trent was part of the Austrian Tyrol, so the sisters spoke a Germanic language that was widespread in Prague.

Chiara's first letter to Anežka was written shortly before she entered religious life, but she may have received it later.

Father Regis speculates that Chiara wrote the second letter to respond to the pope's decree allowing Anežka's monastery to use revenue from the hospice (CA:ED 41). Gregorio wrote to Anežka regarding this on May 18, 1235 (CA:ED 353–54).

Chiara's words to Anežka are from the *Second Letter to Agnes of Prague* (CA:ED 47–49) and the *First Letter to Agnes of Prague* (CA:ED 45–46). The Church Father Saint Jerome wrote that the name "Rachel" means "seeing the beginning" (CA:ED 48 footnote).

44

Messer Giovanni di Maestro Giovanni

Via San Petrignano, Assisi (Late June 1238)

Messer Giovanni di Maestro Giovanni walked beside the litter, carried by two pages, on which lay his motionless, hollow-cheeked son. In the five-year-old's skeletal face, red and burning with fever, huge brown eyes gazed blankly at the sky. On the left side of the child's throat swelled a grotesque scrofula the size of a small, unripe melon. The best doctors and medicines couldn't cure this son. Only prayer remained.

How fiercely Giovanni loved this child, born in his wife's death agony, the last gift of her long life! His other children were adults; this boy, the joy of his father's old age. He could not die.

The steep road sloped toward San Damiano. As procurator for the Poor Ladies, Giovanni had often made this trek on horseback. Just three weeks ago he had executed a legal parchment, signed by all fifty ladies, that granted the power of attorney to Madonna Agnese's father, Messer Oportulo di Bernardo, so that he could sell to the cathedral of Assisi a piece of property belonging to San Damiano.

God, you must let her heal him.

"Her" was Madonna Chiara, who came to the curtained parlor grill when summoned. Extending her hand through the grate, she touched the still child's shoulder. Giovanni heard no words, but tales of her cures circulated everywhere.

God, please, You have to cure him!

HAVE TO?

The gentle internal rebuke caught Giovanni off guard.

He is my life, God!

THEN, GIOVANNI, WHO AM I?

A verse came to mind. "He who loves father or mother more than Me is not worthy of Me; and he who loves son or daughter more than Me is not worthy of Me."

GIOVANNI, DO YOU TRUST ME?

Giovanni laid his hand on the lad's burning forehead. What if the child died? Would he be happier in God's kingdom than in Giovanni's household? Did God know what was best?

Within Giovanni's soul, a struggle arose. Didn't the child belong to God more fully than he belonged to Giovanni? As he curled the boy's thin fingers in his own, silent words cried in the anguish of his soul. *God, heal him, if it be Your will.*

Within moments the boy's fingers felt excruciatingly hot. A tremor shook his body as the child shrieked in sudden agony. As the litter began to quiver, Giovanni threw himself against it to steady it. Chiara's hand was making the sign of the cross over the child.

"Papà?"

Giovanni gasped. He pressed the boy's head, temples, cheeks. They were cool. He felt the child's neck. The scrofula had disappeared. "Praised be God! He is cured! Grazie, Madonna Chiara! Grazie! Grazie!"

NOTES

As procurator for the Damianites, Messer Giovanni di Maestro Giovanni acted as their agent in procuring supplies and in conducting their other business (CA:ED 158 footnote).

A document, dated June 8, 1238, gave Messer Oportulo the power of attorney to sell a piece of property belonging to San Damiano. Fifty sisters signed the document.

Since Messer Giovanni was procurator, he may have helped execute it (CA:ED 429–30).

Through her prayers, Chiara cured Giovanni's unnamed five-year-old son of both fever and scrofula (CA:ED 158, 176). The child was "carried" to Chiara. At this time, carriages were not invented. People used carts to carry goods, but these bumped along over the heavily rutted roads and would have been very uncomfortable for an ill child. A litter would have been a smoother way to carry a sick lad.

Chiara's many healings using the sign of the cross were common knowledge (CA:ED 148, 156, 169, 184).

The Scripture verse about loving God above relatives is from Matthew 10:37.

45

Suor Balvina di Martino

Infirmary, San Damiano (Mid-December 1239)

S uor Balvina di Martino had been in the refectory, pinning together two pieces of fine purple satin to make a priest's stole, when Suor Bonaventura called all the sisters to the infirmary because Suor Chiara wanted to speak to the entire community. Now Balvina sat on the infirmary floor, her bare feet tucked under her ample gown, her dark eyes bright above her very plump cheeks.

Having left her bed in the dormitory, Chiara was seated on a small bench, her usually vivacious face oddly grim. "Sisters, let us begin with prayer." Her voice was quiet, almost flat.

Balvina bowed her head.

"Dear Lord, may we know that You wish us to freely love and serve You. May we accept what we do not understand. May we serve You though all the world . . ." Chiara's voice trembled, halted, ". . . though all the world go astray. Amen."

Balvina raised her head, her soul troubled at the distress in the prayer.

Chiara puckered her lips. "Sisters, this is difficult news." She hesitated, sighed. "Fra Cappellano has just told me that Fra Elia has joined the emperor and has been excommunicated."

A wave of shocked disbelief swept over the sisters. Balvina sat stupefied. Fra Elia! She could picture him preaching: bushy black beard, deep-set dark eyes, almost imperceptible swagger, his expressive voice bellowing.

Elia was brilliant, authoritative. He had been San Francesco's friend from their youth. San Francesco had first made him provincial of Syria, then vicar of the ordine. After caring for Francesco in his final illness, Elia had written a touching letter to the friars and sisters upon Francesco's death. Elia had designed the massive, marvelous Basilica di San Francesco. He'd been elected minister general from 1232 until Pentecost of this year, even though he had asked the friars to select someone else since his health problems made it difficult for him to live the Rule. The friars told him that he could make exceptions as he saw fit, yet when he rode on horseback, kept servants, and ate the choicest foods, the friars complained. They complained, too, that he tried to govern the ordine completely on his own, that he hand-picked provincials and custodians who agreed with his policies, and that he hadn't called a single meeting of the friars since his election. But he had been busy and ill. Besides, he probably trusted the friars he had placed in charge of the many extra provinces he'd created. The complaining friars were too hard on Elia, Balvina had often thought. Perhaps they were jealous.

Because Elia had not called a general chapter meeting, Pope Gregorio did. At this year's Pentecost chapter, Elia had been voted out as minister general and replaced by Fra Alberto da Pisa, provincial of England, whom Francesco had received into the ordine. On his last visit to San Damiano, Elia had explained that he was going to Cortona to be with friends.

"Fra Elia has been visiting the Damianites in their monasteries in Cortona and Arezzo," Chiara was explaining. This was permitted when he was minister general, but now he needed papal permission. "When the Holy Father told Fra Elia to stop his visits, Fra Elia grew angry and joined forces with the emperor."

The superficial reason confounded Balvina. For years, Elia had tried to make peace between Federico II and Lord Pope. He knew that joining the emperor meant automatic excommunication. Why had he done it?

"So, sisters, we must pray for Fra Elia's soul." Chiara's voice was forcefully controlled. "And we must pray for the brothers and the Church, because this is a great and irreparable scandal." Chiara's words trembled. "May no souls be lost through this bad example. May we not lose faith." Chiara, who prized Fra Elia's advice, was blinking fiercely.

She's trying not to cry, Balvina realized.

"Let us fix our gaze on Christ, betrayed by Judas. Though friends disappoint and those we trust fail, God is still in charge."

"But why did he do it?" Balvina blurted out.

"Because God gave Fra Elia, like all of us," Chiara said softly, "the freedom to choose."

Balvina pressed her face into her hands. Some choices were bad ones. *Dear God, save Fra Elia's soul.*

NOTES

None of the primary sources state how Chiara and her sisters received news of Fra Elia's defection nor how they responded to it. But they must have been deeply shaken, as were Francesco's other followers. Having allied with Federico II, Elia spent Christmas of 1239 with him in Pisa (Brooke, *Early Franciscan Government* 39).

Elia's physical description is taken from a 1236 image of him, reproduced as an engraving and printed as a frontispiece to Brooke's book.

PART ELEVEN

The Father of Mercies

46

Suor Cecilia di Gualtieri Cacciaguerra

Refectory, San Damiano (September 1240)

Standing in the refectory of San Damiano, Suor Cecilia stared, befuddled, at the stale half loaf of bread before her. At Chiara's request, she had taken the other half to the brothers who served the monastery. Chiara had told her to cut this half into fifty slices so that each sister might have one. "It would take the miracle of the loaves and the fishes to make fifty slices out of that!" Cecilia had blurted out.

"Go and do as I have told you," Chiara had calmly replied.

There was no other food in the monastery.

Cecilia could hear the sisters filing into the refectory. Better get started. Her thin eyebrows wrinkled and her full lips pursed as she took up the knife. She was so hungry that she could have eaten the entire piece herself.

How could life change so much in two weeks?

Two weeks ago, Cecilia was coughing so violently that she couldn't swallow without fear of suffocating. That Friday almost two weeks ago, when the sisters had been fasting on bread and water, Chiara had led Cecilia into the kitchen, where she had given her a small cake to eat. Cecilia had nibbled the sweet morsel out of obedience. Wondrously, the cake had cured her. She hadn't coughed since.

Two weeks ago, Assisi had been at peace. Now, according to the brothers, the emperor's Saracen soldiers had arrived. None of the sisters had ever met a Saracen. But they had heard rumors about them. The Saracens were from some place called Morocco and other areas around the Holy Land. They followed a prophet called Muhammad. They were fierce and skilled in war. Federico was employing them in his army. He wanted to take the papal states from Lord Pope. His army was here, now, in Umbria, in the papally held Duchy of Spoleto.

Two weeks ago, folks brought alms to San Damiano and the brothers begged food in Assisi. Now Saracen troops were killing papal sympathizers. No one came to San Damiano anymore. No brothers begged. The sisters and brothers had eaten all the garden vegetables and used up all the flour. Only this stale loaf remained.

How ironic! Chiara's bones and body were badly weakened because she had fasted too severely when she was younger. Now, older and wiser, she ate something daily and forbade the sisters to fast as she had done. But there was no food. If this continued, other sisters might end up like Chiara.

Taking a deep breath, Cecilia blessed herself. How thin could she cut without the bread crumbling? She cut one slice. My goodness, it was rather plump. She thought she had cut it almost parchment-thin. Well, she could cut that plump slice into eight parts.

She made another slice. What was wrong with her? This slice was thick, too. Now she had two slices to cut into eighths.

Cecilia held the loaf under her hand and spread her fingers across it to hold it steady. How odd! She had two ample slices of bread on the table and the half loaf was very small. Yet her fingers still spread as widely as they had before she made the first cut. Puzzled, she cut again, very, very carefully. And this slice was plump, too.

Cecilia put the knife down. Was it the blade or her cutting? She now had three fat slices of bread. Forty-seven more to go. She could cut each of the three slices into eighths to make twenty-four parts. Then she would have to cut twenty-six thin slices from the loaf. How could she get twenty-six slices from that?

Taking a slow, deep breath, Cecilia held the loaf firmly and began to cut again. The piece was as thick as the other three. And the loaf was no smaller.

Would it happen again? Quickly she cut a fifth thin—no, it was coming out plump—piece. A sixth. Like a madwoman, she began to slice. Seven. Eight. Nine. *Slice. Slice.* Her mind was reeling, singing. Her hands began to tingle. She began to lose count. She was trembling at what was happening. The slices piling up were already more than she had begun with. What does one do when experiencing a miracle? One keeps on going. *Slice. Slice. Slice.* Until the loaf was done.

Cecilia's heart was dancing as she laid down the knife and flexed her cramped fingers. The bread was heaped up every which way before her. Could there be . . . ? She began to count the slices as she placed them on two large wooden platters. One, two, three . . . twenty, twenty-one . . . thirty-eight, thirty-nine . . . fifty. Cecilia gasped. What was she supposed to do?

Serve the bread, an inner voice said.

Si, Lord. Serve the bread.

She did, one slice for each sister. When Cecilia bit into her portion, the bread was sweeter than the cake that had cured her cough.

NOTES

Cecilia remembered well Chiara's impossible instruction to cut a half loaf of bread into fifty slices and how they multiplied when Cecilia obeyed (CA:ED 170–71). At some unspecified time, Chiara cured Cecilia of a violent, persistent cough (CA:ED 164, 169). In September 1240, Saracens invaded Umbria. Most of those in Federico's employ came from Lucera, having been deported there from Sicily.

47

Suor Illuminata

Dormitory, San Damiano (9:00 a.m., September 1240)

S uor Illuminata stood at one of the dormitory windows of San Damiano, gazing out at the Via Cupo di San Petrignano. She could not be seeing what she was seeing. The shouting that had drawn her to the window had materialized into a horde of Saracen soldiers passing by the monastery. All of Assisi had feared the coming of these troops.

In Pisa, Illuminata had been a saddlemaker's daughter. She had admired the strong knights who patronized her father's business, secretly believing that, like them, she wouldn't flinch in the face of danger. Now her statuesque body was frozen with fear. She wanted to run, but there was nowhere to go.

Suddenly a horrific bashing shook the dormitory. Again.

"Suor Chiara!" The shriek came from Suor Angeluccia, who had just raced up the stairs into the dormitory and thrown herself at Chiara's bedside. "The Saracens are battering the door of the church!"

"Quick, daughters!" Chiara commanded from her sickbed. "Gather the sisters and bolt every door and window. Pull up the infirmary stairs! Have Suor Prassede bring the Body of the Lord! May God protect us!"

Angeluccia darted out of the dormitory and down the stairs, leaving Illuminata to bolt the dormitory windows. Into the dormitory hurried

Francesca, Benvenuta, Lucia. Quickly the women shuttered the windows. One. Another. Another. As Illuminata bolted the last window, she saw Saracen soldiers swarming over the wall and dropping like vicious ants into the enclosure.

Oh, God, no!

Around Chiara's bed, sisters were clustering in anguished terror, hysterical weeping, and stoic heroism.

"Everything is bolted, sister!"

"Suor Chiara, save us!"

"God will protect us. Won't He?"

"Save us!"

Into the dormitory rushed Suor Prassede, bearing in her hands the little ivory-bound silver casket from the oratory. In it resided the Eucharistic Lord. Prassede's heavily lidded eyes were wide with terror, her usually doleful expression horrified.

The dormitory shook again with another loud crash. A shocked hush fell.

Cecilia's voice quivered, "The refectory door."

"Suor Prassede," Chiara said, her words shaking, "go before me. Francesca and Illuminata, help me. We will take the Lord to the refectory door where He will have to protect us."

As the women began to protest, Chiara raised her hand. "Sisters, do not fear. If the Lord is with us, the enemy cannot harm us. Have confidence in our Lord Jesus Christ." She had told them this several times when they had voiced their fears about the Saracens possibly invading Umbria.

"I have told you that if the soldiers came here, you were to place me before them. Now we shall go. The remainder of you pray in the oratory or with the sisters in the infirmary. Suor Illuminata and Suor Francesca, help me, please."

Living this nightmare, Illuminata grasped Chiara beneath one arm while Francesca took her by the other one. As they helped her rise, they heard another crash from the refectory.

"Quickly!" Chiara said.

They were hurrying, supporting Chiara, almost lifting and carrying her, following Prassede and the Eucharistic Lord. When they reached the refectory, Prassede stopped and looked at Chiara as another crash shook the door.

"Right in front of the door, sister."

Quickly Prassede blessed herself and hurried to the door as a man on the other side began to call out strong, commanding words. Facing the door, Prassede knelt, trembling, holding the Eucharist directly in front of the entrance.

Illuminata and Francesca brought Chiara to the entrance, where all three knelt as the door shuddered with another ramming. Immediately Chiara prostrated herself, while Illuminata and Francesca drew closer as if to protect her.

Chiara's prayers were strong, almost demanding. "Lord, we are here trusting in You. You, Lord, are our spouse. Defend us and save us from these evil men."

The door was bashed again.

"Look upon these servants of Yours," Chiara cried, "because I cannot protect them."

In a brief hush, a voice, incredibly sweet and calm, filled the silence. I WILL ALWAYS DEFEND YOU.

Illuminata gasped as the door was rammed yet again. "Lord, there are so many good people in the city," Chiara pleaded. "So many who trust in and serve You. My dear God, please defend the city as well."

The voice came again, gentle, firm. THE CITY WILL ENDURE MANY DANGERS, BUT IT WILL BE DEFENDED.

Chiara raised her head. "Do not be afraid, sisters, because I am a hostage for you so that you will not suffer any harm now nor any other time as long as you wish to obey God's commandments." Then Chiara turned toward the ivory box and pressed her face to the floor before it.

Again, the door shuddered under savage ramming.

NOTES

Both Francesca and Illuminata of Pisa supported Chiara in her confrontation with the Saracens. Both women heard Christ assure Chiara that He would protect San Damiano and Assisi (CA:ED 154, 159, 174–75).

Paintings often depict Chiara holding the Eucharist herself, but she had It brought to the refectory door, where she prostrated herself in prayer before It. The person who carried the Blessed Sacrament isn't named but was likely another sister, although some historians believe it was the monastery chaplain.

Prassede's name appears on the 1238 list of sisters at San Damiano (CA:ED 430). We know nothing else about her.

48

Saracen Troop Petty Officer

Enclosure, San Damiano (9:30 a.m., September 1240)

Under a brilliant blue sky, the swarthy, middle-aged Saracen officer laughed as his men rammed a thick tree trunk into the old wooden door. Behind that door, so he had heard, fifty or more women lived. Only one or two more batterings to collapse the door. He intended to be the first inside.

Emperor Federico's troops, including this one, had spread through the March of Ancona and the Duchy of Spoleto, pillaging, murdering, raping, attempting to take the cities loyal to the papacy. Now they were headed north to quell rebellion in the Romagna and to lay siege to Ravenna, Faenza, Venezia, and Bologna. But first they would have fun with these women!

The young soldiers had initially attempted to gain entrance by breaking down the church door, but the officer had stopped them, for women in these places would not be in the church. Seizing a grappling hook from one of the men, the officer had tossed it high against the pink enclosing wall. When it held fast in a crevice, he had scaled the wall, his troops following him. Having trampled the garden, the men were now swarming and whooping about this door.

"Are you women yourselves?" the officer taunted the battering crew. "Move farther back! Put more force behind you. The wood is rotting. It will shatter soon!"

The bevy of soldiers backed up, carrying the trunk.

From the other side of the door came a woman's voice, strong, unafraid. Then the soldiers ran forward, ramming the door again.

The woman's voice came from behind the door a second time. Why didn't the woman run?

The men rammed the door again. It didn't budge.

The door was old, the hinges weak and rusted, the wood dry. At the bottom and the right side the planks were rotted. The door should have given way.

The woman's voice came a third time. Deep. Fearless. If they broke in, she would be immediately assaulted. Why was she there?

Thick fear rose inside the officer's innards. Those who called upon Allah faced danger as fearlessly as this woman did. She had to be calling upon her god.

Allah brought victory in war and vengeance on enemies. He backed the armies that served him. But he wasn't bringing down a rotting door. Was the woman's god more powerful? Or was her courage stronger than his?

Suddenly fearing to desecrate this place, the officer thrust his fist skyward. "Come!" he cried. "Other troops must be almost in the city! This place has nothing of value. The city has treasure and more women!"

Motioning to the men, he raced to the wall, threw the grappling hook against it, and called the men over.

On sturdy legs the troops pushed up the long hill, falling in with their fellows before the high city walls and strong gates of Assisi.

NOTES

"[C]ertain Saracen troops scaled the walls of the monastery and went down into the enclosure. . . . The strength of [Clare's] prayer was such that the hostile Saracens departed as if driven away without doing any harm nor touching anyone in the house" (CA:ED 159). History doesn't record the Saracen viewpoint on this incident.

49

Suor Cristiana di Bernardo da Suppo

San Damiano (Dusk, June 20, 1241)

T he bell was ringing so wildly at the speaking grill of San Damiano that Suor Cristiana forgot the customary greeting. The breathless, red-faced messenger thrust a tightly rolled parchment through the grill. "My master, Messer Iacopo di Stefano di Presbitero . . ." he puffed, ". . . bid me run here with this urgent message . . ." The youth caught his breath. "Have Madonna Chiara read it and then return it to me. Be quick."

Her doe eyes wide with curiosity and concern, Cristiana raced upstairs with the parchment. Around Chiara's bed, the sisters were folding up altar cloths and vestments they had been stitching. Chiara was winding the final length of flaxen thread that she had spun today on the drop spindle. Swiftly breaking the thread between the spindle and the distaff, she snagged it in a notch on the spindle's end. As Cristiana handed her the parchment, Chiara laid the spindle in a small basket on the floor between the legs of the freestanding distaff. There it would wait until she reconnected the threads and spun again.

Breaking the wax seal, Chiara angled the parchment to catch the light. Her face stiffened. Rolling up the parchment, she handed it to Cristiana. "Return this to the servant. Then call all the sisters to me."

A shiver of fear lanced Cristiana's heart as she hurried downstairs. The youth grabbed the parchment and bolted out of the church.

Lord, bring him safely home, Cristiana prayed as she went to gather the sisters. Some were locking the church for the night; some were clearing the refectory tables of the day's stitching; others were readying supper; a few were tending the infirm. In minutes, all the sisters except the infirm ones were at Chiara's side.

Chiara's expression was grim. "Sisters, I have received correspondence from a knight of Assisi. The emperor is sending his armies to Assisi under Vitale d'Aversa."

A gasp of dismay rushed over the sisters.

Her blue eyes gazing intently at the women, Chiara went on. "The knights are readying for battle, but they fear that their forces cannot withstand the emperor's. The knights say the city must be handed over. Vitale d'Aversa has sworn that he will not leave until Assisi is taken."

Oh, my Lord, no! A scene of unbelievable carnage flashed across Cristiana's mind.

Suor Gregoria fell to her knees. Suor Mattia and Suor Lea, then the others, followed Gregoria's example.

"Messer Iacopo has asked us to pray that this be avoided." Chiara paused. Her voice trembled, her eyes brimming with tears. "We have received many benefits from the city. We should pray that God will protect it."

The sisters nodded.

"Let us remember this intention in Vespers and Compline and pray through the night."

When the Saracens had left San Damiano's enclosure not a year ago, they had marched on Assisi but had not attacked it. However, during the past months, Emperor Federico II, despite a few defeats, had taken city after city loyal to Lord Pope. The brothers had relayed the news to the nuns, who added the inhabitants of the defeated cities to their prayers. Ravenna. The papally held cities of Tuscany. Faenza. Benevento. The brothers had said that, in Pisa, the emperor had imprisoned thousands of church prelates to keep them from going to Rome to depose him. He was boasting that God had smitten the Church. The brothers said that his army was marching south toward Rome, where Lord Pope was deathly ill. They'd have to pass through Assisi to get there.

Other than praying the Office in the choir, Cristiana and nearly all the other sisters spent the night in the oratory, begging God's protection on Assisi. With nearly all the monastery crowded before the Eucharist, the little oratory felt sti-fling in the still June night. The hours slipped on. Cristiana began fighting sleep. Finally, as other sisters had already done, she plodded up the stairs to the dormitory.

There, in the glow of oil lamps, scattered sisters slept on straw mattresses. Someone had moved Chiara's bed to face the unshuttered windows that over-looked Assisi. Chiara, who could no longer walk, was propped up, her hands joined, her cheeks shiny with tears, her gaze on a wide, distant ring of flickering lights. Campfires. The emperor's army had surrounded the comune.

Cristiana fell to her knees by Chiara's cot, hands groping for hands, eyes seeking eyes. Chiara grasped Cristiana's fingers as she mouthed the words "Pray. Pray."

Day dawned clear, harmonious, filled with birdsong. How could peace pre-vail here when Assisi was on the verge of battle?

Chiara called the sisters to her. Someone had brought her ashes from the hearth. Silently, she removed her veil and sprinkled ashes on the crown of her close-cropped head.

"Remove your veils, sisters," Chiara softly instructed. The bareheaded sisters knelt as Chiara placed ashes on each head. "Today we shall fast on bread and water. May God reward those who eat nothing as a penance for Assisi. Go to the chapel, sisters, and beg God to free the city."

Cristiana and the other sisters knelt in the oratory, their eyes on their Eucharistic Lord. All day they prayed—kneeling, prostrate, seated. Through the open windows came distant shouts, shrieks. The pounding of hooves. Battle sounds. During the night, Cristiana, weak from lack of sleep and food, fell asleep while praying. The next day the praying and the fasting continued.

Sometime after the Office of Sext, the sisters heard a wild pounding on the church doors, barred against attack. Unmitigated terror seized Cristiana. She flung herself facedown on the oratory floor and begged for the mercy and pro-tection of God. Almost simultaneously, there was a sharp ringing at the speaking grill. Three rings in a row. The brothers' signal.

Cristiana was answering the bell this week. Her legs weak, she started down-stairs to find Pacifica and Beatrice following her. At the grill, Beatrice clutched Cristiana's hand. "We lived together in the same household, sister. We shall die together." Swiftly the three women embraced; then Cristiana unbolted the little door and squeaked out, "Pace e bene."

"Sister, that knocking was a band of knights from the city." Fra Cappellano's voice was jubilant. "They thank you for your prayers. The knights have defeated Vitale d'Aversa. Today at dawn, the enemy left the comune."

NOTES

In 1220, Madonna Cristiana, daughter of Messer Bernardo da Suppo, entered San Damiano. She had lived with Madonna Chiara's family in Assisi and had seen the open door of the dead that Chiara used on Palm Sunday night in 1212 (CA:ED 185 and footnote).

Vitale d'Aversa threatened Assisi in June 1241. An unnamed messenger brought to San Damiano news of the impending attack. Chiara had Cristiana assemble the sisters (CA:ED 186), then called for ashes to be brought. Covering her own unveiled head with ashes, Chiara then immediately sprinkled them on the sisters' heads and commanded them to pray "so the Lord God would free the city." That night, Vitale left with his army (CA:ED 159, 175–76).

Messer Iacopo di Stefano di Presbitero was a knight of Assisi who so esteemed Chiara that he named her, along with his blood brother, as testamentary executrix of his will (Fortini 364).

Some historians believe that Elia, in league with the emperor, promoted an abortive plot to hand Assisi over to Federico's forces (*Early Franciscan Government* 175). Is this true? If so, was d'Aversa's attack the result of this plot?

We can imagine the sisters' terror at Federico II's victories, especially over the Church prelates, and the Assisian knights' doubts as to their own ability to withstand d'Aversa's massive army. On June 22, "the city people attacked the imperial camp at dawn and put the enemy forces to rout." For centuries, Assisi celebrated this victory with a colorful festival in gratitude for Chiara's prayers and those of her sisters (Fortini 362 and footnote).

Part Twelve

An Increase of Talents

50

Suor Angeluccia di Angelico

Via San Petrignano, Assisi (Sunday Evening, June 30, 1247)

Suor Angeluccia's delicately white skin was warm in the rays of the descending sun. Earlier today, she and Suor Cristi had come to pray at the bedside of the dying Messer Lambertini and to comfort his widow. As on every trip into the city, they'd met beggars who needed bandages, medications, salves, splints, and cleansing agents—not to mention prayers. Now they were on their way back to San Damiano. Tomorrow they would bring the supplies; tonight they would pray for the intentions.

Angeluccia's aging mind was befuddled by too many things to remember. Suor Cristi, daughter of Messer Cristiano di Paride, a consul of the comune, was young and had recently joined the sisters. Although deaf in one ear, she heard most things. She'd remember what needed remembering about the salves and bandages. Cristi's actual name was Cristiana, shortened to distinguish her from the other Cristianas at San Damiano. With her long legs, Suor Cristi walked more quickly than Angeluccia, but praying while they walked slowed her down.

"Let's pray for the emperor," Angeluccia suggested. Praying for the emperor was her personal ministry, begun in earnest when that nasty general—she couldn't remember his name—had attacked Assisi. That general had been killed, the brothers said, but not that wicked emperor and his sons. They were still warring against Lord Pope. But Lord Pope Gregorio had died a long time ago, and now there was Lord Pope Innocenzo IV. The sisters prayed for him every day. He was living someplace in France to get away from that emperor, whom he had deposed. But that Emperor Federico paid no attention. He continued to reign. Lots of people disliked him. Maybe he was the Antichrist!

Poor Emperor Federico. Didn't he care that warring against the Church would cost him salvation? All the rest of the way down the hill, up the ladder, and into the dormitory, Angeluccia and Cristi prayed Our Fathers for Federico's repentance.

Out of the corner of her eye, Angeluccia saw the accident happen. Chiara, who had grown strong enough to tend the door, pushing the heavy door closed. The door wobbling on its hinges, breaking loose, collapsing inward, falling on her. Only Chiara's toes showed under the door.

Angeluccia and Cristi both shrieked. Together they grabbed the door, trying to lift it. It wouldn't budge.

"Suor Chiara!"

No answer.

"Sister! Sister!" Angeluccia screamed.

Cecilia came running. Balvina of Porzano.

The four women pulled and tugged, but the door still wouldn't budge. Cristi ran to get the brothers.

Cecilia, Balvina, and Angeluccia tried again and again to lift the door. Impossible.

Into the dormitory through the doorless doorway scrambled Fra Cappellano, Fra Marco, and Fra Gino. Ordering the women back, they grabbed the door, strained, heaved it off Chiara, and eased it to the monastery floor.

The sisters ran to Chiara's frail, crumpled body.

"Sister! Sister!" they called.

As if being roused from deep slumber, Chiara pushed herself to a sitting position and shook her head. "I'm all right," she said, wondrously. "It was as if a mantle had been thrown over me."

Cappellano helped Chiara to her feet. "Madonna, that door is rotted. We'll replace it tomorrow."

"The night is warm," Gino noted. "Leave the door where it is. Pull up the ladder when we leave and you'll be safe."

"We'll do as you say," Chiara agreed. "Grazie."

As the friars descended the ladder, Angeluccia's heart began to race as if her fear had been suppressed until the danger had passed.

Chiara smiled at the sisters. "Let us go and thank the good God for His blessings."

Together they walked to the oratory to do just that.

NOTES

Angeluccia was present when the monastery door fell on Chiara. Since the sisters couldn't lift it, they called three friars (named in the histories) to do so. Chiara, unharmed, said the door felt like a mantle thrown over her (CA:ED 167, 171, 188, 189). Why did the door fall? How was it repaired? We can only speculate.

The precise time of this accident can be calculated from data given in the *Process of Canonization*, dated October 18, 1253 (CA:ED 143 footnote). The accident happened "about seven years ago, in the month of July, during the octave of Saint Peter" (CA:ED 167), according to the testimony of Suor Cristiana. Suor Angeluccia confirms that it occurred "almost seven years ago . . . during the octave of Saint Peter, a Sunday evening" (CA:ED 188). Saint Peter's feast was celebrated on June 29, which fell on a Saturday in 1247. The octave would follow. Medieval people considered the new day as beginning at sunset, so the evening of June 30 would have been July 1 to Chiara's sisters. The door fell on Chiara on July 1, 1247.

Of the sixteen sisters who testified to Chiara's merits in the process of canonization (CA:ED 143–44, 188, 189, 190), Angeluccia is the only sister who mentions how Chiara admonished the serving sisters always to praise the Lord when they left the monastery (CA:ED 189). Could this mean that Angeluccia was a serving sister who was returning from some errand outside the monastery on a day that Chiara was tending the door?

51

Messer Scherno

Great Hall of a Great House, Pisa, Italy (March 1249)

Seated on a broad bench, muscular Messer Scherno stretched his chilled feet toward the fire snapping in the fireplace of the great hall in a great house in Pisa. Upon his father's death three years ago, Scherno had inherited the house.

Today's hunt had been unbelievably successful. Sixteen deer and eight boar. Enough to feed his entire household for two weeks.

He heard someone enter the room, but he was too cozy to turn to see who it was.

"Messer."

Ah, Mamma.

"I heard that you had a most successful hunt."

He grunted. What was she getting at?

"You now have time to take Madonna Pia to the holy nuns. They say the prayers of Madonna Chiara are most effective . . ."

Scherno swung around. "Mamma, give up! Madonna Pia is a hopeless case. If God wanted to heal her, He could do it here."

"Can't you do this for your sister? Please?"

He sprang to his feet, his toes still icy. "Religion destroyed Madonna Pia's mind. You expect religion to restore it?" This pious sister of his had prayed long hours in the chapel, lingered after Mass, modestly avoided open windows, and had considered becoming a nun. That was before the demons had gotten her.

"Please. I beg you."

Scherno slapped one huge fist into the other. "I will write. That's all."

His mother, much shorter than he, trembled before him. "Grazie. I will send a servant in with parchment."

"Not tonight, Mamma."

"Tonight." The voice was firm.

All right. Tonight.

He took the parchment and reed pen offered him and scrawled: "To Madonna Chiara. My mother asks you to pray for my demon-possessed sister Madonna Pia. Cure her if you can. As if God cares." He thrust the parchment at the servant and turned back to the fire.

Before Scherno had to hunt again, the answer arrived. He was in his counting room, reviewing accounts with the bailiff, when Mamma brought him the parchment. She wouldn't leave until he read it to her.

"It says that Madonna Chiara and her sisters are praying for Madonna Pia," he said, swiftly skimming the finely penned prose. The letter had been written on the parchment he had used—beneath Chiara's words, traces of scraped-off ink revealed his own note.

Mamma smiled widely. "Thanks be to God."

Scherno spat. "The prayers have done no good." Madonna Pia was the same. Her bedroom door was still tightly shut. Servants continued to leave her food at the door because she flung it at them if they entered. He often heard eerie moanings coming from the bedroom and, three days ago, a wild thrashing. Last night, she had passed him in the hall, a thin wraith in a white chemise coming from the direction of the chapel, her auburn hair matted and uncombed, a vacant stare on her face.

Mamma reached for the letter and pressed it to her chest. "Grazie." Silently she left the room.

Scherno returned to his accounts, a bit unsettled. Madonna Chiara had severely admonished him for his lack of faith, had pleaded with him to repent, and had written that she and the sisters were praying with tears for him.

Lent arrived. Easter. Spring crops were planted. Still Pia's bedroom door remained closed, the tray delivered in the hall. The shrieks and thrashing increased. Pia grew worse.

On the feast of Pentecost, Scherno was surveying the great hall, set for a sumptuous banquet. The long head table for the men, the side table for the women. The guests would arrive within the hour. Satisfied, he turned to leave and met Madonna Pia entering.

She was clothed in a saffron gown, her hair caught up in a crispinette of net at her neck, a maroon velvet hat fastened under her chin with a wide band. She seemed as peaceful as she had been before the demons consumed her. Smiling, she placed her thin, pale hand on Scherno's arm.

"My brother, you must write a letter to Madonna Chiara. Her prayers have driven out the demons. There were five of them."

Scherno looked skeptically into his sister's tranquil gray eyes. "Five?" She was still possessed to think that she knew the number of demons!

"They told me their names as they were leaving."

Scherno laughed disdainfully.

Pia patted Scherno's arm. "Scruple. Shame. Self-Hatred. Mistrust of God's Mercy. Refusal to Accept God's Forgiveness."

"What kind of names are those?" Scherno roared.

"They told me the names of your demons," Pia said calmly. "Unbelief. Scorn. Arrogance. Pride. Trust in Oneself. Everyone knew that demons possessed me. You don't know that they possess you."

Scherno stiffened.

"The demons said that Madonna Chiara's prayers were burning them, because the fire of faith is more consuming than the fire of hell. May the fire of faith cast out your demons, my brother."

NOTES

About the year 1249, a pious lady from Pisa came to San Damiano to thank God and Chiara. Chiara's petitions had cast out five demons from the woman, who said that Chiara's prayers "were burning them" (CA:ED 166, 173). No other details are given.

Since parchment was expensive, people commonly scraped ink from it and reused it for another letter. Chiara wrote many letters, but only four are extant—the letters to Anežka of Prague, whose wealth precluded her from having to reuse the parchment.

Chiara wept over worldly people, reproached them, and exhorted them to penance (CA:ED 152).

52

Suor Cristi
(Suor Cristiana di Cristiano di Paride)

Dormitory, San Damiano (September 8, 1252)

On a bench next to Chiara's raised bed, Suor Cristi's long, lean body felt awkwardly tense. She was trying to hem the altar cloth in her lap, but her gentle gray eyes kept glancing from the cloth to Chiara, who was barely clinging to life.

In this week's chapter meeting, Suor Pacifica had assigned Cristi the task of tending Chiara. In her naturally tender way, Cristi had been bathing Chiara's warm forehead, coaxing her to sip a bit of watery broth, turning her body so that she could rest more comfortably.

Beneath the idle distaff, loosely twisted with flaxen fibers, Chiara dozed. She had spun enough thread to make over fifty sets of corporals and their cases. Would she ever spin again?

Chiara had experienced her first grave health crisis last autumn, when Lord Pope and the Curia were still in Lyons. The Damianite sisters had sent word to her fellow religious in area convents, monasteries, and hermitages to pray for Chiara. A comforting but perplexing message had arrived from the Benedictine convent of San Paolo delle Abbadesse in Bastia, where Chiara had lived for a time after being tonsured by San Francesco. While deep in prayer for Chiara, one of the San Paolo sisters had experienced a haunting vision. The sister had felt as if she and the other San Paolo sisters were attending the ill Chiara as she lay on a queenly bed of gold, studded with precious gems. As the sisters had wept, a majestic, strikingly beautiful woman had appeared at the foot of the bed. "Daughters, do not weep over one who is about to be victorious," she consoled. "Suor Chiara cannot die until the Lord comes with His disciples."

Shortly after the vision, in early November, Innocenzo IV and his court had arrived in Perugia, safe now that Emperor Federico had died. Cardinal Rinaldo, protector of the ordine, had hurried to visit gravely ill Chiara. She had begged him to urge Lord Pope to ratify the Form of Life she had written and to confirm the privilege of poverty for San Damiano. Rinaldo had visited Chiara a few times since then. Always she asked the same favor. It had not yet been granted.

An almost imperceptible cough jerked Cristi's attention back to Chiara. Before Cristi could elevate Chiara's head to help her inhale more deeply, Chiara had resumed an easy, shallow breathing pattern.

How ironic that Cristi could hear Chiara's faint choking while just months ago she sometimes couldn't make out her abbess' words! Early in the summer, Chiara had felt a bit stronger. She had resumed her spinning and, one summer day, she asked Cristi about her deaf ear. "It's still deaf," Cristi admitted.

"Why don't you kneel? I'll pray," Chiara suggested. So Cristi had knelt. Chiara prayed silently over her, then made the sign of the cross and touched her deaf ear, which had popped inside. Instantly Cristi could hear with it.

Now Chiara was too weak even to bless herself.

Oh, God! Cristi prayed—as she had prayed every day since Chiara had grown so ill—*Can't You let Lord Pope approve her Form of Life before she dies? It's all she wants for herself, Lord.*

Five years ago, Lord Pope Innocenzo IV had given all the Damianites a Rule. Innocenzo's Rule had stated that monasteries must hold goods in common and that they were permitted to hold property. Dismayed at the mitigation of their vowed poverty, many of the monasteries, including San Damiano, had asked Lord Pope to rescind his order; two years ago, he had. Chiara then began to write her own Form of Life, putting the sisters solidly under the friars, incorporating sections of Innocenzo's Rule and Cardinal Ugolino's, and firmly adhering to poverty. She had sent her Form of Life to Lord Pope. Why was he taking so long to approve it?

Sì, he had other things on his mind. He was struggling against Federico's sons for control of parts of the empire. The Holy Land was largely in enemy hands. The cruel Tartars threatened eastern lands. Heresy persisted. All these must seem more pressing than approving a woman's Form of Life.

The rustle of woolen habits and the sound of bare feet running on the stairs startled Cristi.

"Cardinal Rinaldo has come to visit Suor Chiara!" Venuta's eager whisper was flung Cristi's way as Venuta, along with Balvina, hurried toward the door that opened to the courtyard below. Balvina, still strong despite her age, heaved open the door. Together she and Venuta lowered the staircase. Cristi could hear the stairs creaking under the weight of the ascending cardinal.

Protector of the Order of Saint Damian, Cardinal Rinaldo dei Conti di Segni reminded Cristi of Balvina—elderly, plump, and large. The cardinal's thin legs and small feet, shoved into his riding boots, seemed disproportionate to the rest of his scarlet-clothed bulk. The sisters said he had been thinner when young, but equally handsome.

As the cardinal and Fra Cappellano approached Chiara's bed, Cristi stood to relinquish her seat, but Cardinal Rinaldo waved his big hand, motioning for her to sit, while he and Cappellano each took a spare bench from along the wall and placed them next to Chiara's bed. At once the cardinal beckoned the other sisters to her bedside. Then he deftly straddled his bench, took a good look at Chiara, and bowed his head in prayer.

When he opened his eyes, Chiara had opened hers as well. "Messer Cardinal, how good of you to come," she said weakly.

The Church official patted Chiara's thin hand. "So you are ill again, Madonna Chiara. As soon as I heard of your illness, I determined to visit you. I have had Fra Cappellano bring with him the Body of the Lord. Would you like to receive Him?"

A radiant smile broke over Chiara's pinched face.

Raising his right hand, the cardinal blessed the ill woman and uttered the customary prayers before removing the consecrated Host from the little silver box in Cappellano's hands. With great reverence and with tears streaming down her cheeks, Chiara delicately consumed the Eucharistic Body of the Lord while Cristi bowed her head and prayed for Chiara's welfare.

In such peaceful, prayerful recollection, the minutes slipped by until Chiara broke the silence. "Grazie, Messer Cardinal, for the gift of my Lord. You are so good to me and to my sisters. You are a saint to us."

The distinguished man reddened. "Madonna Chiara, if you wish to speak of saints, let us speak not of me, a sinner, but of Stanisław, bishop of Kraków. Have you perhaps heard of this most holy man?"

No one had, so Rinaldo began to tell them of the holy bishop, martyred two hundred years ago, whom Lord Pope would most likely canonize the following year. He then began a long, obviously extemporaneous homily on the virtues of faith, truth, and martyrdom, exhorting the sisters to hold fast to those values. As always, his words were lofty, his sentences complex—so unlike the simple sermons the brothers preached.

"Therefore, dear women in Christ, although you may be lodged in this enclosure, your good example must penetrate as a light to the darkened world beyond these walls. May final perseverance and a most happy end be given to you all," the cardinal beamed. Then he raised his hand in benediction and blessed them with the sign of the cross. "Now, Madonne, the press of duties calls. I shall bid you farewell with hopes of returning again as my schedule permits."

"Messer Cardinal, before you go, I must ask a favor."

The prelate smiled indulgently. "Of course, Madonna Chiara. What do you wish?"

"Only this, Messer." Down Chiara's hollow cheeks ran little streams of tears. "My sisters believe that I am dying. You are the protector of our ordine. Watch over my soul with your prayers and supplications, and over the souls of my sisters as well."

The tears were coming faster as Rinaldo reached for Chiara's hand.

"And I implore you, Messer, to beg Lord Pope and all the cardinals to quickly confirm the Form of Life that I have sent and to grant us, inviolably and for all time, the privilege of poverty."

Rinaldo patted Chiara's bony hands. "Madonna Chiara, I have been doing all within my power to see that your request is granted. I solemnly promise that

I will make an extra effort to have Lord Pope act soon. May you and your sisters continue to support my efforts with your constant prayers."

"Messer Cardinal," Chiara said with trembling voice, "we pray for nothing more ardently than that Lord Pope allow us for all time to conform ourselves totally to the poor and humble Christ."

NOTES

Chiara was the first woman in history to write a Form of Life for an order. Sometime prior to the events detailed in this chapter, she had completed her *Form of Life* and submitted it to the Holy Father for approval.

An unnamed nun at San Paolo experienced the vision recounted in this chapter (CA:ED 313). Rinaldo visited shortly after (CA:ED 314) on September 8, 1252 (Catherine Bolton Magrini, trans., Editrice Minerva—Assisi, p. 70, footnote). Marco Bartoli (*Clare of Assisi* 177–78) implies that the visit was much earlier, probably at the end of 1251, shortly after the pope's arrival in Perugia on November 5, 1251. It seems likely that Rinaldo visited Chiara more than once during this time since he greatly admired her. This chapter reflects that probability.

Rinaldo is described as being "very fat" (Horace Mann [vol. 15, p. 10]). He exhorted the sisters, gave Chiara the Eucharist, and promised, when asked, to be an advocate for the privilege of poverty (CA:ED 314).

Saint Stanisław's history is found in Butler's *Lives of the Saints*. In 1253, Innocenzo IV canonized Bishop Stanisław of Kraków.

Rinaldo's final blessing is from his 1228 letter to several Damianite monasteries (Armstrong, p. 106).

We have no records of which sisters cared for the ill Chiara. They probably took turns. Chiara cured Cristiana's deafness by making the sign of the cross on her head and touching her ear (CA:ED 166).

53

Suor Gatta

Oratory, San Damiano (December 24, 1252)

Suor Gatta was the current cat in a long string of cats that kept San Damiano free of mice. Years ago, following the death of a previous Suor Gatta, a nobleman had given the sisters this Gatta. Then a gray, orange, and white kitten, she was now old and arthritic.

Right now, Gatta was plodding through the oratory without even nibbling a heel of the kneeling sisters or arching her bony head under any elbow. Long ago Gatta had learned that the sisters who tickled her chin, rubbed her tummy, or cuddled her in other rooms ignored her in this one. So she bounded up the stairs into the dormitory and pounced into the lap of the one sister who would caress her. Chiara.

Tucked under a gray blanket, Chiara was, as always nowadays, lying in bed. On workdays, she would be spinning or embroidering; on prayer days like today she would lie awake, her eyes closed. Gatta curled up in Chiara's lap, purring as Chiara's thin hand stroked her gray fur. Gatta closed her yellow eyes and snoozed.

Sometime later Gatta awoke, her old body stiff. On achy legs, she pushed erect and stretched. Then she jumped off the bed to walk the pains away. Folded near one of the sisters' mats was a small white towel used to bathe Chiara's face.

Gatta caught the towel in her claws and began to stretch the kinks out of her toes.

"Suor Gatta!" Chiara ordered. "Bring that here!" Chiara had taught Gatta the command "Bring." When Gatta obeyed, Chiara would tickle Gatta's chin. Mouthing the cloth, Gatta began to drag it across the floor.

"Oh, you naughty little thing!" Chiara scolded. "You don't know how to bring it. Why are you dragging it along the ground like that?"

Gatta cocked her head. What was wrong? She clawed the cloth into a loose roll and picked it up in her mouth as she would a kitten, carrying it, her head high, to Chiara.

"Good, Suor Gatta!" Chiara took the cloth from Gatta's mouth and tickled her chin. Then she folded the towel and placed it in a basket in which lay a reed pen and parchment.

"Suor Cristi brought our supper while you were asleep." Chiara reached over her bed and plucked a quarter slice of dark brown bread from the dormitory floor. Not very hungry, Gatta sniffed the bread, then sat on her haunches.

Chiara laughed lightly. "So you know that Christmas Eve is a fast day! How smart you are!"

Gatta yawned at the unintelligible praise, then leaped into the basket and curled up on the towel.

"No!" Chiara picked up Gatta with one hand, and with the other, the basket.

"You can't sleep on my letter to Lord Pope. What will he think if I send him a crushed letter asking him to approve our Rule?" Chiara placed the basket by her left side and put Gatta into her lap.

With Chiara smoothing the fur along Gatta's spine, Gatta fell asleep. When she awakened, she padded through the dormitory, now filled with sleeping sisters, and used the flat tub of sand placed in one corner just for her. Then she curled up next to Lucia's face. Lucia's measured breathing warmed Gatta's back.

Lucia's kiss to Gatta's head roused the cat from slumber. Stretching, she opened her eyes and saw the dormitory emptying. Every morning the sisters walked down to that room where they sat on benches and said soft words in unison. Chiara never went there anymore.

Gatta pounced into Chiara's lap and felt thin fingers scratching her head as Chiara spoke softly to two crossed twigs, tied with twine, which she held in her other hand.

"Well, Lord God, it's Christmas, and I have been left here alone with You."

Immediately Gatta heard beautiful music. She pricked her ears to hear better.

"You hear it, too? An organ."

Chiara gasped. She was gazing toward the center of the dormitory. Gatta looked, too. Where had those rows of brothers come from?

Music swelled. The brothers sang. When the song ended, a deep male voice chanted, "Lord, open my lips." The others responded in unison, "And my mouth will declare Your praise." Gatta's old ears were as keen as they'd always been. Through the floor, she could hear the women downstairs saying the same words.

The chanting went on, reading, more chanting. Gatta grew tired and yawned. The brothers blessed themselves and disappeared.

Puzzled, Gatta nestled under Chiara's arm and mewed.

Chiara's cheeks were dripping with tears. "My God, grazie. To have let me see and hear the brothers in the Basilica di San Francesco praying the Offices of Matins and Lauds for Christmas! Oh, my God, how have You done such a thing?"

NOTES

At an unspecified time when Chiara was bedridden and alone, the convent's cat brought a towel to her when she requested it. This chapter exactly follows that incident (CA:ED 177). On the Christmas Eve before her death, Chiara, bedridden and alone, saw and heard the friars in the Basilica di San Francesco praying the Offices of Matins and Lauds (CA:ED 161, 165, 172).

54

Suor Andrea da Ferrara

Infirmary, San Damiano (Late Spring 1253)

On a straw mattress in the infirmary of San Damiano, old, infirm Suor Andrea lay awake, as rigid as a dry stick. Her mind was racing. Would she have another attack? When? How severe would it be? What if she couldn't breathe?

Twenty years ago, middle-aged, limber Andrea had come to San Damiano from Ferrara, a city on the plain around the Po River. With her deep brown eyes dancing in her round face, Andrea had been eager for work and prayer. As she aged, she had maintained her vigor and joy until several months ago, when this insidious illness had struck.

Now when she felt winded after climbing the stairs from the choir, she experienced increased difficulty with breathing. Her throat was constricted with swellings that sometimes blocked her breath. No one's prayers had helped her.

Suddenly a piercing yowl shattered the still night. Old Suor Gatta, sleeping next to Andrea, torn by yet another convulsion! Before Andrea could soothe the cat, the spasm passed. Gatta sighed, arched, curled again into a ball. Andrea was left with a racing heart.

Suor Gatta had her first convulsion weeks ago. Now the spasms came often. As Andrea stroked Gatta's bony gray head, the animal purred.

Without warning, Andrea's throat tightened. She couldn't breathe. *Oh, God, no!* Impulsively, she clutched her blocked throat and squeezed. She would either burst these boils, bring them up through her mouth, or choke herself to death. Death or cure.

"Sister, what are you doing?" The sharp rebuke was followed by Suor Filippa grabbing her hands and pulling them away from her throat. Andrea felt light-headed. She shook her head, opened her eyes.

Suor Filippa, her pretty face wrinkled with age and worry, was kneeling beside her. "Stop choking yourself," Filippa ordered.

"I wasn't choking . . ." Andrea's mouth was moving but no words came out. With horror, she realized that she had damaged her voice box.

"Drink this." Filippa held out an egg whose shell had been slightly cut away on the upright end.

"I can't," Andrea mouthed. She might choke.

"Madonna Chiara told me to boil an egg, bring it to you, and wait until your voice returned. Here." Filippa handed the egg to Andrea.

Incredulous, Andrea began to suck out the egg's warmed, thickened contents. The mass slid easily down her throat.

"Can you speak?" Filippa asked.

"No," Andrea said, her voice startling her. "Sì," she whispered, awed.

Filippa stood. "Then let's go to Suor Chiara."

Chiara? What reproach awaited her? Reluctantly, Andrea followed Filippa into the dormitory.

Chiara was lying on her side, her back to the wall. She beckoned Andrea closer. "What was the matter, sister?" she asked quietly, the light from the oil lamps throwing her aged face into bold relief. She took Andrea's pale, heavily veined hand in her own. "Sister, confess your thoughts to the Lord, for He has told me what you have done. The Lord Jesus will cure this illness, but you must change your life for the better. You are soon to suffer another illness, and you will not rise from that one."

The totally unexpected words knifed Andrea. Like a dry twig, her sanity snapped. She jerked out of Chiara's grasp and bolted for the door. Swiftly she kissed the oratory floor before her Eucharistic Lord, then felt her way down the dark stairs to the burial plot. When her bare feet touched the packed earth at the foot of the stairs, Andrea fell to her knees, her hands pressed against the hard, cold soil. Here were buried Illuminata. Egidia. Marsebilia. Giovanna. And here she, too, would be soon.

Something soft brushed Andrea's thigh. Suor Gatta. In the blackness, Suor Gatta arched her head under Andrea's palm as Andrea settled onto her heels and drew the cat into her lap.

As she stroked the calm, purring animal, Andrea's mind cleared. Who would expect such crazy behavior from someone her age? Chiara must be praying for her right now. She could almost feel the prayers reaching downward like tender arms.

Christ would cure her. But then she would die of another illness. Terror rose in Andrea's soul. When would the illness strike? How long would it last? How painful would it be?

Gatta stiffened, shrieked. Another spasm. Andrea embraced the rigid animal and felt the tremor pass, the body relax. Gatta began to purr.

The purring wove through Andrea's mind. *"Learrrrn. Learrrrn,"* it crooned.

"Learn what?" Andrea whispered, rubbing Gatta's shoulders. "Here you are, purring as if nothing happened."

Her words caught her. Whenever convulsions struck Gatta, she rode them out and forgot them. She didn't worry about them striking again. Gatta lived in the present. She accepted everything as it came. She was at peace.

What mattered was not why one suffered but that one accepted it, learned from it, and lived at peace in the now. God had promised to give His people strength to bear whatever came.

Andrea was tired. And she needed to apologize to Chiara. Gathering Gatta in her arms, Andrea felt her way upstairs. Chiara was lying on the floor, her face downward in prayer or sleep. Andrea would apologize tomorrow.

Quietly Andrea returned to the well-lit infirmary. Cuddling Gatta under her blanket, she lay on her mattress and closed her eyes. *Live . . . this . . . moment,* she thought, as she drifted off to sleep.

NOTES

The *Process* for Chiara's canonization was conducted in November 1253 by Messer Bartholomew, Bishop of Spoleto. The *Process* details the undated incident regarding Suor Andrea, whose boils in the throat were most likely lymph nodes swollen with tuberculosis bacteria (CA:ED 155, 158–59). Messer Bartholomew implies that Andrea also testified briefly to Chiara's healing abilities (CA:ED 169). *The Legend of Saint Clare*, published in 1255, details the incident regarding Andrea and states that, shortly after being cured of the swellings in her throat, she died of a different disease, as Chiara predicted (CA:ED 326–27).

It seems that Andrea was alive at the time of the *Process* but dead when the legend was written.

PART THIRTEEN

To Persevere to the End

55

Suor Francesca di Capitaneo
da Collemezzo

Infirmary, San Damiano (Early August 1253)

On her straw mattress in the infirmary of San Damiano, Suor Francesca was in anguish from the painful throbbing in her head.

From the time Francesca, then Madonna Massariola, had entered San Damiano twenty-one years ago, until five years ago when these headaches began, she had been ill only two days. Of average height yet incredibly strong, Francesca had been as robust as the noblemen in her family—her father, Messer Capitaneo of the castle of Collemezzo; her brother Messer Pietro; her uncles Ugolino, Guido, and Bonifazio, who was Lord Bishop of Todi. None of them, however, ever had headaches like this. It might last for hours or days before disappearing. Then it would return. Right now, she was biting her lower lip to keep from crying out and waking her ill, sleeping sisters.

The headaches had begun just after the vicious wars around Turin had caused the Poor Sisters there to leave their monastery and be dispersed among other Damianites. Even now wars raged. Sì, Federico II had died three years ago, clad as a penitent in a white Cistercian habit and receiving absolution and the last sacraments from Archbishop Berard of Palermo—in answer to the many prayers offered for the emperor's final repentance. Sì, two years ago Pope Innocenzo IV had returned to the papal lands, settling in Perugia instead of in unsafe Rome. But Federico's excommunicated son and heir, King Corrado, still battled Lord Pope for power. Assisi could yet be drawn into the fray. Every day the sisters prayed for peace. Francesca offered every headache for that intention.

The pain in Francesca's head swelled. How could she endure it? Maybe if Chiara prayed for her . . . Chiara's prayers had cured Amata of fever, coughing, pain, and dropsy so severe that her little belly had been horribly swollen. They had cured Balvina of a continuous fever and hideous abscess on her breast and of a throbbing pain in her thigh. They had restored Suor Benvenuta's voice when she had been unable to speak above a whisper for more than two years. Chiara's prayers had cured Cecilia of a persistent cough, Cristi of deafness in one ear, Venuta of a fistula so large you could put five fingers into the pus-filled abscess. They had cured Andrea of the swellings in her throat.

It was the middle of the night! Yet Chiara had told the sisters that they could come to her at any time. Francesca pulled her mantle about her, her head pounding worse for having moved. In agony, she made her way out of the infirmary, through the corridor to the oratory, and up the stairs to the dormitory.

On her raised bed in the corner, Chiara lay perfectly still, her eyes closed. Francesca silently knelt at the bedside to wait until Chiara awakened. If she awakened. Chiara was dying. She had been unable to eat anything for days. Her strength was ebbing away.

Francesca felt a gentle, weak touch on her head. Looking up, she saw Chiara's blue eyes gazing at her from a hollow, gaunt face, felt Chiara's bony hand resting lightly on her scalp.

"What's wrong, sister?" Chiara whispered.

"This headache. Every day I would offer God five hidden deeds of love if I were rid of it."

"Such a beautiful gift!" With trembling hand, Chiara made the sign of the cross over Francesca. Her lips moved slightly as her head bowed in prayer. Francesca felt as peaceful as she had during the festival of Calendemaggio. Then she had seen a great brilliance about Chiara's head while an incredibly beautiful young boy, sitting on Chiara's lap, had leaned against her breast. Surely He was the Christ Child. Francesca had told no one of the vision, nor had she spoken of a second vision she experienced around the feast of Saint Martin three years ago. Then Fra Cappellano had come to the dormitory to give the dying Chiara the Holy Eucharist. Francesca again saw the brilliance about Chiara's head as she received the Lord's Body, which seemed to be that same beautiful Christ Child. After meditating, Chiara had whispered to her sisters, "God has given me such a gift today that heaven and earth could not equal it." Then Chiara's life had been restored.

Francesca shook her head. It no longer hurt. Her headaches never disappeared instantly like this. She was cured.

"Grazie, Suor Chiara."

Chiara patted Francesca's hand.

"What will we do if you die?" Francesca asked softly.

Smiling weakly, Chiara pointed to a basket on the floor near the head of her bed. "There you'll find my final testament. It will tell you what you must do when I'm gone. You may read it."

With eyes smarting with unbidden tears, Francesca plucked the several parchment pages.

"In the name of the Lord! Amen." So began the document.

The document was beautifully written in Chiara's fine hand. She thanked God for their vocation and Francesco for his example and support. She spoke of the beginnings of her community and exhorted the sisters always to embrace holy poverty, never turning aside from their promises. She spoke of the simplicity of their dwellings and the humility of their lives, while reminding the sisters that they must love all with the love of Christ.

Francesca's tears flowed as she read Chiara's exhortation to the abbess. The abbess must be more virtuous than the others and must lead more by love than by authority. She must be a discerning, gentle mother to her daughters, caring for each and being available to all at any time.

> "Let us be very careful, therefore, that, if we have set out on the path of the Lord, we do not at any time turn away from it through our own fault or negligence or ignorance, nor that we offend so great a Lord and His Virgin Mother, and our blessed Father Francis, the Church Triumphant and even the Church Militant. For it is written: 'Those who turn away from your commands are cursed.'

"For this reason I bend my knee to the Father of our Lord Jesus Christ that, through the supporting merits of the glorious and holy Virgin Mary, His Mother, and of our most blessed Father Francis and all the saints, the Lord Himself, who has given us a good beginning, will also give the increase and final perseverance. Amen.

"So that it may be better observed, I leave you this writing, my very dear and beloved sisters, those present and those to come, as a sign of the blessing of the Lord and of our most blessed Father Francis and of my blessing, your mother and servant."

Francesca was trembling as she replaced the parchment in the basket. "How will we ever go on without you?"

Chiara opened her arms and Francesca embraced her tightly. "When I die, you'll continue to follow in the footprints of our Lord Jesus Christ, for He will never die."

NOTES

Francesca's visions and cure, as well as the other cures mentioned in this chapter, are accurate (CA:ED 176–77). Fortini (351) tells of Francesca's background.

Gilliat-Smith, in his book *Clare of Assisi: Her Life and Legislation* (p. 104), mentions that in about 1248, wars caused the Turin sisters to leave their monastery and settle elsewhere.

Quotes are from Chiara's *Testament* (CA:ED 60–65). Chiara's Scripture remembrance about those being cursed who turn from the Lord is a paraphrase of Deuteronomy 11:28.

Scholars dispute whether Chiara wrote her *Form of Life* prior to her *Testament* or vice versa. Some scholars question the authenticity of the *Testament*. Lezlie Knox (*Creating Clare of Assisi*) summarizes the pros and cons of this debate.

Chiara's state of health at this time follows the histories.

56

Sestra Anežka

Kitchen, Damianite Convent, Prague (August 1253)

In the kitchen of the Damianite monastery in Prague, Sestra Anežka plunged a wretched, tattered tunic into a deep basin of hot water and strong soap. On her thin hands, red sores created by the soap stung as she dunked the filthy, foul-smelling garment. Above her dark, almond-shaped eyes, Anežka's beautifully arched eyebrows lifted as she scanned the leper's garb. She would wash it carefully, dry it in the sun, and mend it before sending it back to its owner—along with a loaf of bread baked especially for the poor in the massive outdoor oven outside the refectory.

When the portress called Anežka to the speaking grill, the garment was drying. Friars had brought a letter from Madonna Chiara and the news that Chiara was dying without receiving approval from Lord Pope for her Form of Life.

With promises to pray for Chiara and her sisters, Anežka took the letter and made her way to her small, private oratory. Closing the door, she fell to her knees before the wall crucifix, crying aloud, "She's dying, my God!"

Anežka had experienced death before. Her father. Her mother. Two nephews, one brutally murdered. Her dear cousin Elisabeth, now declared a saint. Their deaths were not as shattering to her as this one. Although Anežka shared her lineage with her relatives, she shared her soul with Chiara. Chiara had encouraged Anežka in her vocation and in her struggle to maintain poverty for the Prague monastery. She had supported her successful bid to separate the Prague monastery from the hospice's support. She had scolded her for fasting too severely and had advised her to remember that her body was made of flesh. Chiara had agreed that she could mitigate certain parts of the Rule due to Bohemia's harsh climate, and Lord Pope had consented.

"Oh, my God! What will I do without her?" Though Anežka had never met Chiara in person, she knew her spirit through the letters they exchanged. The women prayed daily for each other. They would pray for each other until each was in heaven.

Taking a deep, quavering breath, Anežka found a square of linen tucked into the tight sleeve of her undertunic and dabbed her eyes. With shaky hands and a rush of love in her heart, she broke the wax seal on the parchment.

She began to read, her eyes swiftly brimming with tears. Chiara was address-ing her as "half of" Chiara's soul, as "the special shrine" of Chiara's "deepest love," as "the illustrious Queen and Bride of the Lamb, the eternal King." Anežka was filled with love at the affectionate greeting. "May she sing the new song with the other most holy virgins before the throne of God and the Lamb and follow the Lamb wherever He will go."

Anežka continued to read. Chiara apologized for not writing more often because of "the lack of messengers and the obvious dangers of the roads." The emperor's battles and those between Anežka's brother Václav and his son Ottokar had made travel dangerous. But largely through Anežka's prayers and efforts, father and son had agreed to peace. They had made their pact within this monastery's church dedicated to San Francesco, which Anežka had built.

Chiara's love pulsated throughout the letter. She called Anežka to surrender to Christ, writing of Him as one would a lover. She exhorted her to look at Christ as if at a mirror, to see reflected there the holy virtues of poverty, humil-ity, and love, and to adorn herself with those virtues.

Anežka devoured the words. The beautiful, intense prose glowed with ardor as Chiara, like the bride in the biblical Song of Songs, sang to her Lord, "Draw me after you, let us run in the fragrance of your perfumes, O heavenly Spouse."

Anežka's heart was in a turmoil of elation and sorrow. "I have inscribed the happy memory of you indelibly on the tablets of my heart, holding you dearer than all others."

Oh, God! Chiara was telling her goodbye.

"What more? In your love may the tongue of the flesh be silent; may the tongue of the Spirit speak and say this: 'O blessed daughter, because the love that I have for you can never be fully expressed by the tongue of the flesh"—the tears were flowing faster—"what I have written is inadequate. I beg you to receive my words with kindness and devotion, seeing in them at least the motherly affection that in the fire of charity I daily feel toward you and your daughters to whom I warmly commend myself and my daughters in Christ.'"

Oh, my God, let her feel my love for her. Let her know that I am lifting her to Your throne. Oh, my God, if I write to her, will she receive my letter?

The thought came swiftly. SHE WILL BE WITH ME WHEN YOUR LETTER ARRIVES.

My Lord, let her know how much I love her.

THIS SHE ALREADY KNOWS, ANEŽKA.

Will You be with her, Lord, when she dies? Will You comfort and encourage her? Don't let her die alone! Preserve her from the demon in her final hours.

An assurance came. I WILL BE WITH HER. SHE WILL RECEIVE A SPECIAL GRACE.

Anežka's pounding heart slowed. God would be with Chiara. She would know that she was loved. With an aching heart, Anežka found her place in the letter and read it to the end.

"Farewell, my dearest daughter, with your daughters until we meet at the throne of the glory of the great God.... As much as I can, I recommend to your charity the bearers of this letter..."

Anežka smiled thinly. It was so like Chiara, dying herself yet requesting prayers for the brothers who brought the letter. She would enter God's kingdom, loving Him and all those whom she touched by her life and her prayers.

NOTES

Biographies of Anežka (Agnes) of Prague tell how she cooked for the monastery and secretly washed clothing from lepers and her ill sisters, chafing her skin with the strong soaps and bleaches used in those days. In the middle of the night, she would rise and secretly mend the garments.

Since Anežka was princess of Bohemia, she had the funds to build and expand her monastery, adding a private oratory for herself. Her earliest biographer tells how her sisters would hear her speaking to God in the room and would sometimes hear a gentle male voice answering her.

Most historians believe that Chiara and Anežka had an extensive correspondence, written in the common language of Latin, although no letters from Anežka to Chiara have been identified. In the third of her four extant letters to Anežka, Chiara advised her to fast with moderation.

Most historians agree that, shortly before her death, Chiara wrote her *Fourth Letter to Agnes*, portions of which are reproduced verbatim in this chapter (CA:ED 54–58).

57

Suor Venuta (Benvenuta)
di Madonna Diambre

Dormitory, San Damiano (Friday Evening, August 8, 1253)

Leaning against the back wall of the dormitory of San Damiano, Suor Benvenuta di Madonna Diambre struggled against wakefulness. She had been mulling over the events of yesterday—the aristocratic, stooped Pope Innocenzo IV had heard Chiara's confession and the provincial of the brothers had administered the Eucharist to her. They had been part of a steady stream of cardinals, priests, and friars who had visited the dying woman. After Lord Pope's departure, Chiara had spoken joyously to her sisters. "My daughters, praise God because heaven and earth are not enough for such a benefit I have received from God. Today I have received Him in the Blessed Sacrament and I have also seen His Vicar."

Ow! Benvenuta, whom everyone called Venuta, pushed her aching shoulders against the wall. How long had she been dozing? Here around Chiara's bed were the other Poor Sisters, some lying in tired heaps, others sitting bleary-eyed and half awake, a few sobbing. Many sisters were too ill with grief to taste food. No one seemed able to do any decent work. Only prayer went on as usual, broken by sobs and by voices cracked with sorrow.

Chiara had asked for three things.

First, that Suor Benedetta would return to San Damiano to become abbess. Venuta didn't know Benedetta very well. Even before Venuta had entered San Damiano thirty years ago, Benedetta had been often away, establishing other monasteries. The older sisters said she'd been Chiara's childhood friend named Ginevra.

Benedetta had arrived, an answer to Chiara's first prayer. Chiara had made her abbess.

Then Chiara had requested that her blood sister Agnese be summoned from Florence so that she could be with Chiara when she died.

Agnese, accompanied by a few of her extern sisters, had returned to share precious moments with Chiara and Beatrice. Second prayer answered.

Finally, Chiara had prayed that, before she died, she would receive in her hands her Form of Life approved by Lord Pope.

Yesterday, Lord Pope had left, promising again to look at the Form of Life. God would have to act quickly if this third prayer were to be answered.

Now Venuta was fully awake. *Ow!* Aging! As she wiggled her once-stately body into a more erect position, sharp pains shot through her back, shoulders, and thighs. A good stretch would ease the cramps.

But nothing could ease her crushing grief. She'd felt varying degrees of mournful exhaustion whenever one of the sisters died—Ortulana, Egidia, Giovanna, Illuminata, Felicita, others. She had wept when her parents had died—Papà a few years after she'd entered San Damiano, and Mamma not very long ago. She'd felt overwhelming anguish when, a few years after Papà's death, her brother Pietro's home had been burnt with him in it because he wouldn't sell his inheritance.

Worse than any of these tragedies was Chiara's impending death, for Chiara's faith and compassion had carried Venuta through her other losses. Who would carry Venuta through this?

"O Lord, may You who have created me be blessed." Chiara's whisper trailed off even as her lips continued to move. How did she have strength to speak, having eaten nothing for the past two weeks?

Chiara was saying something about the Trinity. Venuta couldn't quite make out the words. She spied a small space on the floor next to Pacifica, between Andrea's pallet and Chiara's. Maybe she'd move there.

"You have a good memory. Remember well what the Lady says."

That was Filippa. She was swabbing Chiara's forehead with a damp cloth.

She's not talking to me, is she? Venuta wondered.

"You will only remember these things I now say," Chiara was whispering, "as long as He who made me say them permits you. Remember, instead, the Passion of our Lord. This is Friday, on which we are bound to contemplate Him Who endured the suffering of the cross for us all, delivering us from the power of the prince of darkness to which we had been enslaved by the disobedience of our first parent, thus reconciling us to God the Father." Chiara's voice faded. Her blue eyes closed. Her breathing grew shallow.

"Sister!" Agnese, seated next to Pacifica, threw herself over Chiara's chest, weeping. Beatrice lightly kissed her hollow cheek.

"Oh, sister, do not abandon us!" Agnese sobbed. "How can I go on without you?"

Chiara's eyes opened. "It is pleasing to God that I depart. But stop crying, because you will come to the Lord a short time after me. And the Lord will console you greatly after I have left you."

Venuta forced back a fresh volley of tears. Agnese, too, would shortly die?

Chiara's eyes closed. Her whispered, unintelligible words faded.

Benedetta, who was kneeling directly across from Pacifica, lifted Chiara's hand and tapped it lightly. No response. Benedetta shook the hand more vigorously. Nothing.

"Suor Chiara!"

Benedetta looked from one sister to the next.

"She is insensible."

Venuta shuddered. Insensibility often came shortly before death.

"Let us pray, sisters, and keep vigil," Benedetta said, placing Chiara's hand on her hollow chest.

The evening wore on. Chiara continued, immovable. Someone rang the bell for Compline. Amata remained with Chiara while Venuta and the others filed downstairs to pray.

When the sisters returned, they found Amata wide-eyed. "You had been gone but a few moments," Amata said excitedly, "when she opened her eyes and looked straight past me up there." Amata pointed to the upper corner of the dormitory. "She smiled and asked, 'Did you see the King of Glory whom I saw?' I saw nothing. She asked me a few more times, 'Did you see the King of Glory whom I saw?' Then she closed her eyes and became insensible again."

Venuta was trying to think this through as she sat on the floor at the outer rim of the sisters gathering around the bed. Chiara had seen Jesus? It sounded like that.

She heard a faint voice. "Go in peace, because you will have a good escort..." Chiara was speaking, softly but clearly. "The One Who created you has already provided for you by being holy. The One Who created you has infused the Holy Spirit in you and guarded you as a mother does her littlest child."

Chiara's eyes were closed, her dry, cracked lips moving ever so imperceptibly.

"Sister," Anastasia asked, taking Chiara's thin right hand, "to whom are you speaking?"

"I am speaking to my blessed soul."

Chiara's voice faded to silence, and she lay as if dead. Then a little breath, a little wheeze, and life continued.

How good and holy Chiara was! God had been so good to bring Venuta here, where Chiara had taught her three lessons that were all one ever needed to learn. To love God. To recognize and confess one's own sinfulness. To follow Christ wherever He led.

Venuta's eyes brimmed with love and gratitude. She thought of the heavenly court preparing for Chiara's coming, of the Blessed Mother gathering some of her own garments to clothe this new saint.

Light bursting through the door startled Venuta. Who had lowered the staircase for these women, each dressed in white and crowned with gold and jewels? Silently the regal, virginal women slipped in among the sisters, but no one but Venuta seemed aware of them.

The tallest woman, who had entered first, held back, watching the others. That woman's gown was more radiant, her face more beautiful than any Venuta had ever seen. She wore a larger, more brilliant crown than the others, above which shimmered a golden thurible, such as a priest might use in a great cathedral to burn incense.

The virginal queen now approached Chiara, the other women moving aside for her. How tenderly, with the help of the other women, did she drape a narrow length of cloth around Chiara's shoulders and across her body! Why, the cloth was a pallium, so fine that Venuta could see Chiara through it. How wondrous! As Lord Pope would embrace an archbishop whom he had just clothed with the pallium as a sign of unity with the Church and the Holy See, so the queen bent over Chiara's breast as if to embrace her. The two women seemed to merge, and then the queen, virgins, pallium, and light were gone.

Venuta was totally awake. She had been totally awake during the entire vision. The praises in honor of the holy virtues, written by San Francesco, flooded Venuta's mind. She couldn't remember the words exactly, but she remembered the important things. *Hail, Queen Wisdom! Hail her Sisters! Simplicity. Poverty. Humility. Charity. Obedience. All the Holy Virtues.*

Had she seen Queen Wisdom, the Mother of Him through Whom all virtues come? Had she seen the personified virtues accompany her, for surely the Blessed Mother was the paragon of all of them? The queen had clothed Chiara as one solidly in union with Christ and His Church. The virtuous women had been in attendance, for Chiara had so perfectly nurtured every virtue. How could Venuta speak of such a vision?

NOTES

Fortini discusses Venuta's family history (350).

Chiara's words in this chapter are taken directly from the histories describing her death: CA:ED 160 (her joyful words following the pope's visit); CA:ED 160 ("O, Lord, may you who have created me . . ."); CA:ED 160 ("You will only remember these things . . ."); CA:ED 315 (her words to Agnese); CA:ED 166 ("Did you see the King of Glory . . . ?"); and CA:ED 181 ("Go in peace . . .").

"The whole night of that day during which she passed from this life, she admonished her sisters by preaching to them" (CA:ED 160). Her preaching was unrecorded. Since this was a Friday, and since Chiara spent every Friday in meditation on the Passion (CA:ED 160), the author has used her words about the Passion (CA:ED 45) as a possible sample of this preaching.

Venuta experienced the vision described (CA:ED 181–82), but whether she recalled Francesco's words about the virtues (FA:ED I 164–65) is conjecture. She told no one of her vision until asked to testify to Chiara's holiness (CA:ED 182).

58

Pope Innocenzo IV

*Convent at the Basilica di San Francesco, Assisi
(Early Morning, Saturday, August 9, 1253)*

Pope Innocenzo IV sat bolt upright in the plush, curtain-draped bed in his private quarters at the convent at the Basilica di San Francesco in Assisi. In a faint glow seeping through open windows, he saw his white overshirt and slipped into it.

An internal pressure had awakened him. APPROVE THE FORM OF LIFE.

Couldn't it wait until dawn?

The pressure was insistent. APPROVE IT.

Innocenzo didn't operate that way, listening to inner promptings. Sì, Cardinal Rinaldo had approved the Form of Life last year. But Innocenzo wasn't comfortable with it. A year ago or longer, while he was in Perugia, a friar had brought him the document. He hadn't had the time to ponder it.

Pope Gregorio IX had died in 1241. His successor—old, ill Cardinal Goffredo da Castiglione, Bishop of Sabina, who had taken the name Celestino IV—had died seventeen days after being elected. Intrigues of Federico II and dissension among the cardinals had delayed the next papal election until 1243 when Innocenzo, the former Sinibaldo Fieschi, son of Count Ugo of Lavagna, had been chosen. Innocenzo considered himself generous, even magnanimous. He always tried to believe the best of everyone. Nevertheless, he'd experienced

Federico's treacheries. Eventually he had excommunicated the emperor, had warred against him, and had fled from him to Lyons.

Federico's death in 1250 had brought no respite. The ruler's excommunicated twenty-five-year-old son, King Corrado, had subdued every city in the lower peninsula except Naples, which was currently under siege. Innocenzo's attempt to offer this kingdom of Apulia, Sicily, and Calabria to Richard, the Earl of Cornwall and brother of England's King Henry III, had been refused. Now he was attempting to make the same offer to Charles of Anjou, the youngest brother of the saintly French King Louis IX.

Besides these matters, Innocenzo was enmeshed in additional worldly concerns: battling heresy, converting the Tartars, raising money, forging alliances, providing for relatives, and sending ambassadors to various potentates—some of whom were Federico II's other crafty, power-hungry sons. In every matter, Innocenzo based his decisions on logic and strategy—backed up, of course, by prayer. Yet two days ago he had visited Chiara, whose decisions were based on prayerful, intuitive following of the Spirit's promptings. He couldn't rule on intuitions and inner proddings, could he? Or should he?

Where was that candlestick? As he reached for it, he knocked it over. The golden candlestand bumped along the floor.

"Messer, is something wrong?"

"What is it, Lord Pope?"

The racket had awakened two aides who slept, keeping guard, on the floor near his bed.

"I need a light," Innocenzo said a bit too gruffly.

"Sì, Lord Pope."

In the blackness, the men scuffled. The door opened, and light from the lamplit corridor flooded in. An aide scooted into the hall with the candlestick and quickly returned with a lit taper.

"Put the candle on my desk," Innocenzo directed, easing into the desk chair.

Candlelight flooded the desk as Innocenzo planted his bare feet on the floor. "Grazie. Go back to sleep. I have work to complete."

The men lay down on their straw mats. Even before Innocenzo found the *Form of Life* among the parchments piled into baskets near his desk, the two men were snoring softly.

Innocenzo unrolled the sheets of parchment and began to read the fine Latin handwriting.

"The Form of Life of the Order of the Poor Sisters that Blessed Francis established is this: to observe the Holy Gospel of our Lord Jesus Christ, by living in obedience, without anything of one's own, and in chastity."

He read on. Chiara promised, for herself and all her sisters forever, "obedience and reverence to the Lord Pope Innocent and his successors canonically elected, and to the Roman Church."

Absentmindedly, Innocenzo stroked his thick white beard, cleft in the center. His gaze moved down the first parchment. All the sisters were to consent to admitting newcomers, who, if they agreed with the Form of Life, were to sell their goods if possible and distribute the money to the poor, then enter the monastery, tonsured and with but three tunics and a mantle, there to remain for a year's formation—after which they would "be received into obedience, promising to observe perpetually the life and form of our poverty."

Poverty. That was the problem. Innocenzo ran his hand across his bald scalp and down to the halo of thick white hair that ringed his head. Poverty of goods, possessions, spirit. In early May, just a few weeks after moving to Assisi to prepare for the dedication of the Upper Basilica di San Francesco, he had visited Chiara. She had been weak but eating. Two days ago, he'd visited her again, blessing her and her sisters but noting that she'd been unable to eat for two weeks. She had, however, that very day, already received the Eucharist from the provincial minister of the friars.

Completely at peace, Chiara had kissed Innocenzo's hand when he offered it and then asked to kiss his foot as well. He had removed his right riding boot and she had kissed, with lips that felt like parchment, first the upper part of his foot and then his sole. With radiant but tired blue eyes, she had gazed at him in gratitude. Embarrassed, Innocenzo had realized that she was honoring Christ in his person.

That was poverty. Poverty of spirit that died to one's own will by living in God's will. Every moment was either a doing of one's own will or a dying to it, Innocenzo thought.

Chiara had asked Innocenzo to absolve her of her sins. Startled by her humility, he had blurted out, "Would that my need of pardon were such as

yours!" Then, dismissing the sisters clustered like chicks around her bed, he had
heard Chiara's confession. Such sorrow for such slight faults! How deeply
Chiara loved God and how fully she sensed His holiness! He had granted her
the gift of perfect absolution and gave her his fullest blessing.

Only then did Chiara ask him, as she had asked in May, to approve her
Form of Life and the privilege of poverty. What a request! No pope had ever
approved a Form of Life written by a woman! Innocenzo's approval would mean
the Church's—Christ's—approval. He paged through the parchments, looking
for troubling passages.

> No heavy debt may be incurred except with the common consent of the sisters
> and by reason of manifest necessity, and let this be done through the procura-
> tor. Let the Abbess and her sisters, however, be careful that nothing is deposited
> in the monastery, for such practices often give rise to troubles and scandals.

That must mean, Innocenzo reasoned, that the monastery was not to
become a place for benefactors to store possessions. That made sense.

> ... by not receiving or having possession or ownership either of themselves or
> through an intermediary, or even anything that might reasonably be called
> ownership, except as much land as necessity requires for the integrity and
> proper seclusion of the monastery ...

So the women didn't want to own anything. He already knew that. But they
wanted to ensure that their monastery's protective grounds couldn't whimsi-
cally be decreased. For their privacy, that was sensible.

> Let the sisters not appropriate anything, neither a house nor a place nor any-
> thing at all; instead, as pilgrims and strangers in this world who serve the Lord
> in poverty and humility, let them confidently send for alms ...

And suppose no one gave them alms? Or not enough? There was that poverty again. That sort of poverty was not sensible.

Innocenzo had dealt with popes beginning with Onorio III, who had summoned him to Rome to be in his service. Then, in 1227, Pope Gregorio IX had
made the then-Sinibaldo cardinal-priest of San Lorenzo in Lucina. Innocenzo
knew Gregorio's concerns about poverty regarding the followers of Francesco
and Chiara. While San Francesco's ordine was mitigating some of its founder's

dictates, Chiara was holding to her original ideals. How could Innocenzo approve her Form of Life? Poverty for enclosed women was illogical. Yet one of the sisters had hinted that Chiara had begged God not to let her die until after she had received such approval.

I can't keep someone from dying, Innocenzo mentally reminded God.

BUT I CAN. The thought discomfited him. Then, again, that insistent command. APPROVE THE FORM OF LIFE, INNOCENZO.

He fingered the parchment. *I disagree with it!*

YOU NEED NOT AGREE. YOU NEED ONLY OBEY. Would God actually say something like this?

This is not logical! Innocenzo protested.

DOESN'T MY LOGIC SUPERSEDE YOURS?

Oh, goodness! Quickly he made the sign of the cross. Swiftly an image came to mind. Jesus, smiling indulgently at him.

All right. He would read it again, try to agree with it. Here. Chiara was discussing the election of an abbess.

> Let her also strive to preside over the others more by her virtues and holy behavior than by her office, so that, moved by her example, the sisters may obey her more out of love than out of fear. . . .
>
> Let her console the afflicted. Let her also be the last refuge for those who are troubled. . . .

He kept reading. About weekly chapter meetings, where the sisters would confess their faults and consult together on the running of the monastery. Recitation of the Divine Office, continual fast except for Christmas and Sundays. Confession twelve times yearly. Silence from the hour of Compline until Terce. Care of the grill and parlor. Work inside the monastery. Serving sisters. Care of the sick. Who may enter the monastery. Correction of and penances for sisters who sin. Custody of the monastery door. Regulations regarding the visitator, chaplain, cardinal protector, and those outsiders who must do work inside the monastery. Then, Chiara's final words, just above Rinaldo's approval:

> Let the sisters be strictly bound always to have as our Governor, Protector, and Corrector that Cardinal of the Holy Roman Church who has been delegated

by Lord Pope for the Lesser Brothers, so that, always submissive and subject at the feet of that same holy Church and steadfast in the Catholic faith, we may observe in perpetuity the poverty and humility of our Lord Jesus Christ and of His most holy Mother and the holy Gospel we have firmly promised. Amen.

If I approve this and they starve . . .

THEY SHALL NOT STARVE.

Lord, they will have nothing.

EXCEPT ME.

Innocenzo sank back in his chair.

I don't like doing things this way.

WHOSE WILL SHALL BE DONE, INNOCENZO? MINE? OR YOURS?

His. It had to be His will.

From the bell tower in the basilica came a sharp tolling. Time for the Office of Lauds already? Indeed, dawn was pinking the sky. Quickly, Innocenzo summoned his aides, dressed, and hurried to the choir to pray the first Office of the day with the friars. When he returned, he sent for his secretary, asking him to bring a large, fresh parchment.

"Write small," Innocenzo told the clerk, a young priest himself. "I'm going to issue a bull that will precede all of this." Innocenzo flipped through Chiara's parchments so the clerk could estimate the length of the text. "You must put the bull and all this text on a single parchment."

Nodding, the clerk sat at Innocenzo's desk and took up a reed pen. Incredulous at what he was doing, Innocenzo began to dictate in Latin. "Innocent, Bishop, Servant of the servants of God, to his beloved daughters in Christ, Clare, Abbess, and the other sisters of the monastery of San Damiano in Assisi, health and apostolic blessing." He continued to dictate at a measured pace. "We confirm by Our Apostolic authority the form of life that Blessed Francis gave you and which you have freely accepted." He dictated a few more lines, then handed the young man the Form of Life, which was prefaced and concluded with Rinaldo's approval.

IT MUST ALL BE COPIED TODAY.

Inside, Innocenzo moaned. "It must be done today."

"Lord Pope, it would take at least two days to write all this well."

"Today. All of it."

"But I cannot write neatly if I write that quickly."

"It is more important that it be finished than that it be neat."

"Sì, Lord Pope."

"Take this to your quarters and begin at once. As soon as you complete it, beckon me, even if it's the middle of the night."

And it was almost the middle of the night when an aide awakened Innocenzo and beckoned him to the scribe's room. The clerk was sitting, hunched and bleary-eyed, at his desk. Innocenzo glanced over the parchment, written straight across in neat rows that grew more smudged with ink blots toward the bottom.

"It's messy, Lord Pope. I was growing so tired."

Innocenzo patted the young man's back. "It's fine. Would you write just a bit more at the very bottom, please?" He began to dictate. The young man stretched his fingers and began to write.

"Therefore, no one is permitted to destroy this document of our confirmation or oppose it recklessly. If anyone shall presume to attempt this, let him know he will incur the wrath of Almighty God and His holy Apostles Peter and Paul. Given at Assisi, the fifth of the Ides of August, in the eleventh year of our Pontificate." He smiled. "That's all," Innocenzo said. "You've done well. Go and have something to eat. Then you may go to bed."

With a grateful bow, the clerk left. In the stillness, Innocenzo began to reflect on what he had done. Had he really issued the bull? How would people respond to his approving a Form of Life written by a woman? And such a Form of Life, with its insistence on highest poverty! He hadn't yet affixed his papal seal. Without it, the document was invalid. But even with his seal, some would question his decision.

Your decision, Innocenzo mentally told his God.

He could counter questions before they arose. Taking the reed pen, Innocenzo began to write, in his small, cramped style, in the left-hand corner of the upper margin. "So be it! S." The S was the initial of his name, Sinibaldo. And then, as an afterthought, he added below it, "For reasons known to me and the protector of the monastery, so be it!"

Taking a deep breath, Innocenzo looked at what he had written. He could burn this Form of Life. Or he could affix the papal seal to it and send the document to San Damiano.

Can't I have a day to think about it?

He sensed Jesus smiling at him. YOU CAN HAVE TONIGHT.

Of course. It was already dark. No one was going anywhere tonight. He could still change his mind. Tomorrow.

NOTES

Innocenzo, who was lodging with the friars at the Basilica di San Francesco, visited Chiara twice during her final illness, the last time being "a few days before her death" (CA:ED 160, 314–15). The parchment on which the papal bull was issued is described accurately—all Poor Clare monasteries have received reproductions of the original, now kept in Assisi. Several scholars reason that the smudges and blots on the *Form of Life* indicate that it was copied hastily. The parchment(s) on which Chiara wrote her *Form of Life* to send to Innocenzo IV have not been preserved. This chapter accurately reproduces some of Chiara's words from this document.

The physical description of Innocenzo IV is taken from historical artwork portraying him. We do not know the mental process by which he approved Chiara's *Form of Life*.

59

Suor Beatrice di Favarone di Offreduccio

Dormitory, San Damiano (Sunday, August 10, 1253)

Suor Beatrice di Favarone sat on the floor next to Chiara's pallet, her head pillowed on her wide hands, Chiara's shallow breathing purring in Beatrice's ear. Beatrice was half asleep, her stocky body tired with waiting and grief. She had seen Papà die, gored by that boar. Mamma die, suddenly struck by an illness that left her unable to speak or move. Friends, relatives, monastery benefactors—so many dead. She knew more people, she thought, who had died than who were still alive. Now Chiara.

Chiara had eaten nothing for sixteen days. She had been unconscious for nearly twenty-four hours until emerging from it yesterday. Today she seemed stronger, but, often just before the end, the body rallied in a frantic, futile effort to live. Death had to be near.

Their blood sister Agnese would die soon, too, if Chiara's prophecy came true. Then Beatrice would die, the last of her immediate family, and the Favarone line of the Offreduccio clan would be gone.

"Pace e bene."

"Pace e bene."

The male voices startled her. When had the friars arrived? Could Beatrice be going deaf? Or had she been so sound asleep that she hadn't heard the ringing of the bell to announce the brothers' arrival?

Beatrice shook the dullness out of her head and smiled at the four men, seated across from her on Chiara's left. How time had flown!

Here was pale Fra Angelo da Rieti, one of San Francesco's constant escorts during the last years of his life. Lithe Angelo's body had grown so frail that it seemed poised to drift into the hereafter.

Dear, meek Fra Leone, still the pure, unpretentious priest. Strong and sturdy, he had accompanied Francesco even to his death. Now Leone was nearly bald, his big broad head hanging forward like that of an exhausted ox.

Small, lively, round-faced Fra Ginepro, whom Francesco praised for his simple humility, his blue eyes still bright but paler, the laugh lines under his eyes deepened with age.

Young, compassionate Rainaldo, who had never known San Francesco, his thick brown beard streaked vertically and horizontally with auburn in the shape of a faint cross, his dark eyes sparkling like a fox's.

How old her family had grown! Once, they had been young like Rainaldo. How long had it been since Chiara had left home to join Francesco? She counted backwards. Forty-one years. Longer than many people live. So many of those who were amazed by Chiara's bold move were clustered about her now. She and her sister Agnese, then called Catarina. Balvina and Amata di Martino. Benedetta, named Ginevra forty-three years ago. Benvenuta di Peroscia. Filippa. Pacifica. Cristiana di Bernardo da Suppo. How could any one of them—how could Chiara—have foreseen what would be? Monasteries of the Poor Sisters now thrived throughout the world. How many monasteries were to come? How long would the Poor Sisters exist? Perhaps, Beatrice shivered with delight, until the end of time? All because of Chiara's "sì" to God.

"Sì" to the living that brought them together and sustained them daily. "Sì" to the dying that would separate them for a time. "Sì" to eternity, where they would be together to praise the God of "sì."

Rainaldo's words broke into Beatrice's musing. "Dear Madonna Chiara, how difficult this prolonged torture must be for you! You must try to be patient during this serious illness, because God will grant you reward because of it."

Chiara laughed weakly. "After I once came to know the grace of my Lord Jesus Christ through his servant Francesco, no pain has been bothersome, no penance too severe; no weakness, dearly beloved brother, has been hard."

"How right you are!" Ginepro agreed. "You have learned what I did when I determined not to speak."

Beatrice smiled to herself. *Here comes that story,* she thought. Poor good-natured Fra Ginepro! He'd grown so absentminded that he repeated himself over and over. The sisters humored him, listening politely as if they were hearing the story for the first time. Ginepro went on to tell how he had decided to keep silent, years ago, for his tongue was his greatest occasion of sin. But how to do it?

"I determined that the first day I would keep silent for love of the heavenly Father. And the second day for the love of Jesus."

Ginepro looked from one sister to the other as he spoke. "The next day for love of the Holy Spirit. And then for the love of the Virgin Mother. And then for love of holy San Francesco, and so on. There are a great many saints," Ginepro noted, nodding wisely, "so I found no difficulty in keeping silent for a different one each day. But one day someone said something—I can't recall now what it was—but, oh, did it anger me! I tried and tried to be quiet," Ginepro explained, squeezing shut his eyes and crinkling his nose, "but it was so difficult. I was putting so much effort into saying nothing that I thought my tongue would jump out of my mouth! Then something popped in my chest and I felt this big rush of blood in my mouth. I was so angry that I spat it out and marched right into the church before the crucifix."

Ginepro put his hands on his hips. "I looked up at our crucified Lord and I said, 'See, my Lord, what I am bearing for love of You.' And then," Ginepro's voice grew soft with wonder, "the Crucified Christ raised His arm from the wood of the cross—although His hand was nailed there, He raised His arm from the nail—and He laid His hand on the wound in His side and He said, very quietly, 'And I, what am I bearing for you?'"

Ginepro hip-hopped from one foot to the other. "I was another man after that. Indeed, not making light of your sufferings, Madonna Chiara, but all we bear in no way compares with the sufferings of our Lord."

"Ah, you are so right," Chiara said with a weak smile. "Your stories always warm our spirits. What else can you share today about the Lord?"

"His Passion, Madonna. Did you not call us to recite His Passion to you and passages of Scripture?"

"Oh, how I wish to hear those!"

From a deep pocket in his tunic, Leone pulled a small, worn volume. Carefully paging through it, he began to read of Jesus at the Last Supper: "And when the hour came, he sat at table, and the apostles with him. And he said to them, 'I have earnestly desired to eat this passover with you before I suffer . . .'" In his rich, gentle voice, Leone slowly read the entire Passion, ending with the burial and resurrection of the Lord.

As Leone closed the book, Angelo turned to Chiara, his large, deep-set eyes glistening with tears. "When good San Francesco was dying," Angelo recalled, his thin voice tremulous, "he asked us to sing 'The Praises of the Lord.' That strengthened him. Would you like us to sing it for you?"

"Oh, sì!"

Leone and Angelo glanced at each other. As one, they began to sing:

"Most High, all-powerful, good Lord, Yours are the praises, the glory, the honor, and all blessing. To You alone, Most High, do they belong, and no one is worthy to mention Your name . . ."

The friars sang on, their voices a bit shaky, until they came to the end:

"Blessed are those whom death will find in Your most holy will, for the second death shall do them no harm."

Their voices swelled with new vigor. *They are singing our faith,* Beatrice realized.

"Praise and bless my Lord and give Him thanks and serve Him with great humility."

The words faded. Silence. Through her tears, Beatrice could see Leone kissing the litter on which Chiara lay and Agnese embracing her and sobbing.

"Truly I can rejoice," Chiara's voice, surprisingly strong, swelled above the grief, "and no one can rob me of such joy, since having at last what under heaven I have desired," she smiled weakly, "that incomparable treasure hidden in the field . . ." Her voice trailed off and Beatrice could not understand what followed. Then she spoke again, in a stronger tone, "Who is there, then, who would not encourage me to rejoice over such marvelous joys?" She beckoned to Benedetta. "Whose feast is today, sister?"

"Saint Lawrence's, the patron of Perugia," Benedetta answered.

"Let us ask Saint Lawrence to intercede for us before the throne of Christ, that the Holy Father might approve our Form of Life." Every day, Chiara asked that day's saint for the same intention. At every Office of Compline, the sisters entreated the day's saint for just such a favor.

The bell rang at the speaking grill. Suor Anna went to answer.

"We must hold to poverty, sisters." How often during this illness had Chiara told them this! "May you cling to His most sweet mother who gave birth to a Son Whom the heavens could not contain, and yet she carried Him in the little cloister of her holy womb." She was smiling again, propped up in bed as she looked from one sister to the next. "So you, too, by following in her footprints, especially those of humility and poverty, can, without any doubt, always carry Him spiritually in your chaste and virginal body." She paused.

"As a poor virgin, embrace the poor Christ."

"Pace e bene," a strange friar said, drawing close to Chiara's bed, Suor Anna beside him. "Lord Pope Innocenzo has sent me to you with this."

The friar handed Chiara a rolled parchment, sealed with the wax seal of Lord Pope.

Chiara's trembling hands fumbled with the seal. "I cannot break this." The words quaked. "Suor Benedetta . . ."

With strong, steady hands, Benedetta broke the seal. She unrolled the document and held it so that Chiara might read it. Beatrice could see Chiara's eyes widening, filling with tears, a radiance spreading across her face. With feeble hands, Chiara reached for the parchment and Benedetta released it into her grasp. The paper rolled itself into a scroll. With great effort, Chiara brought the roll to her lips and kissed it.

"It's a papal bull," Chiara whispered in awe. "Lord Pope has approved our Form of Life and the privilege of highest poverty."

Gasps. Cries of "God be praised!" and "Grazie!" rang out.

"Quick!" Chiara said. "Those of us who cannot rise from our beds must thank God here. The rest of you go into the oratory and fall on your faces before the Lord to thank Him for this wondrous grace. Thank as well all the saints to whom we have prayed. And beseech God's favor upon Lord Pope, who has granted our request."

NOTES

The account of Chiara's death follows the historical record (CA:ED 162, 316–17). We don't have the exact words she used when "she recalled in a praising way the divine blessings while entrusting them [her weeping daughters] with the poverty of the Lord" (CA:ED 316). Her words are taken from her writing: CA:ED 50–51 ("Truly I can rejoice . . ."); CA:ED 51–52 ("May you cling . . ."); and CA:ED 49 ("As a poor virgin . . .").

Angelo is generally assumed to be Angelo da Rieti, although he is not so identified in the stories about Chiara. Fra Ginepro and Leone were early companions of Francesco. No background information exists on Fra Rainaldo.

There is no record that Chiara heard "The Praises of the Lord" on her deathbed.

No record exists of Ortulana's death, although it seems to have occurred before June 8, 1238, since her name is not on a document signed at that time by all the San Damiano sisters (CA:ED 429–30).

Fra Ginepro's stories, including the one about keeping silence, are told in *The Little Flowers of Saint Francis*.

The number of Damianite monasteries at Chiara's death was 147.

The passage Leone reads is Luke 22:14–15, from Luke's account of the Passion of Christ.

60

Suor Agnese di Oportulo di Bernardo

Dormitory, San Damiano (Monday, August 11, 1253)

Suor Agnese di Oportulo di Bernardo was growing accustomed to sleeping sitting up. She had awakened next to Chiara's bed, her lank body more rested than it had been for days. Today in Assisi there would be merry-making, dancing and music, processions and prayers—especially in the church of its patron saint, Saint Rufinus. Perhaps he would cure someone, as he often did on his feast. Chiara, perhaps?

Suor Pacifica was kneeling by Chiara's head, pressing a moist cloth to Chiara's parched lips.

"Sisters, are you here?" Chiara asked weakly, the parchment still clutched in her hands.

"Sì, sister."

"Is Fra Leone here?"

"Sì, Madonna," Leone answered. "Fra Angelo is with me." Keeping vigil.

Chiara's eyes were closed, her voice faint. "My sisters, my brothers, I wish to confess to you all my sins and faults."

A tremor of holy awe passed over Agnese. The sisters always confessed when they sensed that the end was near.

"Fra Leone, please hear my confession. Sisters, would you help me to bless myself?"

Beatrice took Chiara's right hand in hers and guided it through the sign of the cross while Chiara prayed. "I wish to confess all the sins of my past life, Fra Leone. I confess any harshness in the correction of my sisters. All misunderstanding. Times I overworked the sisters. Insensitivity to their pain. To their weakness. Any judgmental attitudes."

Agnese was awed by Chiara's long list of possible offenses, including those that she might have committed as a child or young woman. The list was thorough, yet Agnese could see very few of the failings in Chiara.

"So for all of these, and for all those I have forgotten, I am sorry. May God forgive me, and may you, my sisters and brothers, forgive me as well."

Leone pronounced absolution and gave her a few prayers to say. She prayed them quietly, reverently. He blessed her again, then administered the sacrament of the dying.

"Pray for me, my sisters and brothers," Chiara said softly. "Praise the Lord always. Remember His Passion." She paused. "Sisters," Chiara's voice was faint, her words spoken slowly, "I bless you during my life and after my death, as I am able, out of all the blessings with which the Father of mercies has blessed and will bless His sons and daughters in heaven and on earth . . . and a spiritual father and mother have blessed and will bless their sons and daughters. Amen."

"Amen," the sisters softly echoed.

"Always be lovers of your souls . . . and those of all your sisters," Chiara whispered. "And may you always be eager to observe . . . what you have promised the Lord. . . . May the Lord . . . always be with you." The words seemed to be struggling to emerge from Chiara's parched lips: "And may . . . you always . . . be . . . with Him. . . . Amen."

"Amen," the sisters prayed.

The blessing seemed to have sapped Chiara's strength. She lay still, her breath shallow and intermittent.

Pray the Prayer of the Five Wounds.

It took only the simplest interior prompting to have Agnese pray one of her favorite prayers. She began to pray softly.

LOUDER.

Agnese raised her voice so that Chiara could hear the prayer that she loved and that she frequently, perhaps daily, prayed.

"O Lord Jesus Christ, praise and glory to You for the most sacred wound in Your right hand."

The sisters joined in. Angelo. Leone. Ginepro. Many sobbed out the words. "Because of this sacred wound, grant me the pardon of all the sins I have committed by thought, word, deed, and by omission. Give me the grace to venerate Your most precious death and these Your sacred wounds worthily; and grant that by Your help I may mortify my body and be able to thank You for this great gift, You who live and reign forever. Amen."

Together they all recited the Our Father and the Hail Mary, then began the prayer of the wound of the left hand. They proceeded to the two wounds in the feet and to that in Christ's side. While they prayed, Chiara softly repeated some of the Passion and, every so often, breathed out "Jesus, Lord Jesus," as if riding out a spasm of pain.

"Five wounds of God," Agnese said.

"Be my medicine," the sisters responded.

"By Your five wounds," Agnese intoned.

"Free me, Christ, from my falls."

"Give me peace, O Christ."

"By Your five wounds."

"Let us pray. All-powerful, eternal God, You Who redeemed the human race in the five wounds of Your Son, our Lord Jesus Christ, because of His precious blood, allow those who venerate those wounds each day to escape a sudden and eternal death. Through the same Christ the Lord."

"Amen," Chiara whispered. "Precious . . . in the sight of the Lord . . . is the death . . . of His holy ones."

Agnese began again to say the Prayer of the Five Wounds. She had reached the wound in the side of Christ when she felt a hand resting lightly on her arm. Benedetta, reaching across Chiara's chest.

"Your prayers have given her comfort, sister." Benedetta glanced at Chiara. "She is peacefully gone."

NOTES

No record has been kept of the sins that Chiara confessed. Since Leone and Angelo were with her when she was dying, she may have confessed to Leone, who was a priest.

What words Chiara used to bless her sisters are unknown. Her blessing in this chapter is taken from her written blessing (CA:ED 67).

While Chiara was dying, Agnese, either silently or aloud, prayed the *Prayer of the Five Wounds* (text of this prayer CA:ED 422–24) and remembered Chiara's final words, "Precious in the sight of the Lord . . ." (CA:ED 180).

PART FOURTEEN

The Blessing of the Lord!

61

Iacobello

Bridge outside Narni, Italy (Early Autumn 1253)

The light came slowly, as if the moon were rising. The misty light widened. Iacobello saw leaves drifting. Red. Brown. Yellow. Green. He was dreaming. For the past twelve years, the only time that blind Iacobello could see was in his dreams.

A shadow appeared, became a figure approaching him through the falling leaves.

A beggarwoman, her step firm, her posture straight. He could see her finely patched, rough gray tunic, cinched at her waist with a three-knotted rope that bumped her skirt as she walked soundlessly through the dry leaves. A breeze billowed her thin black veil away from her face, revealing the veil's white lining. The woman's oval face was ageless. She could have been twenty-five years old, like Iacobello. She could have been sixty. The woman's face and tunic were immaculately clean, so unlike a beggar.

Iacobello could see the faint smile on the woman's face, her blue eyes bright with love. Many years ago, Iacobello had seen that look of love on the faces of young noblewomen who came into his master's candlestick shop. The women would ask his master questions about his silver. They would lightly finger the wares, telling of their beloved nobles for whom they wanted to purchase precious silver gifts.

This beggarwoman could have no money. Yet she was noble, regal, serene. "Who are you?" he called out in his dream.

The woman smiled more widely, the smile spreading up to the high cheekbones that emphasized her deep blue eyes. She was so close that Iacobello could smell on her garments the sweet, heavy incense of churches on holy days.

Bending toward Iacobello, the woman gently invited, "Iacobello, why don't you come to me in Assisi and be cured?"

Iacobello awoke with a start. His blind eyes strained into the blackness. Off to his right a river gurgled and splashed. A dry leaf fell against his brow. Near his feet wheezed the measured breathing of the boy Pasquale, who led Iacobello about. A short distance away, two other beggars snorted in their slumber.

Come to Assisi and be cured? Iacobello thought of his arm and his head. Just a few weeks ago, Pasquale, leaving Iacobello at the gates, had entered Terni to beg. That night the boy didn't return. The next morning, when the gates opened, Iacobello had felt his way into Terni, seeking the lad.

Suddenly, swiftly, Iacobello had tripped, bashing his forehead against a rock and breaking his arm. A kind knight had paid a doctor to set his arm and bandage his head and had sent a servant to search for Pasquale, who had become confused by the city and been locked in.

Iacobello's splinted arm now hurt very little. In two weeks, the doctor said, he could remove the splint. The wound on his forehead was nearly healed. Iacobello had removed the bandage a week ago. The beggarwoman couldn't mean that she would cure his arm and his head. They were already practically cured.

Could she mean his blindness?

Iacobello began to tremble. He had given up hope of seeing again. Now he hungered for sight. He wanted to see the river, the leaves, the moon and stars in the black sky. He wanted to shape candlesticks again, to marry, and to bring home his meager pay to a wife as he had brought it to his mother, dead these two years. His mother, who had persistently prayed that the slowly advancing blindness would be cured.

Why had he become blind? Because he had sinned? He remembered some harsh words, some laziness, a few lies, the stealing of two coins he'd secretly repaid. Would God blind him for those sins?

"Iacobello, why don't you come to me in Assisi and be cured?" What did the woman mean by that?

At dawn, when he heard the other beggars stirring awake, Iacobello told them of the noble beggar.

The beggars began to talk excitedly together.

"Assisi."

"Must be that nun. Madonna . . . Madonna . . ."

"Chiara."

"That's it. She died. In August. A saint, they say."

"Lord Pope wants to canonize her."

"Her tomb is honored by the Lord."

"A madman from France was cured there."

"A boy with a demon cured, too. And a cripple."

"Iacobello, you lucky fool. God wants to heal you at the tomb of the holy nun."

Iacobello's mind was reeling. A holy nun, a saint, had appeared to him. God wanted to heal him. Grappling for Pasquale, Iacobello shook the thin, lithe body awake.

"Pasquale! A holy nun wants to heal me! We must go to Assisi!"

All day they traveled and, as night fell, they were near Spoleto. Outside the city walls, they curled up for the night.

The vision came again.

"Iacobello, why don't you come to me in Assisi and be cured?"

The next day, Iacobello urged Pasquale to hurry so they might arrive in Assisi before dusk. Upon their arrival, they inquired where Madonna Chiara was buried and were directed to the Church of San Giorgio. Such a crowd pressed around the doors that Iacobello and Pasquale couldn't get in before the church doors were locked for the night, so they sat at the threshold to sleep.

Iacobello felt a hard lump under his hip. A stone—it would do for a pillow. His heart was pounding. He must get in! Around him he heard snoring and wheezing, but Iacobello was wide awake. He must get in.

Sounds faded. Haze appeared in his darkness. Iacobello saw huge carved doors that slowly opened into a church, into light where the noble beggar stood, smiling.

"The Lord will bless you, Iacobello, if you enter."

Iacobello awoke with a start. He heard a key in a lock. A creaking. The doors of the church were opening.

Iacobello jumped to his feet. The crowd began to surge forward, squeezing him backward. His anguish burst forth.

"Let me in," he shouted like a madman. "The holy nun promised to heal me if I can get in. For the love of God, let me in." His voice cracked into a sob. His face was wet with tears. "I want to see. Dear God, please let me in."

He felt the crowd shifting, felt himself being prodded and pushed. He felt for Pasquale's hand and found other hands, pulling him along, pushing him. Suddenly he was stumbling down a narrow flight of steps, bumping against bodies on the way.

"For the love of God, let me through," he kept pleading. "The nun said she would heal me." The tears were coming faster. The hands were pushing, leading.

"Grazie! Let me in. She promised to heal me."

The pushing stopped. Iacobello was thrust up against a wall. Someone grabbed his hand and stretched it forward. He felt rough, cold stone. He ran his hands along the slab and found a corner. Sides, bottom. A stone casket suspended on an iron grate.

The tomb.

His anguish escaped his lungs in a great sigh. A warmth engulfed him. His clothes seemed aflame. He was melting. He pulled off his mantle. His tunic. His shoes. His stockings. The coolness of the church swept over him, tingling.

Here he was, a sinner, at the tomb of this holy woman. The enormity of his sins swept over him. How could he have thought that little sins were permissible? Little blemishes marred a candlestick as little sins marred his soul. Noblewomen wanted perfection in silver wares; God desired perfection in souls. The holy nun had eradicated every sin from her life. Otherwise, people would not be calling her a saint.

How could he show her, show God, show these people that he was a sinner and that he was sorry?

The laces that had tied his stockings to his legs! Iacobello felt for them, found one. With deep repentance, he tied it about his neck as if it were a noose.

A little murmur shivered through the crowd at this common sign of penitence. Iacobello was kneeling, weeping. Seeing with his eyes did not seem so important now that he could see with his soul.

"I'm sorry, Lord. I'm sorry," he whispered over and over.

All those years, his mother had prayed for him. She must be praying still. The holy nun had the heart of a mother to answer his mother's prayers.

His mind felt so stretched, so weary. He felt a deep, inexplicable peace. He bent to the floor and felt himself drifting to sleep.

He saw a great light and in it the holy nun, her face bright with love as she looked toward the Lord Christ. The lady's gaze was drawing Iacobello's attention to Jesus.

Jesus bore a bloody gash in His forehead. Iacobello remembered. Christ carried His cross. He fell beneath its weight. Several times. He fell, not because He couldn't see but because others were blind. Others like Iacobello.

Iacobello had heard some friars preaching in Spoleto. They said that sins hurt Christ. Iacobello's sins. Yet Christ's gaze was gentle and compassionate, not angry. Like a beggar, Christ extended His hands toward Iacobello, who could see the bloody nail wounds in them.

Suddenly Iacobello knew. His blindness was no punishment for sin. It was to bring him to this moment of interior sight when he could clearly see both his own sins and Christ's mercy. Despite Iacobello's unlovableness, God still loved him. Iacobello touched the wounded palm, putting into it the only alms he had. Himself.

"Get up. Get up, because you have been freed!"

It was the voice of the holy nun.

Iacobello looked from Christ to her. She had disappeared. Then Christ, too, vanished.

Tears were dropping from Iacobello's cheeks to his thighs, running down his legs, etching little rivulets of clean, pale skin against the gray grime. God, his breeches were filthy. His mother never let them get that bad.

Iacobello gasped. He could see his breeches, his thighs, his tears rolling down his legs. The moment seemed suspended in time, as if he could touch it.

He lifted his head. Just in front of him hung a gray casket, suspended on hooks and resting atop an iron grate. On either side, masses of candles blazed.

On the right lay a pile of ragged clothes. His clothes. At his left, a shaggy-haired, grimy boy was staring at him.

"Pasquale?"

The boy squealed.

Iacobello threw his arms around the boy. "Pasquale, I can see!"

God was too good. Iacobello wanted to know God, to know Madonna Chiara, to go to confession. He had to find a priest.

Gathering up his clothes and shoes, Iacobello wedged them between his mending right arm and his body. Then he pushed himself erect and turned to the packed crowd, every face radiant in the candlelight. Taking Pasquale's hand in his own left hand, he began to push through the people. "I can see! Praise God and Madonna Chiara, I can see!"

NOTES

Chiara was buried at San Giorgio in the same place that San Francesco had been buried, the description of which is accurate. Many miracles took place at her tomb and through her intercession (CA:ED 321–28), including Iacobello's cure (CA:ED 323–24).

62

Suor Agnese di Oportulo di Bernardo

Dormitory, San Damiano (Mid-October 1260)

With pains shooting through her shoulders, Suor Agnese stooped to her bed of straw and felt beneath her straw pillow for a simple wooden cross. A bit over fifty years old, she felt herself weakening. Two years ago, Suor Pacifica had died at the age of ninety. Agnese would never reach that age.

Ah, here was the cross. In Agnese's bony, heavily veined hands, the simple cross sang with memories.

How long ago had she made this? Long ago when she and Lucia were children, before San Francesco died. All these years she had fallen asleep praying and clutching the cross.

"Sister, are you ready?"

Young, vibrant Suor Giuseppina was offering Agnese her left hand. Agnese grasped Giuseppina's arm and stood.

Next to Giuseppina stood rosy-cheeked Suor Sofia and, between them, a large two-handled basket, its lid securely tied to it with twine. From within came a plaintive, repetitive yowling. Suor Gatta. Today the sisters were leaving San Damiano, never to return.

With Giuseppina supporting Agnese and Sofia embracing the basket with both arms, the three women moved toward the stairs that led out of the dormitory. Suor Gatta yowled louder.

"The cross means a lot to you, doesn't it?" Giuseppina asked in her sweetly musical voice.

"Sì."

How could Agnese explain? She had wept over this cross when Papà had been excommunicated. She had tried to do penance by wearing Chiara's hairshirt, drinking foul water, and cinching her cord tightly until Chiara had stopped her. One Good Shepherd Sunday, when Agnese had seen the Christ Child at Chiara's side, she had finally understood the profoundness of the cross.

The sisters walked through the oratory. None bent to kiss the floor, because the Body of Christ had been taken to the Monastery of Santa Chiara in Assisi.

Santa Chiara, sì.

Immediately after Chiara's death, Pope Innocenzo IV had begun an inquiry into her sanctity. Upon his death, Cardinal Rinaldo had become pope, taking the name Alessandro IV. He had canonized Chiara in 1255.

The sisters had always known that Chiara was a saint. They had secretly kept her hair, blond at first before turning silver-gray, cut during their periodic tonsurings. They'd also saved her tunic, mantle, and hairshirt. Fra Leone and Fra Angelo had given them Francesco's deacon alb that Chiara had embroidered, as well as his breviary. The sisters were taking all these relics to the Monastery of Santa Chiara.

"Shush, Suor Gatta!" Sofia scolded.

"What number Suor Gatta is she?" Giuseppina asked Agnese, helping her down the narrow stairs that led to the choir.

Agnese had to think. The Suor Gatta when Agnese had entered San Damiano was gray. So was the second. The third, black with white paws, had mysteriously disappeared. Suor Gatta number four had died about the same time as Chiara. "This is Suor Gatta Five," Agnese figured.

"Poor Suor Gatta!" Sofia was speaking to the basket. "Shush now. When we get to the Monastery of Santa Chiara, you will have a much larger place to explore."

So Agnese had heard. Chiara's body had been laid to rest at San Giorgio in the same place that Francesco's body had lain while the Basilica di San Francesco was being built. At the same time, some San Damiano sisters had moved to a temporary monastery at San Giorgio. Abbess Benedetta intended to build a permanent monastery there for the sisters alongside the Basilica di Santa Chiara commissioned by Pope Alessandro IV.

Working with Lord Pope and through the bishop and the Chapter of San Rufino, Benedetta had exchanged the San Damiano complex for the Church of San Giorgio, its adjacent Hospital of San Rufino, and a small amount of land. Then, stubbornly persistent, both she and Lord Pope had overcome tremendous opposition to build a magnificent edifice to house Chiara's body on the site. The disputes over property, rights, and clerics' ideas would have discouraged a lesser person, but Benedetta, a knight's true daughter, had gotten her way.

First the Monastery of Santa Chiara had been built around the Church of San Giorgio. To build the Basilica di Santa Chiara, Benedetta had obtained as architect the highly esteemed Fra Filippo di Campello, designer of the Basilica di San Francesco. As agreed, the outbuildings of San Damiano had been demolished and the stones used to build the Basilica di Santa Chiara. Benedetta had commissioned a painted crucifix, reportedly quite beautiful, to hang in the new church. On October 3, Chiara's body had been transferred from the Church of San Giorgio to the Basilica di Santa Chiara and interred under the high altar. The ceremony, Agnese had heard, had been magnificent, with a joyous, reverent crowd of prelates, abbots, friars, and laity. Benedetta, gravely ill at the Monastery of Santa Chiara, must have been thrilled.

Giuseppina opened the door to the silent, empty choir, guiding Agnese through. To the right lay the empty burial plots. The bodies of the sisters had already been moved to the Monastery of Santa Chiara.

Of all the sisters at San Damiano, only Benedetta and Agnese had known Chiara in the early days. All the others had died. Now Benedetta was dying and Agnese, too.

Into the parlor Agnese shuffled, through the doorway, around the grate, out into the visitors' area in the shadowy church. Above the altar was the empty space where the crucifix that had spoken to San Francesco had hung. With the sisters, that relic was moving today to the new monastery. The dove above the altar, where the Body of Christ had been kept, was empty.

The other sisters waited near the doors of the church. One by one, they ascended the steps to the outer courtyard, Giuseppina helping Agnese while Sofia balanced the wailing basket.

In the blinding sunlight, a male voice questioned, "Are you the last?"

"Sì, Messer," Agnese smiled at the mounted knight, one of many sent by the comune to accompany the sisters. In an oxcart rested the San Damiano crucifix, assorted kitchen vessels, and the relics.

Two young sisters closed the door of the church. A young knight helped Agnese climb into the cart. Sofia wedged the basket between Agnese and the crucifix. As the cart jolted forward, Gatta shrieked. Agnese grabbed the basket to steady it.

Walking and chatting softly among themselves, the youthful sisters followed the rolling cart as it began the ascent up the steep hill at the foot of which lay San Damiano. This hill. Agnese remembered running down it forty years ago, a young girl eager to give herself to God.

Addio, San Damiano, her soul whispered.

"Tell us, Suor Agnese, what was it like when you first came here?" Giuseppina asked.

"Sì, Sister, tell us," the other sisters begged.

What was it like? Agnese had been a curly-haired eleven-year-old who, for months, had begged Papà to live at San Damiano. Oh, the joy, the freshness, the poverty of that beginning, when she, Lucia, Angeluccia, and Venuta were all giddy girls! How all four of them had admired and loved Chiara, who had become their mamma! She had guided all of them through the trials, struggles, and opposition of those early days.

But these young sisters, some of whom hadn't known Chiara and none of whom had known Francesco, had experienced only the glory of the recent years. Now people thought that the Poor Sisters were heroic and angelic. The ordine's founder a saint. Their new dwelling, the Monastery of Santa Chiara and its adjacent basilica, magnificent substitutes for humble San Damiano. Knowing only praise, would these sisters hold to the poverty, humility, and spark of the beginning?

Agnese's gaze shifted to the simple wooden cross. She spoke loudly, to be heard above the gentle plodding of the oxen, the creaking of the cart wheels, and the now subdued meowing. "The beginning was like this," she said, showing the sisters the cross. "Suor Chiara used to say, 'Look upon Him who became contemptible for you, and follow Him, making yourself contemptible in this world for Him. Gaze. Consider. Contemplate desiring to imitate your Spouse. Because of this you shall share always and forever the glory of the kingdom of heaven in place of what is earthly and passing...'"

Her voice trailed off. Speaking loudly was exhausting. For the past forty years, in the silence of San Damiano, she'd spoken softly, almost in a whisper. What could she say that would explain everything?

"We were faithful at the beginning. Faithful to poverty. Joy. Humility. To the cross and to Him Who suffered on it. If we are faithful to the end, we will be His forever."

NOTES

After her death, Chiara's order continued to grow. Giuseppina and Sofia are fictitious sisters who represent two of the many women who entered after Chiara's death and who had never known her.

Despite opposition and obstacles, Benedetta, with the support of the pope and the bishop of Assisi, was instrumental in building the Monastery and Basilica di Santa Chiara. The building sequence in this chapter follows that suggested by Marino Bigaroni in his article "The Church of San Giorgio in Assisi and the First Expansion of the Medieval City Walls." Chiara's body was moved to the basilica on October 3, 1260.

It seems that immediately after Chiara's burial at San Giorgio in 1253, some sisters transferred from San Damiano to San Giorgio to be near her body, where they lived in a temporary monastery built for them.

Historians dispute the year during which the remaining unnamed sisters left San Damiano. Some believe that it was as early as 1257, while others agree with the traditional date, shortly after October 3, 1260 (see Luke Wadding, *The History of the Glorious Virgin Saint Clare*, p. 119). When the last sisters left San Damiano, according to Wadding, they took with them the relics mentioned in this chapter as well as the large, painted crucifix, all of which can today be seen in the Basilica di Santa Chiara in Assisi.

Historians imply that Benedetta, as abbess, ordered the San Damiano crucifix moved to the Monastery of Santa Chiara. Since Benedetta died in 1260 (CA:ED 190), her death may have occurred after the transferal but before the end of the year.

The death dates of the other sisters mentioned in this chapter are as follows:

Agnese di Oportulo died in 1261 (CA:ED 177 footnote).

Pacifica died in about 1258 (CA:ED 144 footnote and *The Collectanea Franciscana Bibliographia Franciscana: 1931–1970* Index).

Lucia died in 1253 (CA:ED 179 footnote).

Angeluccia died sometime after 1253 when she testified in the *Process*.

Venuta (Benvenuta di Madonna Diambre) died sometime after 1253 (CA:ED 180 footnote).

Chiara's words, remembered by Agnese, are from her *Second Letter to Agnes of Prague* (CA:ED 49).

Select Bibliography

This book is the fruit of years of extended study and research on Saint Clare. The full bibliography runs to twenty-two pages. A few of the sources deal more directly with information about Saint Francis and Saint Clare. The author also spent ten days in Assisi, visiting locations associated with the life of Saint Clare, and made a subsequent pilgrimage to Assisi to visit locations associated with the life of Saint Francis. Interviews with Franciscan scholars who were friars at the Basilica di San Francesco or sisters at the Basilica di Santa Chiara provided detailed insights into how these two saints lived.

Translations of Clare's and Francis' Writings and Early Histories and Biographies

Armstrong, Regis J., trans. *Clare of Assisi: Early Documents*. St. Bonaventure, NY: St. Bonaventure University, 1993.

Armstrong, Regis J., ed. *The Lady: Clare of Assisi, Early Documents*, rev. ed. Hyde Park, NY: New City Press, 2006.

Armstrong, Regis J., J.A. Wayne Hellmann, and William J. Short, eds. *Francis of Assisi: Early Documents*. Hyde Park, NY: New City Press (The Franciscan Institute of St. Bonaventure University, St. Bonaventure, NY). 3 vols (1999–2001). This includes: *The Life of Saint Francis* by Friar Thomas of Celano; *The Anonymous of Perugia* by Friar John of Perugia; *The Legend of the Three Companions* by Friars Leo, Angelo, and Rufino; *The Assisi Compi-*

lation seemingly compiled by Friars Leo, Angelo, and Rufino and possibly others; and *The Remembrance of the Desire of a Soul* by Friar Thomas of Celano.

Brown, Raphael, trans. *The Little Flowers of St. Francis.* Garden City, NY: Hanover House, 1958.

Celano, Tommaso. *The Life of St. Clare Virgin.* Translated by Catherine Bolton Magrini. Assisi, Italy: Editrice Minerva, 1994.

Clare and Francis of Assisi. *Francis and Clare: The Complete Works.* Translated by Regis J. Armstrong, OFM Cap., and Ignatius C. Brady, OFM. New York: Paulist Press, 1982.

Dalarun, Jacques. *The Rediscovered Life of Saint Francis of Assisi by Thomas of Celano.* Translated by Timothy J. Johnson. St. Bonaventure, NY: Franciscan Institute Publications, 2016.

Francis of Assisi. *The Prayers of Saint Francis.* Translated by Ignatius Brady, OFM. Ann Arbor, MI: Servant, 1987.

Habig, Marion A., ed. *St. Francis of Assisi: Writings and Early Biographies (English Omnibus of the Sources for the Life of St. Francis).* Quincy, IL: Franciscan Press, 1991.

Wadding, Luke. *The History of the Glorious Virgin Saint Clare.* Adapted from Luke Wadding's *Annals.* Translated into English from the French of Francis Hendricq by Sister Magdalen Augustine, PC, 1635; set into modern English by Celsus O'Brien, 1992. Galway, Ireland: Connacht Tribune, 1992.

Later Biographies

Bartoli, Marco. *Clare of Assisi.* Translated by Frances Teresa, OSC. Quincy, IL: Franciscan Press of Quincy University, 1993.

Brady, Ignatius. *The Legend and Writings of Saint Clare of Assisi.* St. Bonaventure, NY: Franciscan Institute, 1953.

Carney, Margaret. *The First Franciscan Woman: Clare of Assisi and Her Form of Life.* Quincy, IL: Franciscan Press of Quincy University, 1993.

Cunningham, Lawrence, ed. *Brother Francis: An Anthology of Writings by and about Saint Francis of Assisi.* New York: Harper & Row, 1972.

De Robeck, Nesta. *St. Clare of Assisi*. Chicago: Franciscan Herald Press, 1951.

Dhont, Rene-Charles. *Clare Among Her Sisters*. St. Bonaventure, NY: Franciscan Institute, 1987.

Du Puis, Francis. *The Life and Legend of the Lady Saint Clare*. Translated from the French by Charlotte Balfour. New York: Longmans, Green, and Co., 1920.

Englebert, Omer. *Saint Francis of Assisi: A Biography*. Translated by Eve Marie Cooper. Ann Arbor, MI: Servant, 1965.

Fiege, Marianus. *The Princess of Poverty: Saint Clare of Assisi and the Order of Poor Ladies*. Long Prairie, MN: The Neumann Press, 1991. Originally published by the Poor Clares of the Monastery of St. Clare, Evansville, IN, 1900. Republished 1991.

Fortini, Arnaldo. *Francis of Assisi*. Translated by Helen Moak. New York: Crossroad, 1981.

————. *Nova Vita di San Francesco*. 4 vols. Santa Maria degli Angeli Edizioni. Assisi, Italy: Tipografia Porziuncola, 1959.

Garzonio, Chiara Lucia. *Without Turning Back: Life of Saint Agnes of Assisi*. Florence, Italy: Libreria Editrice Fiorentina, 1991.

Peterson, Ingrid J. *Clare of Assisi: A Biographical Study*. Quincy, IL: Franciscan Press, 1993.

Seraphim, Mary. *Clare: Her Light and Her Song*. Chicago: Franciscan Herald Press, 1984.

Franciscan Studies

Armstrong, Regis J. "Starting Points: Images of Women in the Letters of Clare." From *Collectanea Franciscana* 62 (1992): 63–100. *Greyfriars Review* 7.3 (1993): 347–80.

Bezunartea, Jesús María. "Clare of Assisi and the Discernment of Spirits." *Greyfriars Review Supplement* 8 (1994).

Bigaroni, Marino. "The Church of San Giorgio in Assisi and the First Expansion of the Medieval City Walls." Translated by Lori Pieper, SFO, *Greyfriars Review* 8.1 (1994): 57–101.

———. "San Damiano—Assisi: The First Church of Saint Francis." Translated by Agnes Van Baer, OSC. *Franciscan Studies* 47 (1987): 45–97.

Brooke, Rosalind B. *Early Franciscan Government: Elias to Bonaventure*. Cambridge, England: Cambridge University Press, 1959.

Frances Teresa, Sister, OSC. *Living the Incarnation: Praying with Francis and Clare of Assisi*. London: Darton, Longman, & Todd, 1993.

———. *This Living Mirror: Reflections of Clare of Assisi*. Maryknoll, NY: Orbis, 1995.

Gilliat-Smith, Ernest. *St. Clare of Assisi: Her Life and Legislation*. New York: E.P. Dutton & Co., 1914.

Godet, Jean-François. "Clare the Woman, as Seen in Her Writings." Translated by Paul Barrett, OFM Cap. *Greyfriars Review* 4, no. 3 (1990): 7–30.

———. *Clare of Assisi: A Woman's Life: Symbols of the Feminine in Her Writings*. Chicago: Haversack, 1991.

Godet-Calogeras, Jean-François, ed. *Out of the Shadows: Clare and Franciscan Women*. Chicago: Haversack, 1994.

Grau, Englebert. "Saint Clare's *Privilegium Paupertatis*: Its History and Significance." Translated by Sister M. Jane Frances, PCC, from *Wissenschaft und Weisheit* 1, no. 38 (1975): 17–25. *Greyfriars Review* 6, no. 3 (1992): 327–36.

Hone, Mary Frances, gen. ed. *Clare Centenary Series: Towards the Discovery of Saint Clare of Assisi*. St. Bonaventure, NY: The Franciscan Institute. 8 vols (ca. 1992–96).

Hugo, William R., and Joanne Schatzlein: *Studying the Life of Saint Clare of Assisi: A Beginner's Workbook*. Hyde Park, NY: New City Press, 2019.

Knox, Lezlie S. *Creating Clare of Assisi: Female Franciscan Identities in Later Medieval Italy*. Leiden, Netherlands: Brill, 2008.

Lainati, Chiara Augusta. "The Enclosure of St Clare and of the First Poor Clares in Canonical Legislation and in Practice." Pts. 1 and 2. *The Cord* 28, no. 1 (January 1978): 4–15; no. 2 (February 1978): 47–60.

———. "Saint Clare of Assisi, a Beautiful Woman." Translated by Jayme Lee Mathias, OFM Conv. *Greyfriars Review* 7, no. 2 (1993): 151–66.

Lynn, Beth. "Poverty: Thirteenth Century Revitalization in the Writings of Clare of Assisi." *The Cord* 38, no. 1 (January 1988): 19–31.

Maria, Sandra. "Enclosure in the Order of the Poor Sisters of St Clare." *CTC*, no. 18 (June 1994): 48–55.

Moorman, John. *A History of the Franciscan Order from Its Origins to the Year 1517*. Oxford, England: Clarendon, 1968.

Robinson, Paschal. *The Rule of Saint Clare: Its Observance in the Light of Early Documents*. Philadelphia: The Dolphin Press, 1912.

Roggen, Heribert. *The Spirit of St. Clare*. Translated by Paul Joseph Oligny. Chicago: Franciscan Herald Press, 1971.

The First Rule of Saint Clare and The Constitutions of Saint Coletta. Boston, MA: Angel Guardian Press, 1924.

Articles

Brunette, Pierre. "Clare and Francis: A Saintly Friendship." Translated by Paul Barrett, OFM Cap. *Greyfriars Review* 11, no. 2 (1997): 185–227.

Carney, Margaret. "Francis and Clare: A Critical Examination of the Sources." *Laurentianum* 30 (1989): 25–60.

Cirino, Andre R. "Clare and the Rule for Hermitages." *The Cord* 41, no. 7 (July–August 1991): 195–202.

"Concerning Fasting According to the Rule and Mind of St. Clare." *Pro Monialibus* 73 (1979): 7–9.

"Concerning Silence According to the Mind of St. Clare." *Pro Monialibus* 4 (1979): 6–7.

"Concerning the door called 'regular' (prescribed in the Rule) and other doors." *Pro Monialibus* 5 (1968): 2–3.

"Concerning the Grate for Communion at the Time of Saint Clare." *Pro Monialibus* 81 (1980): 4–5.

"Concerning the Parlor and the Grate at the Time of Saint Clare." *Pro Monialibus* 75 (1979): 3–4.

"Concerning the signs by which St. Clare was accustomed to arouse the sisters at night." *Pro Monialibus* 78 (1980): 2–3.

Cristiana dello Spirito, Sister. "The Cost of Radiance: Footprints of Clare's Interior Journey in the Process of Canonization." *CTC*, no. 19 (January 1995): 22–31.

Flury-Lemberg, Mechtild. *Textile Conservation and Research*. Riggisberg, Switzerland: Abegg-Stiftung, n.d. "The Cowl of St. Francis of Assisi," 314–17.

"From what source did St. Clare take the term 'Sisters serving outside the monastery.'" *Pro Monialibus* 86 (1981): 2–3.

Garzonio, Chiara Lucia. "Agnes, (The) Clare's sister and the very first diffusion of her 'charisma.'" *CTC Communion and Communication* 9–10 (April 1990): 8–9.

Godet, Jean-François. "A New Look at Clare's Gospel Plan of Life. 'Progetto evangelico di Chiara oggi.'" *Vita Minorum* 3 (1985): 198–301. Translated by Edward Hagman, OFM Cap. Reprinted *Greyfriars Review Supplement* 5 (1991).

Hanus, Bishop Jerome. "Clare and Chrism." *The Cord* 44, no. 7–8 (July–August 1994): 193–95.

Hone, Mary Francis. "Claire and the Ancren Riwle: A comparative study of the spirituality of Saint Clare of Assisi with the form of anchoritic life composed by Bishop Richard Poore for three anchoresses of the Tarrent in England." Pts. 1–3. *The Cord* 36, no. 7 (July–August 1986): 202–13; no. 9 (October 1986): 275–88; no. 10 (November 1986): 304–12.

Hutchinson, Gloria. "Clare of Assisi: The Anchored Soul." Chapter taken from *Six Ways to Pray from Six Great Saints*. Cincinnati, OH: St. Anthony Messenger Press, 1982.

"Letters of Cardinal Hugolino to Saint Clare and her Sisters." *Pro Monialibus* 17 (1969): 13–16.

"Monasteries at the time of Saint Clare's Death." *Pro Monialibus* 89 (1982): 4–5.

"Not to till the soil except for a garden for the Nuns." *Pro Monialibus* 15 (1969): 3–4.

"Once Again, the Signs or Bell Used by Saint Clare." *Pro Monialibus* 81 (1980): 2–3.

Pit'ha, Petr. "The Canonization of the Czechs' Agnes." *The Cord* 43, no. 1 (January 1993): 23–25.

"Poor Clare Monasteries Founded in St. Clare's Lifetime." *Pro Monialibus* 37 (1973): 6–8.

"Questions Concerning the letters of St. Clare." *Pro Monialibus* 14 (1968): 4–5.

Robinson, Paschal. "The Personality of St. Clare." *The Catholic University Bulletin*, no. 6 (June 1912): 483–93.

Sensi, Mario. "The Women's Recluse Movement in Umbria during the 13th and 14th Centuries." Translated by Edward Hagman, OFM Cap. *Greyfriars Review* 8, no. 3 (1994): 319–39.

Seraphim, Mary. "Clare and Poverty." *The Cord* 21, no. 4 (April 1971): 100–106.

———. "Clare and the Holy Eucharist." *The Cord* 21, no. 1 (January 1971): 5–10.

"The Authentic Mind of St. Clare Regarding the Enclosure." *Pro Monialibus* 73 (1979): 3.

"The Cord in Place of a Belt among Poor Clares and Conteptionists [*sic*]." *Pro Monialibus* 75 (1979): 3.

"The Enclosure at the Time of St. Clare." *Pro Monialibus* 4 (1968): 3–4.

"The Extern Sisters." *Pro Monialibus* 10 (1968): 3.

"The parlor without a grille?" *Pro Monialibus* 80 (1980): 3–4.

"The Vow of Enclosure among the Religious Vows." *Pro Monialibus* 23 (1970): 6–8.

van Boer, Agnes. "Agnes of Prague, Bohemia (1211–1282)." Campbelltown, New South Wales, Australia. *CTC,* no. 19 (January 1995): 1–14.

van Leeuwen, Peter. "Clare's Rule." Translated by Joseph Oudeman, OFM Cap. *Greyfriars Review* 1, no. 1 (1987): 65–76.

"Whether or Not Saint Clare Promised the Enclosure by a Vow." *Pro Monialibus* 78 (1980): 3–4.

"Why and from Whom Blessed Clare Undertook Contemplative Life in the Enclosure." *Pro Monialibus* 72 (1979): 6–7.

"Withdrawal from the World According to the Spirit of St. Francis." *Pro Monialibus* 10 (1968): 8–9.

Other Resources

Aelred of Rievaulx. "Rule of Life for a Recluse." In *Treatises and Pastoral Prayer*, 43–102. Kalamazoo, MI: Cistercian Publications, 1971. Third printing 1995.

Bodo, Murray. *Clare: A Light in the Garden*, rev. ed. Cincinnati, OH: St. Anthony Messenger Press, 1992.

Bonner, Dismas W. *Extern Sisters in Monasteries of Nuns: A Dissertation*. Washington, DC: Catholic University of America, 1963.

Ciani, Marisa. Private translation shared by Sister Mary Francis Hone, OSC, of "La Chiesa e il Francescanesimo femmilile" ["The Church and Franciscan women"] by Raoul Manselli in *Movimento Religioso Femminile e Francescanesimo nel Secolo XIII* [*The movement of Franciscan women religious in the thirteenth century*] Atti del VII Convegno Internazionale, Assisi, 1979: Assisi: Societa Internazionale di Studi Francescani, 1980: 239–261.

Darwin, Francis D.S. *The English Medieval Recluse*. London: Society for Promoting Christian Knowledge, 1958.

Fonck, Benet A. *To Cling with All Her Heart to Him: The Spirituality of St. Clare of Assisi*. Quincy, IL: Franciscan Press, 1996.

Francis, Mother Mary. "Clare of Assisi: Mirror of Humanism." Roswell, NM: Poor Clare Monastery, 1994.

———. "Dance for Exultation: Letters of Saint Clare to Saint Agnes of Prague." Roswell, NM: Poor Clare Monastery, 1997.

———. "The King's Rooms." Roswell, NM: Poor Clare Monastery, 1995.

Franciscan Friar of the Convent of Saint Francis (Prague). *The Life of the Glorious Virgin Sister Agnes*. Prague, 1282? English translation (1983) taken from the Italian as it appeared in *Forma Sororum* (Jan–Feb Issue, 1982), which had been translated from the Latin edition (J.K. Vyskocil, Publisher, Prague, 1932). No translator name, location, or publisher for English version given. Hand-typed anonymous translation.

Garzonio, Chiara Lucia. *Without Turning Back: Life of Saint Agnes of Assisi*. Florence, Italy: Libreria Editrice Fiorentina, 1991.

Georgianna, Linda. *The Solitary Self: Individuality in the Ancrene Wisse*. Boston, MA: Harvard University Press, 1981.

Hickey, Rita M. *Clare of Assisi: Friend of Francis, Bride of Christ*. New Orleans, LA: Saint Clare's Monastery, 1987.

Miller, Ramona. *In the Footsteps of Saint Clare: A Pilgrim's Guide Book*. St. Bonaventure, NY: The Franciscan Institute, 1993.

Morton, James. *The Nun's Rule being the Ancrew Riwle Modernised by James Morton with Introduction by Abbot Gasquet*. New York: Cooper Square Publishers, 1966.

Nugent, Madeline Pecora, CFP. *Antonio: A Story of Saint Anthony of Padua*. Boston, MA: Pauline Books and Media, 2022.

———. *Francesco: A Story of Saint Francis of Assisi*. Boston, MA: Pauline Books and Media, 2022.

Poor Clares from France. *Clare of Assisi: Light for the Way*. Translated by Paul LaChance, OFM. Strasbourg, Cedex 2, France. Éditiones du Signe, 1991.

Pope Urban IV. "The Rule Approved for the Poor Clares by Pope Urban IV." Appendix in *The Rule and General Constitutions for Nuns of the Order of St. Clare*, 215–247. Dublin, 1932.

Saint Sing, Susan. *A Pilgrim in Assisi: Searching for Francis Today*. Cincinnati, OH: St. Anthony Messenger Press, 1981.

Seton, Walter W. *Some New Sources for the Life of Blessed Agnes of Bohemia*. Aberdeen, Scotland: The University Press, 1915.

Soukupová, Helena. *The Convent of St. Agnes in Bohemia*. Prague: The National Gallery, 1993.

Also by Madeline Pecora Nugent

Continue your journey through early Franciscan history with Madeline Nugent's accounts of the lives of Saint Francis and Saint Anthony.

FRANCESCO
A Story of Saint Francis of Assisi

0-8198-2754-1

544 pages

ANTONIO
A Story of Saint Anthony of Padua

0-8198-0878-4

384 pages